ADVANCED BOOKKEEPING

STUDY TEXT

Qualifications and Credit Framework

AQ2016

This Study Text supports study for the following AAT qualifications:

AAT Advanced Diploma in Accounting – Level 3

AAT Advanced Certificate in Bookkeeping – Level 3

AAT Advanced Diploma in Accounting at SCQF – Level 6

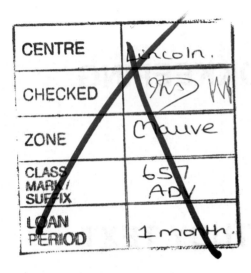

British Library Cataloguing-in-Publication Data

A catalogue record for this book is available from the British Library.

Published by
Kaplan Publishing UK
Unit 2, The Business Centre
Molly Millars Lane
Wokingham
Berkshire
RG41 2QZ

ISBN: 978-1-78415-625-1

This Product includes content from the International Ethics Standards Board for Accountants (IESBA), published by the International Federation of Accountants (IFAC) in 2015 and is used with permission of IFAC.

CONTENTS

INTRODUCTION

HOW TO USE THESE MATERIALS

These Kaplan Publishing learning materials have been carefully designed to make your learning experience as easy as possible and to give you the best chance of success in your AAT assessments.

They contain a number of features to help you in the study process.

The sections on the Unit Guide, the Assessment and Study Skills should be read before you commence your studies.

They are designed to familiarise you with the nature and content of the assessment and to give you tips on how best to approach your studies.

STUDY TEXT

This study text has been specially prepared for the revised AAT qualification introduced in September 2016.

It is written in a practical and interactive style:

- key terms and concepts are clearly defined

- all topics are illustrated with practical examples with clearly worked solutions based on sample tasks provided by the AAT in the new examining style

- frequent activities throughout the chapters ensure that what you have learnt is regularly reinforced

- 'pitfalls' and 'examination tips' help you avoid commonly made mistakes and help you focus on what is required to perform well in your examination

- 'Test your understanding' activities are included within each chapter to apply your learning and develop your understanding.

ICONS

The chapters include the following icons throughout.

They are designed to assist you in your studies by identifying key definitions and the points at which you can test yourself on the knowledge gained.

 Definition

These sections explain important areas of Knowledge which must be understood and reproduced in an assessment.

 Example

The illustrative examples can be used to help develop an understanding of topics before attempting the activity exercises.

 Test your understanding

These are exercises which give the opportunity to assess your understanding of all the assessment areas.

Quality and accuracy are of the utmost importance to us so if you spot an error in any of our products, please send an email to mykaplanreporting@kaplan.com with full details.

Our Quality Co-ordinator will work with our technical team to verify the error and take action to ensure it is corrected in future editions.

UNIT GUIDE

Introduction

This unit is the first of two Advanced level financial accounting units. It develops Foundation level skills, incorporating Advanced Bookkeeping and managing records for non-current assets, in preparation for producing final accounts for unincorporated organisations.

The purpose of this unit is to build on skills and knowledge learned in the Foundation level accounting units and to develop bookkeeping skills, taken to an initial trial balance. This is valuable progress for the student, both in terms of moving towards preparing final accounts and also in terms of offering employers more technical skills at this stage. The bookkeeping skills that students have acquired at an earlier stage will be reinforced and developed in this unit. While the daybooks and some of the ledger accounts may be familiar, the accruals basis of accounting is introduced to underpin many of the adjustments that are commonly found in the workplace, including accruals, prepayments, accounting for irrecoverable and doubtful debts and the period end valuation of inventory. This takes the student to the position of being able to draw up a trial balance using adjusted figures, and to extend it to identify the profit or loss for the period.

Students will study non-current asset accounting in some depth, including the accurate recording and control of the valuable resource of non-current assets which is vital to all organisations. On completion of this unit, students will understand and know how to use the non-current assets register as an important and independent record of the details of each individual non-current asset. The student will know how to use the various ledger accounts required to record the acquisition and disposal of non-current assets, how to calculate the gain or loss on disposal, and how to choose and apply depreciation methods and rates.

Students are expected to know and explain why they follow certain procedures, rather than just knowing that they have to be followed. While recognising that computerised accounts packages and spreadsheets will normally be used in the workplace, this unit helps the student understand the background processes. On completion of this unit, students will also begin to understand how ethical principles apply in the context of their work in this area. This enables the student to be a more independent member of a team and to work intelligently in their role, requiring increasingly less supervision as their knowledge grows and starting to supervise more junior members of the team.

Advanced Bookkeeping is a mandatory unit in this qualification. It follows on from the Foundation level units, Bookkeeping Transactions and Bookkeeping Controls. It is closely linked with the Advanced level unit, Final Accounts Preparation, which is recommended to be delivered after this unit. It also incorporates appropriate parts of Ethics for Accountants. Skills and knowledge from this unit are essential for the Professional level unit, Financial Statements of Limited Companies.

Learning outcomes

On completion of this unit the learner will be able to:

- Apply the principles of advanced double-entry bookkeeping.
- Implement procedures for the acquisition and disposal of non-current assets.
- Prepare and record depreciation calculations.
- Record period end adjustments.
- Produce and extend the trial balance.

Scope of content

To perform this unit effectively you will need to know and understand the following:

Chapter

1   **Apply the principles of advanced double-entry bookkeeping**

1.1   **Demonstrate the accounting equation**   1

Students need to know:

- the importance of the accounting equation for keeping accounting records
- the effect of accounting transactions on elements of the accounting equation.

KAPLAN PUBLISHING

Chapter

1

1.2 Classify assets, liabilities and equity in an accounting context

Students need to know:

- definitions and examples of assets: non-current (tangible, intangible) and current; liabilities: current and non-current; equity and capital; income (revenue); expenses (costs).

Students need to be able to:

- classify general ledger accounts as income (revenue), expense (cost), asset, liability or equity (capital).

1.3 Demonstrate the purpose and use of books of prime entry and ledger accounting

1, 2

Students need to know:

- the different books and records that make up the accounting system: books of prime entry: sales and purchases daybooks, cash book, journal (including narratives), general ledger accounts, memorandum ledgers, control accounts: sales ledger, purchases ledger, value added tax (VAT, may be known by another name in other countries) and payroll

- what information should be recorded in each record

- how these records relate to each other, including dealing with VAT

- the importance of following organisational policies and procedures

- the importance of the integrity and accuracy of records

- why the records need to be kept secure, and how.

Chapter

Students need to be able to:

- write up general ledger accounts correctly and accurately

- close off accounts to the statement of profit or loss, where appropriate

- carry down balances, where appropriate.

1.4 Apply ethical principles when recording transactions   7

Students need to know:

- the meaning of objectivity and its importance in accounting

- the importance of transparency and fairness

- that only valid transactions for the period must be included, and that all relevant transactions must be included.

Students need to be able to:

- apply the ethical principle of confidentiality

- identify whether entries are made with integrity, professional competence and due care

- identify whether transactions are genuine and valid for inclusion in the organisation's records

- identify professional behaviour, including dealing with the pressures of familiarity and authority.

Chapter

1.5   Carry out financial period end routines   1, 10, 11

Students need to know:

- that income or expense accounts will carry a balance prior to closing off to the statement of profit or loss at the end of the financial period.

- which account balances to carry forward and which to close off to the statement of profit or loss at the end of a financial period.

Students need to know how to:

- verify general ledger balances by using other sources of information and performing reconciliations where appropriate: physical checks, inventory records, supplier and bank statements, sales and purchases ledgers (memorandum ledger accounts)

- resolve discrepancies or refer them to the appropriate person

- identify and make corrections in the general ledger, including the journal.

2   Implement procedures for the acquisition and disposal of non-current assets

**2.1   Demonstrate the importance of prior authority for   3
capital expenditure**

Students need to know:

- why authorisation is necessary

- the appropriate person in an organisation to give authority.

Chapter

2.2   Identify capital expenditure   3

Students need to know:

- that International Financial Reporting Standards (IFRS) exist that are relevant to non-current assets

- the definitions of cost, useful life, residual value, depreciable amount, carrying amount

- what can and cannot be included in the cost of non-current assets

- the importance of organisational policy, including applying a given level of materiality

- that revenue expenses should be excluded

- that the depreciable amount of the acquisition should be allocated over its useful life; this is an application of the accrual basis of accounting

- the effect of capitalisation on the statement of profit or loss and statement of financial position.

Students need to be able to:

- treat VAT according to the registration status of the acquiring organisation.

2.3   Differentiate between funding methods for acquisition of non-current assets   3

Students need to know:

- the following funding methods: cash purchase (including purchase on standard commercial credit terms); borrowing, including loans, hire purchase, finance lease (no detailed knowledge of accounting treatment); part-exchange

- the suitability of each of the above in a tightly defined business context.

                                        KAPLAN PUBLISHING

Chapter

2.4 **Record acquisitions and disposals of non-current assets**

3, 5

Students need to know:

- the purpose and content of the non-current assets register, including assisting physical verification and checking general ledger entries and balances

- the carrying amount of an asset that has been disposed of at the end of the period

- the meaning of the balance on the disposals account

- how gains and losses on disposal are treated at the period end.

Students need to be able to:

- update the non-current assets register for acquisitions and disposals make entries in books of prime entry

- record acquisitions and disposals in the general ledger

- account for acquisitions and disposals by part-exchange

- treat VAT, according to the registration status of the acquiring organisation

- use the following accounts: non-current asset at cost (for example, motor vehicles at cost), non-current asset accumulated depreciation, bank/cash, loan, disposals.

Chapter

3   **Prepare and record depreciation calculations**

3.1   **Calculate depreciation**   4

Students need to know:

- how charges are treated at the period end.

Students need to be able to:

- choose and use appropriate methods of depreciation, taking into account the expected pattern of usage of the asset

- choose and use appropriate rates of depreciation, taking into account the estimated useful life of the acquisition

- use the straight-line method of depreciation, using a percentage, fraction or over a period of time, including cases when a residual value is expected, for a full year or pro rata for part of a year, according to organisational policy

- use the diminishing balance method of depreciation for a full year using a percentage

- use the units of production method of depreciation.

3.2   **Record depreciation**   4

Students need to be able to:

- record depreciation in the non-current assets register

- record depreciation in the general ledger, including the journal

- use the following accounts: depreciation charges, non-current asset accumulated depreciation.

Chapter

4 Record period end adjustments

4.1 Record accruals and prepayments in income and expense accounts   12

Students need to know:

- that adjustments for accruals and prepayments are an application of the accrual basis of accounting

- how opening and closing accruals and prepayments affect income and expense accounts.

Students need to be able to:

- explain the difference between the amount paid or received and the amount recognised in the accounts

- account for accruals and prepayments by making a double-entry in the current period and reversing it in the future period

- recognise the reversal of a previous period adjustment in the ledger accounts

- calculate adjustments pro rata

- enter adjustments in the general ledger, including the journal

- calculate the amount transferred to the statement of profit or loss

- use the following accounts: accruals/accrued expenses, accrued income, prepayments/prepaid expenses, prepaid income.

Chapter

4.2 **Record irrecoverable debts and allowances for doubtful debts**　9

Students need to know:

- the differences between irrecoverable debts, allowances for specific doubtful debts and general allowances

- that allowances for doubtful debts are an application of the accrual basis of accounting (recognition only).

Students need to be able to:

- calculate new allowances for doubtful debts in accordance with organisational policy

- calculate adjustments for an existing general allowance for doubtful debts

- account for the recovery of an irrecoverable debt previously written off

- use the journal to record irrecoverable debts and allowances for doubtful debts (VAT implications are not required)

- use the following accounts: irrecoverable debts (statement of profit or loss), sales ledger control account, allowance for doubtful debts account (statement of financial position), allowance for doubtful debts adjustment account (statement of profit or loss).

Chapter

8

4.3 Record inventory

Students need to know:

- that IFRS exist that are relevant to inventory valuation

- the meaning of net realisable value

- that valuation must be at the lower of cost and net realisable value on an individual item basis

- the principles of different methods of valuation (calculations not required)

- what can and cannot be included in the valuation of inventory

- that accounting for inventory is an application of the accrual basis of accounting.

Student need to be able to:

- determine the correct closing inventory figure in accordance with current accounting standards

- calculate the cost of inventory from selling price when VAT or an element of profit is included (calculations involving an understanding of mark-up or sales margin will not be required)

- make entries in the journal

- use the following accounts: closing inventory – statement of profit or loss; closing inventory – statement of financial position.

Chapter

4.4   Record period end adjustments   7, 14

Student need to know:

- that, when making period end adjustments, there is scope to significantly affect the reported results of the organisation

- the effects of including misleading or inaccurate period end adjustments (non-compliance with regulations, misinformed decision making by users of the final accounts).

Students need to be able to:

- respond appropriately to period end pressures (time pressure, pressure to report favourable results, pressure from authority).

5   Produce and extend the trial balance

5.1   Prepare a trial balance   1, 6, 13, 14

Students need to know:

- that certain accounts can carry either a debit or a credit balance (in particular: VAT, disposals, allowance for doubtful debts adjustment, bank, loan, irrecoverable debts)

- the importance of the trial balance for the preparation of final accounts.

Students need to be able to:

- transfer balances from ledger accounts, a list of balances or written data into correct debit or credit columns of the trial balance

- correct any errors that are not shown by the trial balance

- use and clear the suspense account.

5.2   Carry out adjustments to the trial balance   6, 13, 14

Students need to be able to:

- place the following adjustments correctly in the extended trial balance: closing inventory, accruals, prepayments, corrections of errors/omissions, depreciation, irrecoverable debts, allowances for doubtful debts.

 KAPLAN PUBLISHING

		Chapter
5.3	**Complete the extended trial balance**	6, 14

Student need to be able to:

- extend figures in the ledger balances and adjustments columns correctly into the statement of profit or loss and statement of financial position columns

- make the extended columns balance

- correctly label the balancing figure line as profit or loss.

Delivering this unit

Unit name	Content links	Suggested order of delivery
Final Accounts Preparation	Advanced Bookkeeping gives students underlying knowledge that may support their study of Final Accounts Preparation.	It is recommended that Advanced Bookkeeping is delivered before Final Accounts Preparation.
Ethics for Accountants	Advanced Bookkeeping touches on ethical matters in the context of bookkeeping.	Not applicable for this unit.
Indirect Tax	Advanced Bookkeeping requires knowledge of how VAT is treated.	Early delivery of Indirect Tax may enhance understanding of the VAT elements of the Bookkeeping units.

THE ASSESSMENT

Test specification for this unit assessment

Assessment type	Marking type	Duration of exam
Computer based unit assessment	Computer marked	2 hours

The assessment for this unit consists of 5 compulsory, independent, tasks.

The competency level for AAT assessment is 70%.

Learning outcomes		Weighting
1	Apply the principles of advanced double-entry bookkeeping	24%
2	Implement procedures for the acquisition and disposal of non-current assets	20%
3	Prepare and record depreciation calculations	13%
4	Record period end adjustments	20%
5	Produce and extend the trial balance	23%
Total		100%

UNIT LINK TO SYNOPTIC ASSESSMENT

AAT AQ16 introduced a Synoptic Assessment, which students must complete if they are to achieve the appropriate qualification upon completion of a qualification. In the case of the Advanced Diploma in Accounting, students must pass all of the mandatory assessments and the Synoptic Assessment to achieve the qualification.

As a Synoptic Assessment is attempted following completion of individual units, it draws upon knowledge and understanding from those units. It may be appropriate for students to retain their study materials for individual units until they have successfully completed the Synoptic Assessment for that qualification.

With specific reference to this unit, the following learning objectives are also relevant to the Advanced Diploma in Accounting Synoptic Assessment.

LO1 Apply the principles of advanced double-entry bookkeeping.

LO2 Implement procedures for the acquisition and disposal of non-current assets.

LO3 Prepare and record depreciation calculations.

LO4 Record period end adjustments.

LO5 Produce and extend the trial balance.

STUDY SKILLS

Preparing to study

Devise a study plan

Determine which times of the week you will study.

Split these times into sessions of at least one hour for study of new material. Any shorter periods could be used for revision or practice.

Put the times you plan to study onto a study plan for the weeks from now until the assessment and set yourself targets for each period of study – in your sessions make sure you cover the whole course, activities and the associated Test your understanding activities.

If you are studying more than one unit at a time, try to vary your subjects as this can help to keep you interested and see subjects as part of wider knowledge.

When working through your course, compare your progress with your plan and, if necessary, re-plan your work (perhaps including extra sessions) or, if you are ahead, do some extra revision/practice questions.

Effective studying

Active reading

You are not expected to learn the text by rote, rather, you must understand what you are reading and be able to use it to pass the assessment and develop good practice.

A good technique is to use SQ3Rs – Survey, Question, Read, Recall, Review:

1   **Survey the chapter**

    Look at the headings and read the introduction, knowledge, skills and content, so as to get an overview of what the chapter deals with.

2   **Question**

    Whilst undertaking the survey ask yourself the questions you hope the chapter will answer for you.

3   Read

Read through the chapter thoroughly working through the activities and, at the end, making sure that you can meet the learning objectives highlighted on the first page.

4   Recall

At the end of each section and at the end of the chapter, try to recall the main ideas of the section/chapter without referring to the text. This is best done after short break of a couple of minutes after the reading stage.

5   Review

Check that your recall notes are correct.

You may also find it helpful to re-read the chapter to try and see the topic(s) it deals with as a whole.

Note taking

Taking notes is a useful way of learning, but do not simply copy out the text.

The notes must:

- be in your own words
- be concise
- cover the key points
- be well organised
- be modified as you study further chapters in this text or in related ones.

Trying to summarise a chapter without referring to the text can be a useful way of determining which areas you know and which you don't.

Three ways of taking notes:

1   Summarise the key points of a chapter

2   Make linear notes

A list of headings, subdivided with sub-headings, listing the key points.

If you use linear notes, you can use different colours to highlight key points and keep topic areas together.

Use plenty of space to make your notes easy to use.

3 Try a diagrammatic form

The most common of which is a mind map.

To make a mind map, put the main heading in the centre of the paper and put a circle around it.

Draw lines radiating from this to the main sub-headings which again have circles around them.

Continue the process from the sub-headings to sub-sub-headings.

Annotating the text

You may find it useful to underline or highlight key points in your study text – but do be selective.

You may also wish to make notes in the margins.

Revision phase

Kaplan has produced material specifically designed for your final examination preparation for this unit.

These include pocket revision notes and an exam kit that includes a bank of revision questions specifically in the style of the new syllabus.

Further guidance on how to approach the final stage of your studies is given in these materials.

Further reading

In addition to this text, you should also read the 'Accounting Technician' magazine every month to keep abreast of any guidance from the examiners.

KAPLAN PUBLISHING

Double entry bookkeeping

1

Introduction

A sound knowledge of double entry underpins many of the learning outcomes and skills required for Advanced Bookkeeping. It is essential knowledge in order to pass this unit and candidates will be assessed on double entry bookkeeping in the examination and so this must be very familiar ground. Although much of the content of this chapter should be familiar, it is essential that it is covered in order to build upon this basic knowledge in later chapters and for the Final Accounts Preparation unit.

ASSESSMENT CRITERIA	CONTENTS
Demonstrate the accounting equation (1.1)	1 Principles behind double entry bookkeeping
Classify assets, liabilities and equity in an accounting context (1.2)	2 Overview of the accounting system
Demonstrate the purpose and use of books of prime entry and ledger accounting (1.3)	3 Rules of double entry bookkeeping
Carry out financial period end routines (1.5)	4 Double entry – cash transactions
Prepare a trial balance (5.1)	5 Double entry – credit transactions
	6 Balancing a ledger account
	7 Ledger accounting and the trial balance

1 Principles behind double entry bookkeeping

1.1 Introduction

Double entry bookkeeping is based upon three basic principles:

- the dual effect principle
- the separate entity principle
- the accounting equation.

1.2 The dual effect

 Definition – The dual effect principle

The principle of the dual effect is that each and **every** transaction that a business makes has **two** effects.

For example if a business buys goods for cash then the two effects are that cash has decreased and that the business now has some purchases. The principle of double entry bookkeeping is that each of these effects must be shown in the ledger accounts by a **debit entry** in one account and an equal **credit entry** in another account.

Each and every transaction that a business undertakes has **two equal and opposite effects.**

1.3 The separate entity concept

 Definition – The separate entity concept

The separate entity concept is that the business is a completely separate accounting entity from the owner.

Therefore if the owner pays his personal money into a business bank account this becomes the capital of the business which is owed back to the owner. Similarly if the owner takes money out of the business in the form of drawings then the amount of capital owed to the owner is reduced.

The business itself is a completely separate entity in accounting terms from the owner of the business.

KAPLAN PUBLISHING

1.4 The accounting equation

At its simplest, the accounting equation simply says that:

Assets = Liabilities

If we treat the owner's capital as a special form of liability then the accounting equation is:

Assets = Liabilities + Capital

Or, rearranging:

Assets – Liabilities = Capital

Profit will increase the proprietor's capital and drawings will reduce it, so that we can write the equation as:

Assets – Liabilities = Capital + Profit – Drawings

1.5 Definitions

 Definition – Asset

An asset is an item of value controlled by a business. Assets may be tangible physical items or intangible items with no physical form, that add value to the business. For example, a building that is owned and controlled by a business and that is being used as part of the business activities would be classed as an asset.

 Definition – Liability

A liability is an obligation to something of value (such as an asset) as a result of past transactions or events. For example, owing a balance to a credit supplier is a liability.

 Definition – Equity

This is the 'residual interest' in a business and represents what is left when the business is wound up, all the assets sold and all the outstanding liabilities paid. It is effectively what is paid back to the owners when the business ceases to trade.

Definition – Income

This is the recognition of the inflow of economic benefit to the entity in the reporting period. This can be achieved, for example, by earning sales revenue.

Definition – Expense

This is the recognition of the outflow of economic benefit from an entity in the reporting period. This can be achieved, for example, by purchasing goods or services.

Test your understanding 1

Heather Simpson notices an amount of £36,000 on the trial balance of her business in an account called 'Capital'. She does not understand what this account represents.

Briefly explain what a capital account represents.

Test your understanding 2

Musgrave starts in business with capital of £20,000, in the form of cash £15,000 and non-current assets of £5,000.

In the first three days of trading he has the following transactions:

- Purchases inventory £4,000 on credit terms, supplier allows one month's credit.

- Sells some inventory costing £1,500 for £2,000 and allows the customer a fortnight's credit.

- Purchases a motor vehicle for £6,000 and pays by cheque.

The accounting equation at the start would be:

Assets less liabilities	=	Ownership interest
£20,000 – £0	=	£20,000

Required:

Re-state in values the accounting equation after all the transactions had taken place.

KAPLAN PUBLISHING

2 Overview of the accounting system

2.1 Overview of the accounting system

A business may enter into a large number of transactions on a daily basis. It is quite clear that keeping track of all transactions can be a detailed process.

To ensure that a business does keep track of all sales earned, purchases and expenses incurred, the transactions are recorded in an accounting system.

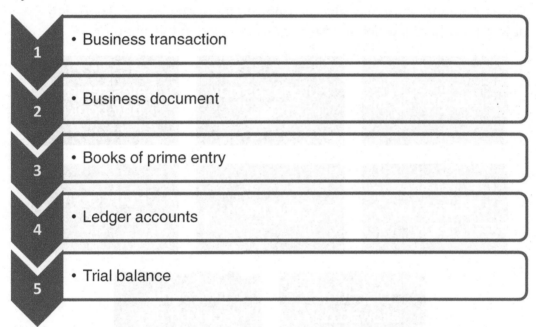

1. • Business transaction
2. • Business document
3. • Books of prime entry
4. • Ledger accounts
5. • Trial balance

(1) Initially a **business transaction** will take place; a credit sale, a credit purchase, a cash sale, a cash purchase, another expense either paid from the bank or by cash, cash paid into the bank, withdrawal of cash from the bank and owner's drawings.

(2) A **business document** will be produced e.g. an invoice.

(3) The transaction and details from the business document will be entered into the **books of prime entry**. A book of prime entry is where a transaction is first recorded. There are several books of prime entry which may also be referred to as 'day books'.

(4) The transactions that have been recorded in the books of prime entry are transferred into **ledger accounts** as part of the **general ledger** on a regular basis. Ledger accounts are used as part of the double entry accounting system.

(5) A **trial balance** is a list of all of the ledger accounts in the accounting system and is used as a control to check that transactions have been recorded correctly in the double entry system prior to the preparation of the financial statements.

2.2 Books of prime entry

A book of prime entry is the place where the transaction (which is detailed on a business document) is first recorded in the books of the business. Books of prime entry may also be referred to as day books. There are several day books which will be briefly reviewed in this chapter:

Sales day book	Purchases day book	Sales returns day book
Purchases returns day book	Cash book	Petty cash book
	Discounts allowed day book	Discounts received day book

🔍 **Definition – Sales day book**

The sales day book is simply a list of the sales invoices that are to be processed for a given period (e.g. a week).

🔍 **Definition – Sales returns day book**

The sales returns day book is simply a list of the credit notes that are to be processed for a given period (e.g. a week).

Definition – Purchases day book

The purchases day book is simply a list of the purchases invoices that are to be processed for a given period (e.g. a week).

 Definition – Purchases returns day book

The purchases returns day book is simply a list of the credit notes that have been received from suppliers for a given period (e.g. a week).

 Definition – Cash book

A cash book is a record of cash receipts and payments that can form part of the double entry bookkeeping system as well as being a book of prime entry.

Definition – Discounts allowed day book

The discounts allowed day book is used to record the discounts that have not been deducted at the point of the invoice being recorded within the sales day book but instead were offered on a conditional basis i.e. prompt payment discounts.

Definition – Discounts received day book

The discounts received day book is used to record the discounts that have not been deducted at the point of the invoice being recorded in the purchases day book but instead were offered on a conditional basis i.e. prompt payment discounts.

 Definition – Petty cash book

A petty cash book is one in which all petty or small payments made through the petty cash fund are recorded systematically.

2.3 The general ledger

 Definition – General ledger

A general ledger contains all the ledger accounts for recording transactions occurring within an entity.

Note: The AAT's preferred term is 'general ledger' but the general ledger may also be referred to as the 'main' or 'nominal' ledger.

2.4 The subsidiary ledger

 Definition – Subsidiary ledger

A subsidiary ledger provides details behind the entries in the general ledger. Subsidiary ledgers are maintained for individual receivables and payables.

 Definition – Subsidiary sales ledger

A subsidiary sales ledger is more commonly referred to as the 'sales ledger'. It is a set of accounts for individual receivables.

 Definition – Subsidiary purchases ledger

A subsidiary purchases ledger is more commonly referred to as the 'purchases ledger'. It is a set of accounts for individual payables.

3 Rules of double entry bookkeeping

3.1 Double entry bookkeeping rules

There are a number of rules that can help to determine which two accounts are to be debited and credited for a transaction:

- When money is paid out by a business this is a credit entry in the cash or bank account.

- When money is received by a business this is a debit entry in the cash or bank account.

- An asset or an increase in an asset is always recorded on the debit side of its account.

- A liability or an increase in a liability is always recorded on the credit side of its account.

- An expense is recorded as a debit entry in the expense account.

- Income is recorded as a credit entry in the income account.

3.2 The golden rule

Every debit has an equal and opposite credit.

Ledger account	
A debit entry represents	**A credit entry represents**
An increase to an asset	An increase to a liability
A decrease to a liability	A decrease to an asset
An item of expense	An item of income

For increases we can remember this as DEAD CLIC

Ledger account	
Debits increase:	Credits increase:
Expenses	Liabilities
Assets	Income
Drawings	Capital

4 Double entry – cash transactions

4.1 Introduction

For this revision of double entry bookkeeping we will start with accounting for cash transactions – remember that money paid out is a credit entry in the cash account and money received is a debit entry in the cash account.

Cash/Bank account	
DEBIT	**CREDIT**
Money in	Money out

💡 Example 1

Dan Baker decides to set up in business as a sole trader by paying £20,000 into a business bank account. The following transactions are then entered into:

(i) purchase of a van for deliveries by writing a cheque for £5,500

(ii) purchase of goods for resale by a cheque for £2,000

(iii) payment of shop rental in cash, £500

(iv) sale of goods for cash of £2,500

(v) Dan took £200 of cash for his own personal expenses.

Note that cash received or paid is normally deemed to pass through the bank account.

State the two effects of each of these transactions and record them in the relevant ledger accounts.

Solution

Money paid into the business bank account by Dan:

• increase in cash

• capital now owed back to Dan.

Double entry:

- a debit to the bank account as money is coming in
- a credit to the capital account.

Bank account

	£		£
Capital	20,000		

Capital account

	£		£
		Bank	20,000

(i)   Purchase of a van for deliveries by writing a cheque for £5,500

- cash decreases
- the business has a non-current asset, the van.

Double entry:

- a credit to the bank account as cash is being paid out
- a debit to an asset account, the van account.

Bank account

	£		£
Capital	20,000	Van	5,500

Van account

	£		£
Bank	5,500		

(ii) Purchase of goods for resale by a cheque for £2,000

- decrease in cash
- increase in purchases.

Double entry:

- a credit to the bank account as money is paid out
- a debit to the purchases account, an expense account.

Purchases of inventory are always recorded in a purchases account and never in an inventory account. The inventory account is only dealt with at the end of each accounting period and this will be dealt with in a later chapter.

Bank account

	£		£
Capital	20,000	Van	5,500
		Purchases	2,000

Purchases account

	£		£
Bank	2,000		

(iii)   Payment of shop rental in cash, £500

- decrease in cash

- expense incurred.

Double entry:

- a credit to the bank account as money is paid out

- a debit to the rent account, an expense.

Bank account

	£		£
Capital	20,000	Van	5,500
		Purchases	2,000
		Rent	500

Rent account

	£		£
Bank	500		

(iv)   Sale of goods for cash of £2,500

- cash increases

- sales increase.

Double entry:

- a debit to the bank account as money is coming in

- a credit to the sales account, income.

Bank account

	£		£
Capital	20,000	Van	5,500
Sales	2,500	Purchases	2,000
		Rent	500

Sales account

	£		£
		Bank	2,500

(v) Dan took £200 of cash for his own personal expenses

- cash decreases

- drawings increase (money taken out of the business by the owner).

Double entry:

- a credit to the bank account as money is paid out

- a debit to the drawings account.

Bank account

	£		£
Capital	20,000	Van	5,500
Sales	2,500	Purchases	2,000
		Rent	500
		Drawings	200

Drawings account

	£		£
Bank	200		

5 Double entry – credit transactions

5.1   Introduction

We will now introduce sales on credit and purchases on credit and the receipt of money from receivables and payment of money to payables. For the sales and purchases on credit there is no cash increase or decrease therefore the cash account rule cannot be used. Remember though that increase in income is always a credit entry and an increase in an expense is a debit entry.

Example 2

Dan now makes some further transactions:

(i)   purchases are made on credit for £3,000

(ii) sales are made on credit for £4,000

(iii) Dan pays £2,000 to the credit suppliers

(iv) £2,500 is received from the credit customers

(v)   Dan returned goods costing £150 to a supplier

(vi) goods were returned by a customer which had cost £200.

State the two effects of each of these transactions and write them up in the appropriate ledger accounts.

Solution

(i)   Purchases are made on credit for £3,000

- increase in purchases

- increase in payables (PLCA).

Double entry:

- a debit entry to the purchases account, an expense

- a credit to the payables account, a liability.

Purchases account

	£		£
Bank	2,000		
Payables	3,000		

Payables account (PLCA)

	£		£
		Purchases	3,000

(ii) Sales are made on credit for £4,000

- increase in sales

- increase in receivables.

Double entry:

- a credit entry to the sales account, income

- a debit entry to the receivables account, an asset.

KAPLAN PUBLISHING

Sales account

	£		£
		Bank	2,500
		Receivables	4,000

Receivables account (SLCA)

	£		£
Sales	4,000		

(iii) Dan pays £2,000 to the suppliers

- decrease in cash
- decrease in payables.

Double entry:

- a credit entry to the bank account as money is paid out
- a debit entry to payables as the liability is reduced.

Bank account

	£		£
Capital	20,000	Van	5,500
Sales	2,500	Purchases	2,000
		Rent	500
		Drawings	200
		Payables	2,000

Payables account (PLCA)

	£		£
Bank	2,000	Purchases	3,000

(iv) £2,500 is received from the credit customers

- increase in cash
- decrease in receivables.

Double entry:

- a debit entry in the bank account as money is received
- a credit entry to receivables as they are reduced.

Bank account

	£		£
Capital	20,000	Van	5,500
Sales	2,500	Purchases	2,000
Receivables	2,500	Rent	500
		Drawings	200
		Payables	2,000

Receivables account (SLCA)

	£		£
Sales	4,000	Bank	2,500

(v)   Dan returned goods costing £150 to a supplier

- purchases returns increase

- payables decrease.

Double entry:

- a debit entry to the payables account as payables are now decreasing

- a credit entry to the purchases returns account (the easiest way to remember this entry is that it is the opposite of purchases which are a debit entry).

Payables account (PLCA)

	£		£
Bank	2,000	Purchases	3,000
Purchases returns	150		

Purchases returns account

	£		£
		Payables	150

(vi)   Goods were returned by a customer which had cost £200

- sales returns increase

- receivables decrease.

Double entry:

- a credit entry to the receivables account as receivables are now decreasing

- a debit entry to sales returns (the opposite to sales which is a credit entry).

Receivables account (SLCA)

	£		£
Sales	4,000	Bank	2,500
		Sales returns	200

Sales returns account

	£		£
Receivables	200		

6 Balancing a ledger account

6.1 Introduction

Once the transactions for a period have been recorded in the ledger accounts it is likely that the owner will want to know certain matters, such as how much cash there is in the bank account, or how much has been spent on purchases? This can be found by balancing the ledger accounts.

6.2 Procedure for balancing a ledger account

The following steps should be followed when balancing a ledger account:

Step 1

Total both the debit and credit columns to find the higher total – enter this figure as the total for both the debit and credit columns.

Step 2

For the side that does not add up to this total put in the figure that makes it add up and call it the balance carried down, or 'bal c/d.'

Step 3

Enter the balance brought ('bal b/d') down on the opposite side below the totals.

Example 3

We will now balance Dan's bank account

Bank account

	£		£
Capital	20,000	Van	5,500
Sales	2,500	Purchases	2,000
Receivables	2,500	Rent	500
		Drawings	200
		Payables	2,000

Bank account

	£		£
Capital	20,000	Van	5,500
Sales	2,500	Purchases	2,000
Receivables	2,500	Rent	500
		Drawings	200
		Payables	2,000
		Balance c/d **Step 2**	14,800
Step 1	25,000	**Step 1**	25,000
Balance b/d **Step 3**	14,800		

Test your understanding 3

(a) Show by means of ledger accounts how the following transactions would be recorded in the books of Bertie Dooks, a seller of second-hand books:

   (i)   paid in cash £5,000 as capital

   (ii)   took the lease of a stall and paid six months' rent – the yearly rental was £300

   (iii) spent £140 cash on the purchase of books from W Smith

   (iv) purchased on credit from J Fox books at a cost of £275

   (v)   paid an odd-job man £25 to paint the exterior of the stall and repair a broken lock

(vi)   put an advertisement in the local paper at a cost of £2

(vii) sold three volumes containing The Complete Works of William Shakespeare to an American for £35 cash

(viii) sold a similar set on credit to a local schoolmaster for £3

(ix)   paid J Fox £175 on account for the amount due to him

(x)   received £1 from the schoolmaster

(xi)   purchased cleaning materials at a cost of £2 and paid £3 to a cleaner

(xii) took £5 from the business to pay for his own groceries.

(b)   Balance off the ledgers, clearly showing balance carried down (c/d) and balance brought down (b/d).

7   Ledger accounting and the trial balance

7.1   Introduction

 Definition – Trial balance

A trial balance is the list of the balances on all of the ledger accounts in an organisation's general (main, nominal) ledger.

7.2   Trial balance

The trial balance will appear as a list of debit balances and credit balances depending upon the type of account. If the double entry has been correctly carried out then the debit balance total should be equal to the credit balance total (this will be dealt with in more detail in a later chapter).

A trial balance lists all of the ledger account balances in the general ledger.

7.3 Preparing the trial balance

When all of the entries have been made in the ledger accounts for a period, the trial balance will then be prepared.

Step 1

Balance off each ledger account and bring down the closing balance.

Step 2

List each balance brought down as either a debit balance or a credit balance.

Step 3

Total the debit balances and the credit balances to see if they are equal.

Example 4

Given below are the initial transactions for Mr Smith, a sole trader. Enter the transactions in the ledger accounts using a separate account for each receivable and payable. Produce the trial balance for this sole trader at the end of 12 January 20X1.

On 1 Jan 20X1   Mr Smith put £12,500 into the business bank account.

On 2 Jan 20X1   He bought goods for resale costing £750 on credit from J Oliver. He also bought on the same basis £1,000 worth from K Hardy.

On 3 Jan 20X1   Sold goods for £800 to E Morecombe on credit.

On 5 Jan 20X1   Mr Smith returned £250 worth of goods bought from J Oliver, being substandard goods.

On 6 Jan 20X1   Sold goods on credit to A Wise for £1,000.

On 7 Jan 20X1   Mr Smith withdrew £100 from the bank for his personal use.

On 8 Jan 20X1   Bought a further £1,500 worth of goods from K Hardy, again on credit.

On 9 Jan 20X1   A Wise returned £200 worth of goods sold to him on the 6th.

On 10 Jan 20X1   The business paid J Oliver £500 by cheque, and K Hardy £1,000 also by cheque.

On 12 Jan 20X1   Mr Smith banked a cheque for £800 received from E Morecombe.

Solution

Step 1

Enter the transactions into the ledger accounts and then balance off each ledger account. Use a separate ledger account for each receivable and payable. (Note that in most examinations you will be required to complete the double entry for receivables and payables in the receivables and payables ledger control accounts, but for practice we are using the separate accounts.)

Step 2

Balance off each of the ledger accounts.

Capital account

	£			£
		1 Jan	Bank	12,500

Sales account

	£			£
		3 Jan	E Morecombe	800
Balance c/d	1,800	6 Jan	A Wise	1,000
	1,800			1,800
			Balance b/d	1,800

Purchases account

		£			£
2 Jan	J Oliver	750			
2 Jan	K Hardy	1,000			
8 Jan	K Hardy	1,500	Balance c/d		3,250
		3,250			3,250
	Balance b/d	3,250			

Purchases returns account

	£			£
		5 Jan	J Oliver	250

Sales returns account

		£			£
9 Jan	A Wise	200			

Drawings account

		£			£
7 Jan	Bank	100			

Bank account

		£			£
1 Jan	Capital	12,500	7 Jan	Drawings	100
12 Jan	E Morecombe	800	10 Jan	J Oliver	500
				K Hardy	1,000
				Balance c/d	11,700
		13,300			13,300
	Balance b/d	11,700			

E Morecombe account

		£			£
3 Jan	Sales	800	12 Jan	Bank	800

A Wise account

		£			£
6 Jan	Sales	1,000	9 Jan	Sales returns	200
				Balance c/d	800
		1,000			1,000
	Balance b/d	800			

J Oliver account

		£			£
5 Jan	Purchases returns	250	2 Jan	Purchases	750
10 Jan	Bank	500			
		750			750

K Hardy account

	£			£
10 Jan Bank	1,000	2 Jan	Purchases	1,000
Balance c/d	1,500	8 Jan	Purchases	1,500
	———			———
	2,500			2,500
	———			———
			Balance b/d	1,500

Note that accounts with only one entry do not need to be balanced as this entry is the final balance on the account.

Step 3

Produce the trial balance by listing each balance brought down as either a debit balance or a credit balance.

Make sure that you use the balance brought down below the total line as the balance to list in the trial balance.

Step 4

Total the debit and credit columns to check that they are equal.

Trial balance as at 12 January 20X1

	Debits	Credits
	£	£
Capital		12,500
Sales		1,800
Purchases	3,250	
Purchases returns		250
Sales returns	200	
Drawings	100	
Bank	11,700	
A Wise	800	
K Hardy		1,500
	———	———
	16,050	16,050
	———	———

NB: E Morecombe and J Oliver have a nil balance so have not appeared in the trial balance.

7.4   Purpose of the trial balance

One of the main purposes of a trial balance is to serve as a check on the double entry. If the trial balance does not balance, i.e. the debit and credit totals are not equal then some errors have been made in the double entry (this will be covered in more detail in a later chapter).

The trial balance can also serve as the basis for preparing an extended trial balance (see later in this text) and finally the financial statements of the organisation.

 Test your understanding 4

Enter the following details of transactions for the month of May 20X6 into the appropriate books of account. You should also extract a trial balance as at 1 June 20X6. Open a separate ledger account for each receivable and payable, and also keep separate 'cash' and 'bank' ledger accounts. Balance off each account and prepare a trial balance.

20X6

1 May	Started in business by paying £6,800 into the bank.
3 May	Bought goods on credit from the following: J Johnson £400; D Nixon £300 and J Agnew £250.
5 May	Cash sales £300.
6 May	Paid rates by cheque £100.
8 May	Paid wages £50 in cash.
9 May	Sold goods on credit: K Homes £300; J Homes £300; B Hood £100.
10 May	Bought goods on credit: J Johnson £800; D Nixon £700.
11 May	Returned goods to J Johnson £150.
15 May	Bought office fixtures £600 by cheque.
18 May	Bought a motor vehicle £3,500 by cheque.
22 May	Goods returned by J Homes £100.
25 May	Paid J Johnson £1,000; D Nixon £500, both by cheque.
26 May	Paid wages £150 by cheque.

7.5 Debit or credit balance?

When you are balancing a ledger account it is easy to see which side, debit or credit, the balance brought down is on. However if you were given a list of balances rather than the account itself then it is sometimes difficult to decide which side the balance should be shown in the trial balance, the debit or the credit?

There are some rules to help here:

- assets are debit balances
- expenses are debit balances
- liabilities are credit balances
- income is a credit balance.

This can be remembered using the 'DEAD CLIC' mnemonic.

Test your understanding 5

The following balances have been extracted from the books of Fitzroy at 31 December 20X2:

Prepare a trial balance at 31 December 20X2.

	£	*Debit*	*Credit*
Capital on 1 January 20X2	106,149		
Freehold factory at cost	360,000		
Motor vehicles at cost	126,000		
Inventories at 1 January 20X2	37,500		
Receivables	15,600		
Cash in hand	225		
Bank overdraft	82,386		
Payables	78,900		
Sales	318,000		
Purchases	165,000		
Rent and rates	35,400		
Discounts allowed	6,600		
Insurance	2,850		
Sales returns	10,500		
Purchase returns	6,300		
Loan from bank	240,000		
Sundry expenses	45,960		
Drawings	26,100		
		_____	_____
TOTALS			
		_____	_____

Test your understanding 6

(1) The bank account for January is as follows:

Bank account

	£		£
Balance b/d	1,900	Payables	7,000
Receivables	2,500		
Cash sales	500		
	———		———
	———		———

At the end of the month there is a **debit/credit** balance of **£7,000/4,900/2,100.**

Circle the correct answer

(2) True or false, to increase a liability a debit entry is made.

> True
> False

Tick the correct answer for task 2

Circle the correct answer for task 3, 4, 5, 6 and 7

(3) When a sole trader uses goods for resale for his own personal use the drawings account is **Debited / Credited** and the purchases account is **Debited / Credited**.

(4) When a supplier is paid the bank account is **Debited / Credited** and the supplier account is **Debited / Credited**.

(5) When goods are sold to a receivable, the sales account is **Debited / Credited** and the receivable account is **Debited / Credited**.

(6) A bank overdraft is a **Debit / Credit** account in the trial balance.

(7) Discounts received are a **Debit / Credit** balance in the trial balance.

Test your understanding 7

Tony

Tony started a business selling tapes and CDs. In the first year of trading he entered into the following transactions:

(a) Paid £20,000 into a business bank account.

(b) Made purchases from Debbs for £1,000 cash.

(c) Purchased goods costing £3,000 from Gary for cash.

(d) Paid £200 for insurance.

(e) Bought storage units for £700 cash from Debbs.

(f) Paid £150 cash for advertising.

(g) Sold goods to Dorothy for £1,500 cash.

(h) Paid the telephone bill of £120 in cash.

(i) Sold further goods to Dorothy for £4,000 cash.

(j) Bought stationery for £80 cash.

(k) Withdrew £500 cash for himself.

Required:

Show how these transactions would be written up in Tony's ledger accounts and balance off the accounts. Note you should enter bank and cash transactions into one ledger account.

 Test your understanding 8

Dave

Dave had the following transactions during January 20X3:

1 Introduced £500 cash as capital.

2 Purchased goods on credit from A Ltd worth £200.

3 Paid rent for one month, £20.

4 Paid electricity for one month, £50.

5 Purchased a car for cash, £100.

6 Sold half of the goods on credit to X Ltd for £175.

7 Drew £30 for his own expenses.

8 Sold the remainder of the goods for cash, £210.

Required:

Write up the relevant ledger accounts necessary to record the above transactions and balance off the accounts.

Test your understanding 9

Audrey Line

Audrey Line started in business on 1 March, opening a toy shop and paying £6,000 into a business bank account. She made the following transactions during her first six months of trading:

	£
Payment of six months' rent	500
Purchase of shop fittings	600
Purchase of toys on credit	2,000
Payments to toy supplier	1,200
Wages of shop assistant	600
Electricity	250
Telephone	110
Cash sales	3,700
Drawings	1,600

All payments were made by cheque and all inventories had been sold by the end of August.

Required:

Record these transactions in the relevant accounts.

8 Summary

In this opening chapter the basic principles of double entry bookkeeping have been revised from your basic accounting studies.

The basic principles of double entry are of great importance for this unit and in particular all students should be able to determine whether a particular balance on an account is a debit or a credit balance in the trial balance.

Test your understanding answers

Test your understanding 1

The balance on the capital account represents the investment made in the business by the owner. It is a special liability of the business, showing the amount payable to the owner at the statement of financial position date.

Test your understanding 2

Assets		
	Non-current assets (5,000 + 6,000)	11,000
	Cash (15,000 – 6,000)	9,000
	Inventory (4,000 – 1,500)	2,500
	Receivables	2,000
		―――――
		24,500
		―――――

Assets – Liabilities = Ownership interest

£24,500 – £4,000 = £20,500

Ownership interest has increased by the profit made on the sale of inventory.

Test your understanding 3

Ledger accounts

Cash account

	£		£
Capital account (i)	5,000	Rent (six months) (ii)	150
Sales (vii)	35	Purchases (iii)	140
Receivables (x)	1	Repairs (v)	25
		Advertising (vi)	2
		Payables (ix)	175
		Cleaning (xi)	5
		Drawings (xii)	5
		Balance c/d	4,534
	———		———
	5,036		5,036
	———		———
Balance b/d	4,534		

Payable account (J Fox)

	£		£
Cash (ix)	175	Purchases (iv)	275
Balance c/d	100		
	———		———
	275		275
	———		———
		Balance b/d	100

Receivable account (School master)

	£		£
Sales (viii)	3	Cash (x)	1
		Balance c/d	2
	———		———
	3		3
	———		———
Balance b/d	2		

Capital account

	£		£
Balance c/d	5,000	Cash (i)	5,000
	5,000		5,000
		Balance b/d	5,000

Sales account

	£		£
		Cash (vii)	35
Balance c/d	38	Receivables (Schoolmaster) (viii)	3
	38		38
		Balance b/d	38

Purchases account

	£		£
Cash (iii)	140	Balance c/d	415
Payable (J Fox) (iv)	275		
	415		415
Balance b/d	415		

Rent account

	£		£
Cash (ii)	150	Balance c/d	150
	150		150
Balance b/d	150		

Repairs account

	£		£
Cash (v)	25	Balance c/d	25
	25		25
Balance b/d	25		

Advertising account

	£		£
Cash (vi)	2	Balance c/d	2
	2		2
Balance b/d	2		

Cleaning account

	£		£
Cash (xi)	5	Balance c/d	5
	5		5
Balance b/d	5		

Drawings account

	£		£
Cash (xii)	5	Balance c/d	5
	5		5
Balance b/d	5		

Test your understanding 4

Cash account

	£		£
5 May Sales	300	8 May Wages	50
		31 May Balance c/d	250
	300		300
1 June Balance b/d	250		

Bank account

	£			£
1 May Capital	6,800	6 May	Rates	100
		15 May	Office fixtures	600
		18 May	Motor vehicle	3,500
		25 May	J Johnson	1,000
			D Nixon	500
		26 May	Wages	150
		31 May	Balance c/d	950
	6,800			6,800
1 June Balance b/d	950			

J Johnson account

	£			£
11 May Purchase returns	150	3 May	Purchases	400
25 May Bank	1,000	10 May	Purchases	800
31 May Balance c/d	50			
	1,200			1,200
		1 June	Balance b/d	50

D Nixon account

	£			£
25 May Bank	500	3 May	Purchases	300
31 May Balance c/d	500	10 May	Purchases	700
	1,000			1,000
		1 June	Balance b/d	500

J Agnew account

	£			£
31 May Balance c/d	250	3 May	Purchases	250
		1 June	Balance b/d	250

K Homes account

		£			£
9 May	Sales	300	31 May	Balance c/d	300
		300			300
1 June	Balance b/d	300			

J Homes account

		£			£
9 May	Sales	300	22 May	Sales returns	100
			31 May	Balance c/d	200
		300			300
1 June	Balance b/d	200			

B Hood account

		£			£
9 May	Sales	100	31 May	Balance c/d	100
1 June	Balance b/d	100			

Capital account

		£			£
31 May	Balance c/d	6,800	1 May	Bank	6,800
			1 June	Balance b/d	6,800

Purchases account

		£			£
3 May	J Johnson	400			
	D Nixon	300			
	J Agnew	250			
10 May	J Johnson	800			
	D Nixon	700	31 May	Balance c/d	2,450
		2,450			2,450
1 June	Balance b/d	2,450			

Sales account

	£			£
		5 May	Cash	300
		9 May	K Homes	300
			J Homes	300
31 May Balance c/d	1,000		B Hood	100
	———			———
	1,000			1,000
	———			———
		1 June	Balance b/d	1,000

Rates account

	£			£
6 May Bank	100	31 May	Balance c/d	100
	———			———
1 June Balance b/d	100			

Wages account

	£			£
8 May Cash	50			
26 May Bank	150	31 May	Balance c/d	200
	———			———
	200			200
	———			———
1 June Balance b/d	200			

Purchase returns account

	£			£
31 May Balance c/d	150	11 May	J Johnson	150
	———			———
		1 June	Balance b/d	150

Office fixtures account

	£			£
15 May Bank	600	31 May	Balance c/d	600
	———			———
1 June Balance b/d	600			

Motor vehicle account

	£			£
18 May Bank	3,500	31 May	Balance c/d	3,500
	———			———
1 June Balance b/d	3,500			

Sales returns account

	£			£
22 May J Homes	100	31 May	Balance c/d	100
	———			———
1 June Balance b/d	100			

Trial balance as at 30 May 20X6

	Dr £	Cr £
Cash	250	
Bank	950	
J Johnson		50
D Nixon		500
J Agnew		250
K Homes	300	
J Homes	200	
B Hood	100	
Capital		6,800
Purchases	2,450	
Sales		1,000
Rates	100	
Wages	200	
Purchase returns		150
Office fixtures	600	
Motor vehicles	3,500	
Sales returns	100	
	———	———
	8,750	8,750
	———	———

Test your understanding 5

Trial balance at 31 December 20X2

	Dr £	Cr £
Capital on 1 January 20X2		106,149
Freehold factory at cost	360,000	
Motor vehicles at cost	126,000	
Inventories at 1 January 20X2	37,500	
Receivables	15,600	
Cash in hand	225	
Bank overdraft		82,386
Payables		78,900
Sales		318,000
Purchases	165,000	
Rent and rates	35,400	
Discounts allowed	6,600	
Insurance	2,850	
Sales returns	10,500	
Purchase returns		6,300
Loan from bank		240,000
Sundry expenses	45,960	
Drawings	26,100	
	831,735	831,735

✎ Test your understanding 6

(1) The bank account for January is as follows:

Bank account

	£		£
Balance b/d	1,900	Payables	7,000
Receivables	2,500		
Cash sales	500		
Balance c/d	**2,100**		
	———		———
	7,000		7,000
	———		———
		Balance b/d	**2,100**

The correct answer is **CREDIT** of **£2,100**.

(2) False.

(3) When a sole trader uses goods for resale for his own personal use the drawings account is **Debited** and the purchases account is **Credited**.

(4) When a supplier is paid the bank account is **Credited** and the supplier account is **Debited**.

(5) When goods are sold to a receivable, the sales account is **Credited** and the receivable account is **Debited**.

(6) A bank overdraft is a **Credit** balance in the trial balance.

(7) Discounts received are a **Credit** balance in the trial balance.

Test your understanding 7

Tony

Cash

	£		£
Capital (a)	20,000	Purchases (b)	1,000
Revenue (g)	1,500	Purchases (c)	3,000
Revenue (i)	4,000	Insurance (d)	200
		Storage units (e)	700
		Advertising (f)	150
		Telephone (h)	120
		Stationery (j)	80
		Drawings (k)	500
		Balance c/d	19,750
	25,500		25,500
Balance b/d	19,750		

Capital

	£		£
Balance c/d	20,000	Cash (a)	20,000
	20,000		20,000
		Balance b/d	20,000

Purchases

	£		£
Cash (b)	1,000	Balance c/d	4,000
Cash (c)	3,000		
	4,000		4,000
Balance b/d	4,000		

Insurance

	£		£
Cash (d)	200	Balance c/d	200
	200		200
Balance b/d	200		

Storage units – cost

	£		£
Cash (e)	700	Balance c/d	700
	700		700
Balance b/d	700		

Advertising

	£		£
Cash (f)	150	Balance c/d	150
	150		150
Balance b/d	150		

Telephone

	£		£
Cash (h)	120	Balance c/d	120
	120		120
Balance b/d	120		

Revenue

	£		£
Balance c/d	5,500	Cash (g)	1,500
		Cash (i)	4,000
	5,500		5,500
		Balance b/d	5,500

Stationery

	£		£
Cash (j)	80	Balance c/d	80
	80		80
Balance b/d	80		

Drawings

	£		£
Cash (k)	500	Balance c/d	500
	500		500
Balance b/d	500		

Test your understanding 8

Dave

Cash

	£		£
Capital	500	Rent	20
Revenue	210	Electricity	50
		Drawings	30
		Car	100
		Balance c/d	510
	710		710
Balance b/d	510		

Capital

	£		£
Balance c/d	500	Cash	500
	500		500
		Balance b/d	500

Purchases

	£		£
Payables (A Ltd)	200	Balance c/d	200
	200		200
Balance b/d	200		

Payables

	£		£
Balance c/d	200	Purchases	200
	200		200
		Balance b/d	200

Revenue

	£		£
Balance c/d	385	Receivables (X Ltd)	175
		Cash	210
	385		385
		Balance b/d	385

Receivables

	£		£
Revenue	175	Balance c/d	175
	175		175
Balance b/d	175		

Electricity

	£		£
Cash	50	Balance c/d	50
	50		50
Balance b/d	50		

Rent

	£		£
Cash	20	Balance c/d	20
	20		20
Balance b/d	20		

Motor car

	£		£
Cash	100	Balance c/d	100
	100		100
Balance b/d	100		

Drawings

	£		£
Cash	30	Balance c/d	30
	30		30
Balance b/d	30		

Test your understanding 9

Audrey Line

Cash

	£		£
Capital	6,000	Rent	500
Revenue	3,700	Shop fittings	600
		Payables	1,200
		Wages	600
		Electricity	250
		Telephone	110
		Drawings	1,600
		Balance c/d	4,840
	———		———
	9,700		9,700
	———		———
Balance b/d	4,840		

Capital

	£		£
		Cash	6,000

Revenue

	£		£
		Cash	3,700

Shop fittings

	£		£
Cash	600		

Rent

	£		£
Cash	500		

Telephone

	£		£
Cash	110		

Drawings

	£		£
Cash	1,600		

Purchases

	£		£
Payables	2,000		

Payables

	£		£
Cash	1,200	Purchases	2,000
Balance c/d	800		
	2,000		2,000
		Balance b/d	800

Wages

	£		£
Cash	600		

Electricity

	£		£
Cash	250		

Accounting for VAT and payroll

Introduction

When dealing with the accounts of sole traders and partnerships it is highly likely that they will be registered for sales tax (called VAT in the UK) unless they are a very small sole trader. Therefore at this stage it is important to consider the accounting for VAT and the rules that apply.

The payroll function and the accounting entries required for the wages and salaries cost and appropriate payroll deductions are also reviewed within this chapter.

ASSESSMENT CRITERIA
Describe the purpose and use of books of prime entry and ledger accounting (1.3)

CONTENTS

1 The operation of VAT (sales tax)
2 VAT and discounts
3 Payroll

1 The operation of VAT (sales tax)

1.1 Introduction

This chapter will begin with just a brief reminder of how the VAT (sales tax) system operates.

1.2 What is VAT (sales tax)?

VAT is:

- an indirect tax,

- charged on most goods and services supplied within the UK,

- is borne by the final consumer, and

- collected by businesses on behalf of HM Revenue and Customs.

VAT is an indirect tax because it is paid indirectly when you buy most goods and services, rather than being collected directly from the taxpayer as a proportion of their income or gains.

VAT is charged by **taxable persons** when they make **taxable supplies** in the course of their business. VAT is not generally charged on non business transactions.

1.3 Taxable persons

 Definition – Taxable person

Taxable persons are businesses which are (or should be) registered for VAT (sales tax).

1.4 Registration and non-registration for VAT (sales tax)

When a business reaches a set annual turnover level, then it must register for VAT (sales tax). If turnover is below this limit, the business can, if it wishes, register voluntarily. If a business is registered it must:

- charge VAT on its sales or services to its customers

- recover the VAT charged on its purchases and expenses rather than having to bear these costs as part of the business.

In such cases, as the VAT charged and incurred is neither revenue nor expense, the revenues and costs of the business are entered in books at their net of VAT value, and the VAT is entered in the VAT account.

If the business is not registered for VAT then the cost of purchases and expenses must include the VAT as these amounts are said to be irrecoverable. Thus, the costs of the business are entered in the books at their gross (VAT inclusive value) and there is no VAT account.

A person can be an individual or a legal person such as a company.

1.5 Taxable supplies

Taxable supplies or outputs, are most sales made by a taxable person. Taxable supplies can also include gifts and goods taken from the business for personal use.

1.6 Output VAT

 Definition – Output VAT

The VAT charged on sales or taxable supplies is called **output VAT**.

1.7 Input VAT

When a business buys goods or pays expenses (inputs), then it will also be paying VAT on those purchases or expenses.

 Definition – Input VAT

VAT paid by a business on purchases or expenses is called **input VAT**.

Businesses are allowed to reclaim their input tax. They do this by deducting the input tax they have paid from the output tax which they owe, and paying over the net amount only. If the input tax exceeds the output tax, then the balance is recoverable from HMRC.

1.8 Rates of VAT

In the UK, VAT is currently charged at two main rates, the standard rate of 20% and the zero rate 0%. The zero rate of VAT applies to items such as food, drink, books, newspapers, children's clothes and most transport.

1.9 Standard rated activities

Any taxable supply which is not charged at the zero or reduced rates is charged at the standard rate.

This is calculated by taking the VAT exclusive amount and multiplying by 20%.

If you are given the VAT inclusive rate then calculate the VAT amount by **20/120.**

The following VAT structure can also be used to calculate VAT, VAT inclusive or VAT exclusive figures.

	%
VAT inclusive	120
VAT	20
VAT exclusive	100

·Ọ· Example 1

Suppose that a business makes sales on credit of £1,000 and purchases on credit of £400 (both amounts exclusive of any VAT). How would these be accounted for in the ledger accounts?

Solution

The sales and purchases must be shown net and the VAT entered in the VAT account. As the sales and purchases were on credit the full double entry would be as follows:

Dr	Receivables account	£1,200
Cr	Sales account	£1,000
Cr	VAT control account	£200

Dr	Purchases account	£400
Dr	VAT control account	£80
Cr	Payables account	£480

Sales account

	£		£
		Receivables	1,000

Receivables account

	£		£
Sales and VAT	1,200		

Purchases account

	£		£
Payables	400		

Payables account

	£		£
		Purchases	480

VAT control account

	£		£
Payables	80	Receivables	200
Balance c/d	120		
	────		────
	200		200
	────		────
		Balance b/d	120

The amount due to HM Revenue and Customs is the balance on the VAT account, £120. We know it is due to HM Revenue Customs as it is brought down on the credit side of the VAT control account – representing a liability.

If a business is not registered for VAT then it will not charge VAT on its sales, and its expenses must be recorded at the gross amount (inclusive of VAT).

If a business is registered for VAT then it will charge VAT on its sales, although they will be recorded as sales at their net amount, and its expenses will also be recorded at the net amount. The output and input VAT is recorded in the VAT account and the difference paid over to HM Revenue and Customs.

1.10 Zero-rated activities

If a business is registered for VAT and sells zero-rated products or services then it charges no VAT on the sales but can still reclaim the input VAT on its purchases and expenses. Such a business will normally be owed VAT by HM Revenue and Customs each quarter.

Example 2

Suppose that a business makes sales on credit of £1,000 plus VAT and purchases on credit of £400 plus VAT. How would these be accounted for if the rate of VAT on the sales was zero, whereas the purchases were standard rated?

Solution

Dr	Receivables	£1,000
Cr	Sales	£1,000
Dr	Purchases	£400
Dr	VAT (400 × 20%)	£80
Cr	Payables	£480

This would leave a debit balance on the VAT control account which is the amount that can be claimed back from HM Revenue and Customs by the business. A debit balance on the VAT control account represents a receivable i.e. a refund is due from HM Revenue and Customs.

1.11 Exempt activities

Certain supplies are exempt from VAT such as financial and postal services.

If a business sells such services then not only is no VAT charged on the sales of the business but also no input VAT can be reclaimed on purchases and expenses.

 Example 3

Suppose that a business makes sales on credit of £1,000 plus VAT and purchases on credit of £400 plus VAT. How would these be accounted for if the sales are exempt activities, whereas the purchases were standard-rated?

Solution

Dr	Receivables	£1,000
Cr	Sales	£1,000
Dr	Purchases	£480
Cr	Payables	£480

There is no VAT on sales due to HM Revenue and Customs and the business cannot claim the £80 from HM Revenue and Customs. However, the seller of the purchases should pay the £80 of VAT over to HM Revenue and Customs.

Test your understanding 1

A business that is registered for VAT makes credit sales of £110,000 in the period and credit purchases of £75,000. Each of these figures is net of VAT at the standard rate of 20%.

Show how these transactions should be entered into the ledger accounts and state how much VAT is due to HM Revenue and Customs.

1.12 Differences between zero rated and exempt supplies

You must be careful to distinguish between traders making zero rated and exempt supplies.

	Exempt	Zero rated
Can register for VAT?	No	Yes
Charge output VAT to customers?	No	Yes at 0%
Can recover input tax?	No	Yes

 Test your understanding 2

Robbie's business bank account shows administrative expenses of £27,216 which is inclusive of VAT at the standard rate 20%.

Calculate the administrative expenses to be included in the trial balance.

Calculate the VAT figure on administrative expenses for inclusion in the VAT control account.

Update the VAT control account below and find the closing balance figure for VAT.

VAT control account

	£		£
VAT on purchases	35,000	Balance b/d	5,000
Paid to HMRC	5,000	VAT on sales	26,250
	———		———
	———		———

2 VAT and discounts

2.1 Discounts

A discount is a reduction to the price of the sales of goods or services. There are different types of discounts that may be offered for different reasons. Before we see how discounts impact the calculation of VAT we will review the different types of discounts.

Trade discount

Bulk discount

Prompt payment discount

2.2 Trade discounts

 Definition – Trade discount

A trade discount is a definite amount that is deducted from the list price of the goods for the supplies to some customers, with the intention of encouraging and rewarding customer loyalty.

The actual calculation of the trade discount on the face of the invoice should be checked and it should be agreed that the correct percentage of trade discount has been deducted. The deduction of a trade discount will appear on the invoice.

2.3 Bulk discounts

 Definition – Bulk discount

A bulk discount is similar to a trade discount in that it is deducted from the list price of the goods and disclosed on the invoice. However, a bulk discount is given by a supplier for sales orders above a certain quantity.

A bulk discount must be checked to the agreement between customer and supplier, to ensure that the correct discount has been deducted. The deduction of a bulk discount will appear on the invoice.

2.4 Prompt payment discount

 Definition – Prompt payment discount

Prompt payment discounts (also known as settlement or cash discounts) are offered to customers in order to encourage early payment of invoices.

The details of the prompt payment discount will normally be shown at the bottom of the sales invoice and it is up to the customer to decide whether to pay the invoice early enough to benefit from the prompt payment discount or whether to delay payment and ignore the prompt payment discount. No deduction will occur for a prompt payment discount on the invoice, it will just be offered to the customer.

The agreement between the customer and supplier should be checked to confirm that the correct percentage of prompt payment discount according to the terms has been offered.

A trade discount or a bulk discount is a definite reduction in price from the list price whereas a prompt payment discount is only a reduction in price if the organisation decides to take advantage of it by making early payment.

2.5 VAT calculations and discounts

VAT is calculated after trade and bulk discounts have been deducted from the original list price.

Prompt payment discounts are only offered on an invoice so it does not impact the VAT calculation at the point of the invoice preparation.

If the customer goes on to take advantage of a prompt payment discount offered, the VAT amount is adjusted.

3 Payroll

3.1 Overview of the payroll function

The responsibilities of payroll staff within an organisation include:

- calculating correctly the amount of pay due to each employee,

- ensuring each employee is paid on time with the correct amount,

- ensuring amounts due to external parties such as HM Revenue and Customs are correctly determined and paid on time.

 Definition – Gross pay

Gross pay is the wage or salary due to the employee for the amount of work done in the period.

Once the gross pay for each employee has been determined then a number of deductions from this amount will be made to arrive at the net pay for the employee.

 Definition – Net pay

Net pay is the amount that the employee will actually receive after appropriate deductions have been made.

Some deductions are compulsory or statutory:

- Income tax in the form of PAYE

 Definition – PAYE

The PAYE scheme is a national scheme whereby employers withhold tax and other deductions from their employees' wages and salaries when they are paid. The deductions are then paid over monthly to HM Revenue and Customs by the employer.

- National Insurance Contributions (NIC) which can also be referred to as social security payments

Definition – National Insurance

National Insurance is a state scheme run by HM Revenue and Customs which pays certain benefits including; retirement pensions, widow's allowances and pensions, jobseeker's allowance, incapacity benefit and maternity allowance. The scheme is funded by people who are currently in employment and have earnings above a certain level.

Other deductions are at the choice of the employer or employee and are therefore non-statutory:

- Save as you earn
- Give as you earn
- Pension contributions

Once the net pay has been determined then each employee must be paid the correct amount, by the most appropriate method at the correct time.

Employers deduct income tax and NIC from each employee's wages or salaries and the employer must also pay its own NIC contribution for each employee. This is done by making payment to HM Revenue and Customs on a regular basis and this is therefore another responsibility of the payroll function.

The payroll staff must ensure that the calculations are made with total accuracy. Not only is the amount that each individual will be paid dependent upon these calculations but there is a statutory duty to make the correct deductions from gross pay and to pay these over to HM Revenue and Customs.

Payroll staff deal with confidential and sensitive information about individuals such as the rate of pay for an individual. It is of the utmost importance that such details are kept confidential and are not made public nor allowed to be accessed by unauthorised personnel.

3.2 Ledger accounts for wages and salaries

The ledger accounts used to record wages and salaries are:

The **wages and salaries control account** which acts as a control over the entries in the accounts. All transactions for payroll pass through this account. The control account should have a nil balance when all entries have been dealt with.

The **wages expense account** which shows the full cost of employing the staff – the employees' gross pay, the employer's National Insurance Contributions and the employer's pension and voluntary contributions (if applicable).

The **HMRC liability account** which shows the amount to be paid to HM Revenue and Customs for income tax (PAYE) and National Insurance Contributions.

The **pension liability account** which records amounts payable to external pension funds – may include both employee and employer contributions.

Note that in the event of there being any other voluntary deductions such as trade union fees there would also be a payable account to reflect this.

3.3 Accounting entries for wages and salaries

Payroll transactions are recorded by journal entries which traces the accounting entry from the payroll record to the journal book to being entered into the general ledger.

The accounting entries for wages and salaries are as follows:

1   Dr Wages expense account

      Cr Wages and salaries control account

      with the total expenses relating to the business (gross pay plus employer's NIC).

2   Dr Wages and salaries control account

      Cr Bank account

      with the net wages paid to the employees.

3   Dr Wages and salaries control account

      Cr HMRC liability

      with those deductions made from the employees which are payable to the HM Revenue and Customs.

If applicable it may also be necessary to record a payable to the pension fund and any other voluntary deductions that are made.

> 4   Dr Wages and salaries control account
>
> Cr Pension/Other voluntary deduction liability
>
> with those deductions made from the employees which are payable to the pension fund or other voluntary deduction.

Example 4

The wages and salaries information for an organisation for a week is given as follows:

	£
Gross wages	40,000
PAYE deducted	(8,400)
NIC deducted	(6,600)
Net pay	25,000
Employer's NIC	8,800

Write up the relevant ledger accounts in the general ledger to reflect this.

Solution

Wages and salaries control account

		£			£
2	Bank account	25,000	1	Wages expense account	48,800
3	HMRC Liability (PAYE)	8,400			
3	HMRC Liability (ees NIC)	6,600			
3	HMRC Liability (ers NIC)	8,800			
		48,800			48,800

Wages expense account

		£			£
1	Wages and salaries control	48,800			
				Bal c/d	48,800
		48,800			48,800

HMRC Liability

	£			£
		3	Wages and salaries control	8,400
		3	Wages and salaries control	6,600
Bal c/d	23,800	3	Wages and salaries control	8,800
	———			———
	23,800			23,800
	———			———
			Bal b/d	23,800

(a)   The wages and salaries control account controls the total gross wages plus the employer's NIC and the amounts paid to the employees, and other organisations (e.g. HM Revenue and Customs for PAYE and NIC). The total gross pay is taken from the company payroll as are the deductions. Assuming that the payroll schedule reconciles and no errors are made when posting the payroll totals to the account, the account should have a nil balance.

(b)   The wages expense account shows the total cost to the employer of employing the workforce (£48,800). This is the gross wages cost plus the employer's own NIC cost.

(c)   The HMRC Liability account shows the amount due to be paid over to HMRC, i.e. PAYE, employee's NIC plus the employer's NIC.

🖉 Test your understanding 3

Given below is a summary of an organisation's payroll details for a week.

	£
Gross wages	54,380
PAYE	11,760
Employee's NIC	8,930
Employer's NIC	12,470

You are required to prepare the journals to enter the figures in the general ledger accounts and to state the balance on the control account, once the net amount has been paid to the employees.

Test your understanding 4

Rena earns £39,000 per annum. Her deductions for the month are:

	£
PAYE	560
Employee's NIC	285
Employer's pension contributions	120
Employee contribution to pension	110
Employer's NIC	320

Based on the information given, write up the wages expense, wages control, HMRC liability and pension liability accounts.

4 Summary

For this unit in most cases you will be dealing with VAT registered businesses and therefore you will need to be able to account for VAT and deal with the amount of VAT that is due either to or from HM Revenue and Customs.

In particular you must understand what is meant by the balance on the VAT control account in the trial balance.

We have also reviewed the payroll function and what accounting entries are required.

Test your understanding answers

Test your understanding 1

Sales account

	£		£
		SLCA	110,000

Sales ledger control account

	£		£
Sales + VAT (110,000 + 22,000)	132,000		

Purchases account

	£		£
PLCA	75,000		

VAT control account

	£		£
PLCA (75,000 × 20/100)	15,000	SLCA (110,000 × 20/100)	22,000
Balance c/d	7,000		
	22,000		22,000
		Balance b/d	7,000

Purchases ledger control account

	£		£
		Purchases + VAT (75,000 + 15,000)	90,000

The amount due to HM Revenue and Customs is the balance on the VAT control account, £7,000.

Test your understanding 2

1   The amount that should be included in the trial balance is the net
     amount. As £27,216 is the VAT inclusive amount, the net is
     calculated as follows:

     £27,216 × 100/120 = £22,680 (or £27,216/1.2)

2   The VAT can be calculated using the gross figure £27,216 ×
     20/120 = £4,536

3   The VAT control would be completed as follows:

VAT control account

	£		£
VAT on purchases	35,000	Balance b/d	5,000
Paid to HMRC	5,000	VAT on sales	26,250
VAT on expenses	4,536	**Balance c/d**	**13,286**
	——		——
	44,536		44,536
	——		——
Balance b/d	**13,286**		

A debit balance represents a refund due from HMRC.

 Test your understanding 3

1   Dr Wages expense account

     Cr Wages and salaries control account

With the total expense of £66,850

2   Dr Wages and salaries control account

     Cr HMRC Liability account

with the PAYE of £11,760, and with the employee's NIC of £8,930 and

with the employer's NIC of £12,470

Once the net amount to be paid to the employee has been posted by
debiting the wages and salaries control account and crediting the bank
account with £33,690 the balance on the control account will be nil.

Test your understanding 4

Solution

Wages and salaries control account

	£		£
Bank account	2,295	Wages expense account	3,690
HMRC Liability (PAYE + both NIC)	1,165		
Pension	230		
	3,690		3,690

Wages expense account

	£		£
Wages and salaries control (Gross + Er's NIC + Er's pension)	3,690		
		Bal c/d	3,690
	3,690		3,690

HMRC liability

	£		£
		Wages and salaries control	1,165
Bal c/d	1,165		
	1,165		1,165

Pension liability

	£		£
		Wages and salaries control	230
Bal c/d	230		
	230		230

Capital and revenue expenditure

3

Introduction

A large proportion of the Advanced Bookkeeping syllabus is accounting for non-current assets. The Advanced Bookkeeping assessment covers all areas of accounting for non-current assets including acquisition, depreciation and disposal.

In this chapter we will start to look at the details of authorising and accounting for capital expenditure.

ASSESSMENT CRITERIA	CONTENTS
Demonstrate the importance of prior authority for capital expenditure (2.1)	1 Capital and revenue expenditure
Identify capital expenditure (2.2)	2 Recording the purchase of non-current assets
Differentiate between funding methods for acquisition of non-current assets (2.3)	3 Types of non-current assets
Record acquisitions of non-current assets (2.4)	4 Non-current asset register

1 Capital and revenue expenditure

1.1 Introduction

In the statement of financial position, assets are split between non-current assets and current assets.

1.2 Non-current assets

 Definition – Non-current asset

The non-current assets of a business are the assets that were purchased with the intention of long term-use within the business.

Examples of non-current assets include buildings, machinery, motor vehicles, office fixtures and fittings and computer equipment.

1.3 Capital expenditure

 Definition – Capital expenditure

Capital expenditure is expenditure on the purchase or improvement of non-current assets.

The purchase of non-current assets is known as capital expenditure. This means that the cost of the non-current asset is initially taken to the statement of financial position rather than the statement of profit or loss. We will see in a later chapter how this cost is then charged to the statement of profit or loss over the life of the non-current asset by the process of depreciation.

1.4 Revenue expenditure

 Definition – Revenue expenditure

Revenue expenditure is all other expenditure incurred by the business other than capital expenditure.

When determining whether a purchase should be treated as capital or revenue expenditure it is important to consider how significant the cost is i.e. materiality. For example, an item of stationery such as a stapler may be used for a long time within a business but the cost is rather insignificant.

Revenue expenditure is charged as an expense to the statement of profit or loss in the period that it is incurred.

Capital expenditure is shown as a non-current asset in the statement of financial position.

1.5   Authorising capital expenditure

There are different factors that need to be considered with capital expenditure:

Non-current assets can be expensive – Many types of non-current assets are relatively expensive. Most non-current assets will be used to generate income for the business for several years into the future. Therefore they are important purchases.

Funding options – Timing may also be critical. It may be necessary to arrange a bank overdraft or a loan, or alternatively capital expenditure may have to be delayed in order to avoid a bank overdraft. Financing options are considered in section 2.9.

Process for authorisation – For these reasons, most organisations have procedures whereby capital expenditure must be authorised by an appropriate person such as a director.

The method of recording the authorisation is also likely to vary according to the nature and size of the organisation, and according to the type of non-current asset expenditure it normally undertakes. In a small business, there may be no formal record other than a signature on a cheque.

In a large company, the directors may record their approval of significant expenditure in the minutes of a board meeting. Other possibilities include the use of requisition forms and signing of the invoice.

In most organisations, disposals of non-current assets must also be authorised in writing.

Where standard forms are used, these will vary from organisation to organisation, but the details for acquisition of an asset are likely to include:

- date
- description of asset
- reason for purchase
- supplier

- cost/quotation
- details of quotation (if applicable)
- details of lease agreement (if applicable)
- authorisation
- method of financing.

Levels of authorisation – In small organisations, most non-current asset purchases are likely to be authorised by the owner of the business. In large organisations, there is normally a system whereby several people have the authority to approve capital expenditure up to a certain limit which depends on the person's level of seniority. The number of signatures required will vary according to the organisation's procedures.

 Test your understanding 1

When authorising the purchase of a new machine, choose the most suitable policy.

New machinery purchases should be authorised by:

(a) The office assistant

(b) The accounting technician

(c) The machine operator

(d) A partner of the business

2 Recording the purchase of non-current assets

2.1 Introduction

We have seen that the cost of a non-current asset will appear in the statement of financial position as capitalised expenditure. Therefore it is important that the correct figure for cost is included in the correct ledger account.

IAS 16 – Property, Plant & Equipment

This standard sets out the accounting treatment for property, plant and equipment. It is important to know what can be included in the cost of a non-current asset and what cannot.

Key features of IAS 16 include the definition of terms that you will encounter throughout your studies of non-current assets including depreciation.

2.2 Cost

The cost figure that will be used to record the non-current asset is the full purchase price of the asset. Care should be taken when considering the cost of some assets, in particular motor cars, as the invoice may show that the total amount paid includes some revenue expenditure, for example petrol and road fund licences. These elements of revenue expenditure must be written off to the statement of profit or loss and only the capital expenditure included as the cost of the non-current asset.

 Definition – Cost

Cost should include the cost of the asset and the cost of getting the asset to its current location and into working condition. Therefore cost is:

Purchase price + additional costs*

*Additional costs may include delivery costs, legal and professional fees, installation costs (site preparation and construction) and test runs.

2.3 Ledger accounts

If a non-current asset is paid for by cheque then the double entry is:

Dr   **Non-current asset account**
Cr   **Bank account**

If the non-current asset was bought on credit the double entry is:

Dr   **Non-current asset account**
Cr   **Payables/loan account**

In practice most organisations will have different non-current asset accounts for the different types of non-current assets, for example:

- land and buildings account
- plant and machinery account
- motor vehicles account
- office fixtures and fittings account
- computer equipment account.

 Test your understanding 2

When a company purchases disks for the new computer, the amount of the purchase is debited to computer equipment (cost) account.

(a)   Is this treatment correct?

(b)   If so, why; if not, why not?

 Test your understanding 3

Stapling machine

When a company purchases a new stapler so that accounts clerks can staple together relevant pieces of paper, the amount of the purchase is debited to the fittings and equipment (cost) account.

(a)   Is this treatment correct?

(b)   If so, why; if not; why not?

 Test your understanding 4

Office equipment

A company bought a small item of computer software costing £32.50. This had been treated as office equipment. Do you agree with this treatment?

Give brief reasons.

Test your understanding 5

Engine

If an airline replaces one of its plane's engines, which are depreciated at a different rate to the rest of the plane's components, at a cost of £1,800,000 would this represent capital or revenue expenditure? Give brief reasons.

2.4 Purchase of non-current assets and VAT

When most non-current assets are purchased VAT will be added and this can normally be recovered from HMRC as input VAT. Therefore the cost of the non-current asset is the amount net of VAT.

 Test your understanding 6

A piece of machinery has been purchased on credit from a supplier for £4,200 plus VAT.

How will this purchase be recorded?

	Account name	Amount £
Dr	Machinery/Building/Fixtures	4,200/5,040
Dr	Machinery/VAT/Payables	5,040/840
Cr	Bank /Payables/VAT	4,200/5,040

Circle the correct account name and the amount.

2.5 Purchase of cars and VAT

As a general rule, when new cars are purchased it is not possible for the VAT to be recovered, unless it is an excepted car. Therefore the cost to be capitalised for the car must include the VAT.

An excepted car is one used exclusively for business use and is not available for any private use.

Example 1

Raymond has just purchased a new car for his business by cheque and an extract from the invoice shows the following:

	£
Cost of car	18,000
Road fund licence	155
	18,155
VAT on cost of car (£18,000 × 20%)	3,600
Total cost	21,755

Record this cost in the ledger accounts of the business.

Motor cars account

	£		£
Bank (18,000 + 3,600)	21,600		

Motor expenses account

	£		£
Bank	155		

Bank account

	£		£
		Motor vehicle + expenses	21,755

Note that only the motor cars account balance would appear in the statement of financial position, i.e. be capitalised, while the motor expenses account balance would appear in the statement of profit or loss as an expense for the period.

2.6 Transfer journal

Non-current asset acquisitions do not normally take place frequently in organisations and many organisations will tend to record the acquisition in the transfer journal.

 Definition – Transfer journal

The transfer journal is a primary record which is used for transactions that do not appear in the other primary records of the business.

The transfer journal will tend to take the form of an instruction to the bookkeeper as to which accounts to debit and credit and what this transaction is for.

An example of a transfer journal for the purchase of a non-current asset is given below.

Journal entry			No: 02714
Date	20 May 20X1		
Prepared by	C Jones		
Authorised by	F Peters		
Account	**Code**	**Debit** £	**Credit** £
Computers: Cost	0120	5,000	
VAT	0138	1,000	
Bank	0163		6,000
Totals		6,000	6,000

A transfer journal is used for entries to the ledger accounts that do not come from any other primary records.

Test your understanding 7

Below is an invoice for the purchase of a motor car purchased on the 1 June 20X1. The payment was made by cheque.

The business's year end is 31 December 20X1

	£
Cost of car	20,000
Road fund licence	165
	20,165
VAT on cost of car (£20,000 × 20%)	4,000
	24,165

Note that in the assessment you may be given different forms to fill in for journal entries, and may be told to ignore any reference columns for the entry. Complete the journal entries to record the purchase of the asset.

Ref	Account name	Dr (£)	Cr (£)

2.7 Non-current assets produced internally

In some instances a business may make its own non-current assets. For example a construction company may construct a new head office for the organisation.

Where non-current assets are produced internally then the amount that should be capitalised as the cost is the production cost of the asset.

 Definition – Production cost

Production cost is the direct cost of production (materials, labour and expenses) plus an appropriate amount of the normal production overheads relating to production of this asset.

2.8   Capitalising subsequent expenditure

It is frequently the case that there will be further expenditure on a non-current asset during its life in the business. In most cases this will be classed as revenue expenditure and will therefore be charged to the statement of profit or loss. However in some cases the expenditure may be so major that it should also be capitalised as an addition to the cost of the non-current asset.

IAS 16 Property, Plant and Equipment states that subsequent expenditure should only be capitalised in three circumstances:

*   where it enhances the value of the asset
*   where a major component of the asset is replaced or restored
*   where it is a major inspection or overhaul of the asset.

2.9   Financing non-current asset acquisitions

Non-current assets generally cost a lot of money and are purchased with the intention that they be used over a period of years. For most businesses the full purchase cost cannot be funded from cash available in the business, and so other financing methods must be found, including the following:

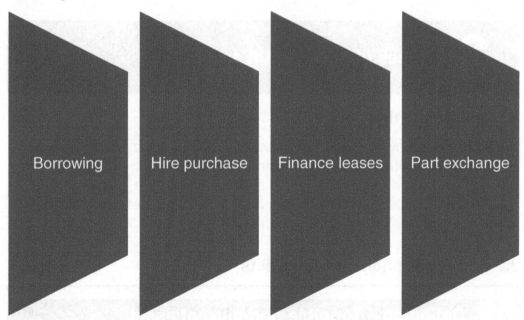

Borrowing   Hire purchase   Finance leases   Part exchange

Borrowing – a bank or other lender lends the business cash to pay for the asset, at a negotiated interest rate. Often the loan will be secured on the asset, so that it can be sold directly for the benefit of the bank or lender in the event of non-payment or liquidation.

Hire purchase – the business makes regular payments to the finance company (comprising capital amounts plus interest) but the asset remains the finance company's property until the last regular payment is made, when the business can elect to take over the asset's full ownership. This method can be used for machinery, vehicles and computer equipment.

Finance leases – with a leasing agreement, an asset owned by a finance company (the lessor) is leased to a business (the lessee) which has use of the asset. The lessee makes regular rental payments to the lessor over a period of time. The lease agreement duration tends to be for the majority of its economic life. Finance leases are commonly chosen for machinery, vehicles and computer equipment. Normally, legal ownership does not transfer to the lessee at the end of the lease agreement.

Part exchange – part of the purchase price of the asset is satisfied by transferring ownership of another asset to the seller. This is frequently seen in the case of motor vehicles, and represents a disposal of the old asset and a purchase of the new asset at the same time. (This will be covered in chapter 5.)

You may be asked to assess the suitability of a choice of funding methods. To do so you would assess factors such as the availability of finance, the overall cost of each finance method, the cash flow requirements to meet repayments and any required security for the debt.

3 Types of non-current assets

3.1 Introduction

We have seen how the non-current assets of a business will be classified between the various types, e.g. buildings, plant and machinery, etc. However there is a further distinction in the classification of non-current assets that must be considered. This is the distinction between tangible non-current assets and intangible non-current assets.

3.2 Tangible non-current assets

 Definition – Tangible non-current asset

Tangible non-current assets are assets which have a tangible, physical form.

Tangible non-current assets therefore are all of the types of assets that we have been considering so far such as machinery, cars, computers, etc.

KAPLAN PUBLISHING

3.3 Intangible non-current assets

 Definition – Intangible non-current asset

Intangible non-current assets are assets for long-term use in the business that have no physical form e.g. patents, licences and goodwill.

Definition – Goodwill

Goodwill is the asset arising from the fact that a going concern business is worth more in total than the total value of its tangible net assets. Goodwill can arise from many different factors including good reputation, good location, quality products and quality after sales service.

4 Non-current asset register

4.1 Introduction

The non-current assets of a business will tend to be expensive items that the organisation will wish to have good control over. In particular the organisation will wish to keep control over which assets are kept where and check on a regular basis that they are still there.

Therefore most organisations that own a significant number of non-current assets will tend to maintain a non-current asset register as well as the ledger accounts that record the purchase of the non-current assets. The non-current asset register forms a record from which control can be maintained through physical verifications and reconciliations with the ledger accounts.

4.2 Layout of a non-current asset register

The purpose of a non-current asset register is to record all relevant details of all of the non-current assets of the organisation. The format of the register will depend on the organisation, but the information to be recorded for each non-current asset of the business will probably include the following:

- asset description
- asset identification code/barcode

- asset location/member of staff the asset has been issued to
- date of purchase
- purchase price
- supplier name and address
- invoice number
- any additional enhancement expenditure
- depreciation method
- estimated useful life
- estimated residual value
- accumulated depreciation to date
- carrying amount
- disposal details.

A typical format for a non-current asset register is shown below.

4.3 Example of a non-current asset register

Date of purchase	Invoice number	Serial number	Item	Cost	Accum'd depreciation b/f at 1.1.X8	Date of disposal	Dep'n charge in 20X8	Accum'd depreciation c/f	Disposal proceeds	Loss/ gain on disposal
				£	£		£	£	£	£
3.2.X5	345	3488	Chair	340						
6.4.X6	466	–	Bookcase	258						
10.7.X7	587	278	Chair	160						
				——						
				758						
				——						

There may also be a further column or detail which shows exactly where the particular asset is located within the business. This will facilitate checks that should be regularly carried out to ensure all of the assets the business owns are still on the premises.

KAPLAN PUBLISHING

Test your understanding 8

Record the cost of the motor car in the non-current asset register below for the previous Activity 7.

Date of purchase	Invoice number	Serial number	Item	Cost	Accum'd depreciation b/f at 1.1.X8	Date of disposal	Depreciation charge in 20X8	Accum'd depreciation c/f	Disposal proceeds	Loss/gain on disposal
				£	£		£	£	£	£
			—							
			—							

 Test your understanding 9

1   Purchase of a motor van is classified as **revenue / capital** expenditure?

2   Decorating the office is an example of **revenue / capital** expenditure.

3   Other than its actual purchase price, what additional costs can be capitalised as part of the cost of the non-current asset?

4   What are the three occasions where subsequent expenditure on a non-current asset can be capitalised according to IAS 16?

5   Goodwill is an example of **a tangible asset / a current asset / an intangible asset**?

5   Summary

In this chapter we have considered the acquisition of non-current assets. The acquisition of a non-current asset must be properly authorised and the most appropriate method of funding used. The correct cost figure must be used when capitalising the non-current asset and care should be taken with VAT and the exclusion of any revenue expenditure in the total cost. The details of the acquisition of the asset should also be included in the non-current asset register.

Test your understanding answers

 ### Test your understanding 1

The answer is D

 ### Test your understanding 2

(a)   No.

(b)   Although, by definition, the computer disks may be considered as non-current assets, their treatment would come within the remit of the concept of materiality and would probably be treated as office expenses – revenue expenditure.

 ### Test your understanding 3

Stapling machine

(a)   No.

(b)   Although, by definition, since the stapler will last a few years, it might seem to be a non-current asset, its treatment would come within the remit of the concept of materiality and would probably be treated as office expenses.

 ### Test your understanding 4

Office equipment

The item will have value in future years and could therefore be regarded as a non-current asset. However, the stronger argument is that this is not justified by the relatively small amount involved and the concept of materiality would suggest treatment as an expense of the year.

Test your understanding 5

Engine

This would typically represent capital expenditure. As the engine is being depreciated separately from the rest of the plane it is effectively an asset in its own right. Therefore the replacement of the separate component is like the purchase of a new asset.

If, on the other hand, the engine was depreciated as part of the plane as a whole it is likely that the replacement cost would simply be treated as a repair/refurbishment cost and would be accounted for as an expense.

 Test your understanding 6

	Account name	Amount £
Dr	Machinery	4,200
Dr	VAT	840
Cr	Payables	5,040

 Test your understanding 7

Ref	Account name	Dr (£)	Cr (£)
	Motor car	24,000	
	Motor expenses	165	
	Bank		24,165

Test your understanding 8

Date of purchase	Invoice number	Serial number	Item	Cost	Accum'd depreciation b/f at 1.1.X8	Date of disposal	Depreciation charge in 20X8	Accum'd depreciation c/f	Disposal proceeds	Loss/gain on disposal
				£	£		£	£	£	£
1 Jun X1			Motor car	24,000						
				———						
				24,000						
				———						

Test your understanding 9

1 Capital expenditure.

2 Revenue expenditure.

3 The full purchase price of the asset plus the cost of getting the asset to its location and into working condition.

4 Where the expenditure enhances the economic benefits of the asset.

Where the expenditure is on a major component which is being replaced or restored.

Where the expenditure is on a major inspection or overhaul of the asset.

5 Intangible asset.

Depreciation

Introduction

Depreciation features prominently within the assessment of Advanced Bookkeeping. This chapter reviews how to prepare and record depreciation calculations.

You need to be able to:

- understand the purpose of depreciation

- choose and use appropriate methods and rates of depreciation, taking into account the expected pattern of usage of the asset and the estimated useful life of the acquisition

- record depreciation in the non-current assets register and the general ledger using the following accounts: depreciation charges, non-current asset and non-current asset accumulated depreciation.

ASSESSMENT CRITERIA	CONTENTS
Calculate depreciation (3.1) Record depreciation (3.2)	1 The purpose of depreciation 2 Calculating depreciation 3 Accounting for depreciation 4 Assets acquired during an accounting period 5 Depreciation in the non-current asset register

1 The purpose of depreciation

1.1 Introduction

We have already seen that non-current assets are capitalised in the accounting records which means that they are treated as capital expenditure and their cost is initially recorded in the statement of financial position and not charged to the statement of profit or loss. However this is not the end of the story and this cost figure must eventually go through the statement of profit or loss by means of the annual depreciation charge.

1.2 Accruals concept

The accruals concept states that the costs incurred in a period should be matched with the income produced in the same period. When a non-current asset is used it is contributing to the production of the income of the business. In accordance with the accruals concept some of the cost of the non-current asset should be charged to the statement of profit or loss each year that the asset is used.

1.3 What is depreciation?

Definition – Depreciation

Depreciation is the measure of the cost of the economic benefits of the tangible non-current assets that have been consumed during the period.

Consumption includes the wearing out, using up or other reduction in the useful economic life of a tangible non-current asset whether arising from use, effluxion of time or obsolescence through either changes in technology or demand for the goods and services produced by the asset.

(IAS 16 Property, Plant and Equipment.)

This demonstrates the purpose of depreciation is to charge the statement of profit or loss with the amount of the cost of the non-current asset that has been used up during the accounting period.

1.4 How does depreciation work?

The basic principle of depreciation is that a proportion of the cost of the non-current asset is charged to the statement of profit or loss each period and deducted from the cost of the non-current asset in the statement of financial position. Therefore as the non-current asset gets older its value in the statement of financial position reduces and each year the statement of profit or loss is charged with this proportion of the initial cost.

🔍 Definition – Carrying amount

The carrying amount is the cost of the non-current asset less the accumulated depreciation to date.

	£
Cost	X
Less: Accumulated depreciation	(X)
Carrying amount	X

The aim of depreciating non-current assets is to show the cost (capital expenditure) of the asset that has been consumed during the year. It is not to show the true or market value of the asset.

The carrying amount will probably have little relation to the actual market value of the asset at each statement of financial position date. The important aspect of depreciation is that it is a charge to the statement of profit or loss for the amount of the non-current asset consumed during the year.

2 Calculating depreciation

2.1 Introduction

The calculation of depreciation can be done by a variety of methods, although there are three methods that are required by the assessment criteria of Advanced Bookkeeping:

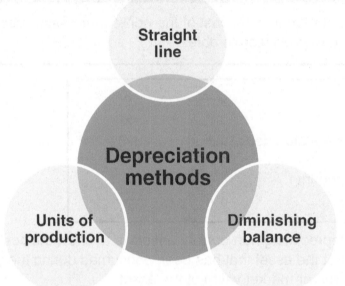

Each of these methods will be reviewed within this chapter. The principles behind each method are relatively the same.

2.2 Factors affecting depreciation

There are three factors that affect the depreciation of a non-current asset:

- the **cost** of the asset (dealt with in Chapter 3 Capital and Revenue Expenditure)

- the length of the **useful economic life** of the asset

- the **estimated residual value** of the asset.

2.3 Useful economic life

 Definition – Useful economic life

The useful economic life of an asset is the estimated life of the asset for the current owner. This can be defined in time (number of years) or in output (activity).

This is the estimated number of years or estimated activity level that the business will be using the asset for and therefore the number of years / output level over which the cost of the asset must be spread via the depreciation charge.

The length of the useful economic life of the asset for the straight line and diminishing balance method is considered to be in terms of time. For the units of production method, the length of the useful economic life is in terms of output i.e. activity level. This will be reviewed in more detail later in the chapter.

One particular point to note here is that land is viewed as having an infinite life and therefore no depreciation charge is required for land. However, any buildings on the land should be depreciated.

2.4 Estimated residual value

Many assets will be sold for a form of scrap value at the end of their useful economic lives.

 Definition – Residual value

The estimated residual value of a non-current asset is the amount that is estimated the asset will be sold for when it is no longer of use to the business.

The aim of depreciation is to write off the cost of the non-current asset less the estimated residual value over the useful economic life of the asset.

 Definition – Depreciable amount

The depreciable amount is the cost of an asset less any residual value. This is the amount that will be depreciated in full by the end of the estimated useful life.

2.5 The straight line method of depreciation

 Definition – Straight line method

The straight line method calculates a consistent amount of depreciation over the life of the asset.

The method of calculating depreciation under this method is:

$$\text{Annual depreciation charge} = \frac{\text{Cost} - \text{estimated residual value}}{\text{Useful economic life}}$$

It should be noted that it is possible to multiply the depreciable amount by a percentage, e.g. instead of dividing by four years you can multiply by 25%; instead of dividing by five years you can multiply by 20%.

Example 1

An asset has been purchased by an organisation for £400,000 and is expected to be used in the organisation for 6 years. At the end of the six-year period it is currently estimated that the asset will be sold for £40,000.

What is the annual depreciation charge using the straight line basis?

Solution

$$\text{Annual depreciation charge} \quad = \quad \frac{400,000 - 40,000}{6}$$

$$= \quad £60,000$$

2.6 The diminishing (reducing) balance method

 Definition – Diminishing balance method

The diminishing balance method of depreciation allows a higher amount of depreciation to be charged in the early years of an asset's life compared to the later years. This reflects the increased levels of usage of such assets in the earlier periods of their lives.

The depreciation is calculated using this method by multiplying the carrying amount of the asset at the start of the year by a fixed percentage.

Annual depreciation charge = Carrying amount × %

Example 2

A non-current asset has a cost of £100,000.

It is to be depreciated using the diminishing balance method at 30% over its useful economic life of four years, after which it will have an estimated residual value of £24,000.

Show the amount of depreciation charged for each of the four years of the asset's life.

Solution

	£
Cost	100,000
Year 1 depreciation 30% × 100,000	(30,000)
Carrying amount at the end of year 1	70,000
Year 2 depreciation 30% × 70,000	(21,000)
Carrying amount at the end of year 2	49,000
Year 3 depreciation 30% × 49,000	(14,700)
Carrying amount at the end of year 3	34,300
Year 4 depreciation 30% × 34,300	(10,290)
Carrying amount at the end of year 4	24,010

 Test your understanding 1

A business buys a motor van for £20,000 and depreciates it at 10% per annum using the diminishing balance method.

Calculate:

- The depreciation charge for the second year of the motor van's use.

- Calculate the carrying amount at the end of the second year.

Solution

£

Cost

Year 1 depreciation

_____

Carrying amount at the end of year 1

Year 2 depreciation

_____

Carrying amount at the end of year 2

_____

2.7 The units of production method

Definition – Units of production method

The units of production method of depreciation is based on the actual usage of the asset. Higher depreciation is charged when there is higher activity and less is charged when there is a lower level of operation. This method is similar to the straight-line method except that the life of the asset is estimated in terms of number of operations or number of machine hours etc.

Time is not important when using the units of production method but activity level is – that is how the useful life is defined. Activity could be defined as units produced, miles driven, litres of liquid pumped or machine hours worked. The depreciation charge will vary each year dependent on how much activity occurs (is consumed) in a year.

The method of calculating depreciation under this method is:

Annual depreciation charge =

$$(\text{Cost} - \text{estimated residual value}) \times \frac{\text{current year's activity}}{\text{expected activity in useful life}}$$

The units of production method is appropriate where the activity level of an asset impacts its physical wear and tear. As no depreciation is charged when an asset remains idle, it would not be appropriate for depreciating assets that suffer a significant decrease in their earning potential with the passage of time for reasons such as technological obsolescence.

Example 3

A non-current asset has a cost of £32,000.

It is to be depreciated using the units of production method based on machine hours. The asset has an estimated useful life of 56,000 machine hours and has an estimated residual value of £4,000.

In year 1, 13,000 machine hours were used. In year 2 6,000 machine hours were used.

Show the amount of depreciation charged for years 1 and 2 of the asset's life.

Solution

Year 1 depreciation

$$(\pounds32,000 - \pounds4,000) \times \frac{13,000}{56,000} = \pounds6,500$$

Year 2 depreciation

$$(\pounds32,000 - \pounds4,000) \times \frac{6,000}{56,000} = \pounds3,000$$

 Test your understanding 2

Oil Ltd installs a crude oil processing plant costing £10 million. It has an estimated capacity to process 40 million barrels of crude oil during its entire life. Production during year 1 is 5 million barrels. Expected residual value of the processing plant is £1 million.

Calculate:

• The depreciation charge for the first year.

Solution

2.8 Choice of method

Whether a business chooses the straight line method of depreciation, the diminishing balance method or the units of production method (or indeed any of the other methods which are outside the scope of this syllabus) is the choice of the management. An assessment of suitability should be made.

The straight line method is the simplest method to use. Often, the diminishing balance method is chosen for assets which do in fact reduce in value more in the early years of their life than the later years. This is often the case with cars and computers and the diminishing balance method is often used for these assets. The units of production method considers output rather than the passing of time.

Once the method of depreciation has been chosen for a particular class of non-current assets then this same method should be used each year in order to satisfy the accounting objective of comparability. The management of a business can change the method of depreciation used for a class of non-current assets but this should only be done if the new method shows a truer picture of the consumption of the cost of the asset than the previous method.

🔍 Test your understanding 3

Give one reason why a business might choose diminishing balance as the method for depreciating its delivery vans?

(a) It is an easy method to apply.

(b) It is the method applied for non-current assets that lose more value in their early years.

(c) It is the method that is most consistent.

3 Accounting for depreciation

3.1 Introduction

Now we have seen how to calculate depreciation we must now learn how to account for it in the ledger accounts within the general ledger.

3.2 Dual effect of depreciation

The two effects of the charge for depreciation each year are:

- there is an expense to the statement of profit or loss and therefore a debit entry to a depreciation charges account

- there is a requirement to create a provision for accumulated depreciation by crediting this account.

Definition – Provision for accumulated depreciation

The provision for accumulated depreciation account (sometimes referred to as accumulated depreciation) is used to reduce the value of the non-current asset in the statement of financial position.

 Example 4

An asset has been purchased by an organisation for £400,000 and is expected to be used in the organisation for six years.

At the end of the six year period it is currently estimated that the residual value will be £40,000.

The asset is to be depreciated on the straight line basis.

Show the entries in the ledger accounts for the first two years of the asset's life and how this asset would appear in the statement of financial position at the end of each of the first two years.

Solution

Step 1

Record the purchase of the asset in the non-current asset account.

Non-current asset account

	£		£
Year 1 Bank	400,000		

Step 2

Record the depreciation expense for Year 1.

$$\text{Depreciation charge} = \frac{£400,000 - £40,000}{6}$$

$$= £60,000 \text{ per year}$$

Dr   Depreciation charges account

Cr   Accumulated depreciation account

Depreciation charges account

	£		£
Year 1	60,000		
Accumulated depreciation			

Accumulated depreciation account

	£		£
		Dep'n charges	60,000

Note the statement of financial position will show the cost of the asset and the accumulated depreciation is then deducted to arrive at the carrying amount of the asset.

Step 3

Show the entries for the year 2 depreciation charge

Depreciation charges account

	£		£
Year 2	60,000		
Accumulated depreciation			

Accumulated depreciation account

	£		£
		Balance b/d	60,000
		Dep'n charges	60,000

Note that the expense account has no opening balance as this was transferred to the statement of profit or loss at the end of year 1.

However the accumulated depreciation account being a statement of financial position account is a continuing account and does have an opening balance being the depreciation charged so far on this asset.

Step 4

Balance off the accumulated depreciation account and show how the non-current asset would appear in the statement of financial position at the end of year 2.

Accumulated depreciation account

	£		£
		Balance b/d	60,000
Balance c/d	120,000	Dep'n charges	60,000
	———		———
	120,000		120,000
	———		———
		Balance b/d	120,000

Statement of financial position extract

	Cost £	Accumulated depreciation £	Carrying amount £
Non-current asset	400,000	120,000	280,000

Q Test your understanding 4

The following task is about recording non-current asset information in the general ledger.

A new asset has been acquired. VAT can be reclaimed on this asset.

- The cost of the asset excluding VAT is £85,000 and this was paid for by cheque.

- The residual value is expected to be £5,000 excluding VAT.

- The asset is to be depreciated using the straight line basis and the assets useful economic life is 5 years.

Make entries to account for:

(a) The purchase of the new asset.

(b) The depreciation on the new asset.

Asset at cost account

£		£
————		————
————		————

Accumulated depreciation

£		£
————		————
————		————

Depreciation charges

£		£
————		————
————		————

🔍 Test your understanding 5

At 31 March 20X3, a business owned a motor vehicle which had a cost of £12,100 and accumulated depreciation of £9,075.

Complete the statement of financial position extract below.

	Cost	Accumulated depreciation	Carrying amount
Motor vehicle			

3.3 Carrying amount

As you have seen from the statement of financial position extract the non-current assets are shown at their carrying amount. As previously stated, the carrying amount is made up of the cost of the asset less the accumulated depreciation on that asset or class of assets.

The carrying amount is purely an accounting value for the non-current asset. It is not an attempt to place a market value or current value on the asset and it in fact often bears little relation to the actual value of the asset.

3.4 Ledger entries for diminishing balance and units of production method

No matter what method of depreciation is used whether it is straight line, diminishing balance or based on units of production, the ledger entries are always the same.

 Example 5

On 1 April 20X2 a machine was purchased for £12,000 with an estimated useful life of 4 years and estimated scrap value of £4,920. The machine is to be depreciated at 20% diminishing balance.

The ledger accounts for the years ended 31 March 20X3, 31 March 20X4 and 31 March 20X5 are to be written up.

Show how the non-current asset would appear in the statement of financial position at each of these dates.

Solution

Step 1

Calculate the depreciation charge.

			£
Cost			12,000
Year-end March 20X3 – depreciation	12,000 × 20%	=	2,400
			9,600
Year-end March 20X4 – depreciation	9,600 × 20%	=	1,920
			7,680
Year-end March 20X5 – depreciation	7,680 × 20%	=	1,536
			6,144

Step 2

Enter each year's figures in the ledger accounts bringing down a balance on the machinery account and accumulated depreciation account but clearing out the entry in the expense account to the statement of profit or loss.

Machinery account

	£		£
April 20X2 Bank	12,000	Mar 20X3 Balance c/d	12,000
April 20X3 Balance b/d	12,000	Mar 20X4 Balance c/d	12,000
April 20X4 Balance b/d	12,000	Mar 20X5 Balance c/d	12,000
April 20X5 Balance b/d	12,000		

Depreciation charges account

	£		£
Mar 20X3 Accumulated dep'n a/c	2,400	Mar 20X3 SPL	2,400
Mar 20X4 Accumulated dep'n a/c	1,920	Mar 20X4 SPL	1,920
Mar 20X5 Accumulated dep'n a/c	1,536	Mar 20X5 SPL	1,536

Machinery: accumulated depreciation account

		£			£
Mar 20X3	Balance c/d	2,400	Mar 20X3	Depreciation charges	2,400
			Apr 20X3	Balance b/d	2,400
Mar 20X4	Balance c/d	4,320	Mar 20X4	Depreciation charges	1,920
		4,320			4,320
			Apr 20X4	Balance b/d	4,320
Mar 20X5	Balance c/d	5,856	Mar 20X5	Depreciation charges	1,536
		5,856			5,856
			Apr 20X5	Balance b/d	5,856

Statement of financial position extract

Non-current assets		Cost £	Accumulated depreciation £	Carrying amount £
At 31 Mar 20X3	Machinery	12,000	2,400	9,600
At 31 Mar 20X4	Machinery	12,000	4,320	7,680
At 31 Mar 20X5	Machinery	12,000	5,856	6,144

Make sure that you remember to carry down the accumulated depreciation at the end of each period as the opening balance at the start of the next period.

 Test your understanding 6

ABC Co owns the following assets as at 31 December 20X6:

	£
Plant and machinery	5,000
Office furniture	800

Depreciation is to be provided as follows:

(a)   plant and machinery, 20% diminishing balance method

(b)   office furniture, 25% on cost per year, straight line method.

The plant and machinery was purchased on 1 January 20X4 and the office furniture on 1 January 20X5.

Required:

Show the ledger accounts for the year ended 31 December 20X6 necessary to record the transactions.

4   Assets acquired during an accounting period

4.1   Introduction

So far in our calculations of the depreciation charge for the year we have ignored precisely when in the year the non-current asset was purchased. Pro rata calculations for the straight line method of depreciation will be required only when the organisational policy stipulates.

There are two main methods of expressing a depreciation policy and both of these will now be considered.

4.2   Calculations on a monthly basis

The policy may state that depreciation is to be charged on a monthly basis. This means that the annual charge will be calculated using the depreciation method given and then pro-rated for the number of months in the year that the asset has been owned.

 Example 6

A piece of machinery is purchased on 1 June 20X1 for £20,000. It has a useful life of 5 years and zero scrap value. The organisation's accounting year ends on 31 December.

What is the depreciation charge for 20X1? Depreciation is charged on a monthly basis using the straight line method.

Solution

Annual charge $= \dfrac{£20,000}{5} = £4,000$

Charge for 20X1: £4,000 × 7/12 (i.e. June to Dec) = £2,333

Test your understanding 7

A business buys a machine for £40,000 on 1 January 20X3 and another one on 1 July 20X3 for £48,000.

Depreciation is charged at 10% per annum on cost, and calculated on a monthly basis.

What is the total depreciation charge for the two machines for the year ended 31 December 20X3?

4.3 Acquisition and disposal policy

The second method of dealing with depreciation in the year of acquisition is to have a depreciation policy as follows:

'A full year's depreciation is charged in the year of acquisition and none in the year of disposal.'

Ensure that you read the instructions in any question carefully as in the exam you will always be given the depreciation policy of the business.

 Test your understanding 8

A business purchased a motor van on 7 August 20X3 at a cost of £12,640.

It is depreciated on a straight-line basis using an expected useful economic life of five years and estimated residual value of zero.

Depreciation is charged with a full year's depreciation in the year of purchase and none in the year of sale.

The business has a year end of 30 November.

Required:

What is the carrying amount of the motor van at 30 November 20X4?

What does this amount represent?

5 Depreciation in the non-current asset register

5.1 Introduction

In the previous chapter we considered how the cost of non-current assets and their acquisition details should be recorded in the non-current asset register.

5.2 Recording depreciation in the non-current asset register

Let us now look at recording depreciation in the non-current asset register.

Example 7

Date of purchase	Invoice number	Serial number	Item	Cost	Accum'd depreciation b/f at 1.1.X8	Date of disposal	Depreciation charge in 20X8	Accum'd deprec-iation c/f	Disposal proceeds	Loss/ gain on disposal
				£	£		£	£	£	£
3.2.X5	345	3488	Chair	340						
6.4.X6	466	–	Bookcase	258						
10.7.X7	587	278	Chair	160						
				———						
				758						
				———						

Using the example from the previous chapter, reproduced above, we have now decided that fixtures and fittings (including office furniture) should be depreciated at 10% per annum using the straight-line method.

A full year's depreciation is charged in the year of purchase and none in the year of disposal.

The current year is the year to 31 December 20X8.

The chair acquired on 10.7.X7 was sold on 12.7.X8. A new table was purchased for £86 on 30.8.X8.

Do not worry at this stage about the disposal proceeds. We will look at disposals in the next chapter.

Solution

Date of purchase	Invoice number	Serial number	Item	Cost	Accum'd depreciation b/f at 1.1.X8	Date of disposal	Depreciation charge in 20X8	Accum'd deprec-iation c/f	Disposal proceeds	Loss/ gain on disposal
				£	£		£	£	£	£
3.2.X5	345	3488	Chair	340	102 (W1)		34	136		
6.4.X6	466	–	Bookcase	258	52 (W2)		26	78		
10.7.X7	587	278	Chair	160	16 (W3)	12.7.X8	– (W4)	–		
30.8.X8	634	1,228	Table	86			9	9		
				———	———		———	———		
				844	170		69	223		
				———	———		———	———		

Workings:

(W1) 3 years' depreciation   –   £340 × 10% × 3 years = £102

(W2) 2 years' depreciation   –   £258 × 10% × 2 years = £52

(W3) 1 year's depreciation   –   £160 × 10%   = £16

(W4) No depreciation in year of sale

Note how the depreciation charge is calculated for each asset except the one disposed of in the year as the accounting policy is to charge no depreciation in the year of sale. If the policy was to charge depreciation even in the year of disposal, then the charge would be calculated and included in the total.

The total accumulated depreciation should agree with the balance carried forward on the accumulated depreciation ledger account in the general ledger.

Test your understanding 9

A business called Stig Trading has asked your advice on improving their accounting system. They would like your advice on how to improve the records of non-current assets.

The business produces fashion clothing. They have the following information on the sewing machines in the business.

Machine number	Cost £
SEW 789367	15,500
ING 401388	25,000
MAC 402765	21,500

(a) Which accounting record would you suggest that the business should keep to record the details of these machines?

(b) Name three additional items that you would suggest to the business that they should keep a record of, regarding the machines?

(c) Name one advantage of recording the machines in the record that you have suggested in part (a).

Test your understanding 10

Mead is a sole trader with a 31 December year end. He purchased a car on 1 January 20X3 at a cost of £12,000. He estimates that its useful life is four years, after which he will trade it in for £2,400. The annual depreciation charge is to be calculated using the straight line method.

Task

Write up the motor car cost and accumulated depreciation accounts and the depreciation charges account for the first three years, bringing down a balance on each account at the end of each year.

 Test your understanding 11

S Telford purchases a machine for £6,000. He estimates that the machine will last eight years and its scrap value then will be £1,000.

Tasks

(1) Prepare the machine cost and accumulated depreciation accounts for the first three years of the machine's life, and show the statement of financial position extract at the end of each of these years charging depreciation on the straight line method.

(2) What would be the carrying amount of the machine at the end of the third year if depreciation was charged at 20% on the diminishing balance method?

Test your understanding 12

Hillton

(a) Hillton started a veggie food manufacturing business on 1 January 20X6. During the first three years of trading he bought machinery as follows:

January	20X6	Chopper	Cost	£4,000
April	20X7	Mincer	Cost	£6,000
June	20X8	Stuffer	Cost	£8,000

Each machine was bought for cash.

Hillton's policy for machinery is to charge depreciation on the straight line basis at 25% per annum. A full year's depreciation is charged in the year of purchase, irrespective of the actual date of purchase.

Required:

For the three years from 1 January 20X6 to 31 December 20X8 prepare the following ledger accounts:

(i) Machinery account

(ii) Accumulated depreciation account (machinery)

(iii) Depreciation charges account (machinery)

Bring down the balance on each account at 31 December each year.

Tip – *Use a table to calculate the depreciation charge for each year.*

(b) Over the same three year period Hillton bought the following motor vehicles for his business:

January 20X6	Metro van	Cost £3,200
July 20X7	Transit van	Cost £6,000
October 20X8	Astra van	Cost £4,200

Each vehicle was bought for cash.

Hillton's policy for motor vehicles is to charge depreciation on the diminishing balance basis at 40% per annum. A full year's depreciation is charged in the year of purchase, irrespective of the actual date of purchase.

Required:

For the three years from 1 January 20X6 to 31 December 20X8 prepare the following ledger accounts:

(i) Motor vehicles account

(ii) Accumulated depreciation account (motor vehicles)

(iii) Depreciation charges account (motor vehicles).

Bring down the balance on each account at 31 December each year.

Tip – *Use another depreciation table.*

🔍 Test your understanding 13

On 1 December 20X2 Infortec Computers owned motor vehicles costing £28,400. During the year ended 30 November 20X3 the following changes to the motor vehicles took place:

		£
1 March 20X3	Sold vehicle – original cost	18,000
1 June 20X3	Purchased new vehicle – cost	10,000
1 September 20X3	Purchased new vehicle – cost	12,000

Depreciation on motor vehicles is calculated on a monthly basis at 20% per annum on cost.

Complete the table below to calculate the total depreciation charge to profits for the year ended 30 November 20X3.

	£
Depreciation for vehicle sold 1 March 20X3	
Depreciation for vehicle purchased 1 June 20X3	
Depreciation for vehicle purchased 1 September 20X3	
Depreciation for other vehicles owned during the year	
Total depreciation for the year ended 30 November 20X3	

6 Summary

This chapter considered the manner in which the cost of non-current assets is charged to the statement of profit or loss over the life of the non-current assets, known as depreciation.

There are a variety of different methods of depreciation; the straight-line, diminishing balance and units of production methods are required for Advanced Bookkeeping.

The accounting entries in the general ledger are the same regardless of the method of depreciation selected. The statement of profit or loss recognises an expense for the depreciation charge and the statement of financial position recognises the accumulated depreciation over the life of the asset to date.

The accumulated balance is netted off against the cost of the non-current asset in the statement of financial position in order to show the non-current asset at its carrying amount.

Finally, the depreciation must also be entered into the non-current asset register each year.

Test your understanding answers

Test your understanding 1

	£
Cost	20,000
Year 1 depreciation	(2,000)
Carrying amount at the end of year 1	18,000
Year 2 depreciation	(1,800)
Carrying amount at the end of year 2	16,200

Test your understanding 2

Depreciation charge for year 1:

$$(\pounds10,000,000 - \pounds1,000,000) \times \frac{5,000,000}{40,000,000}$$

$$= \pounds1,125,000$$

Test your understanding 3

The answer is B

The diminishing balance method is used to equalise the combined costs of depreciation and maintenance over the vehicle's life (i.e. in early years, depreciation is high, maintenance low; in later years, depreciation is low, maintenance is high).

The diminishing balance method is also used for non-current assets that are likely to lose more value in their early years than their later years such as cars or vans.

Test your understanding 4

$$\text{Annual depreciation charge} \quad = \quad \frac{85{,}000 - 5{,}000}{5}$$

$$= \quad £16{,}000$$

Asset at cost account

	£		£
Bank	85,000	Balance c/d	85,000
	85,000		**85,000**

Accumulated depreciation

	£		£
Balance c/d	16,000	Depreciation charges	16,000
	16,000		**16,000**

Depreciation charges

	£		£
Accumulated depreciation	16,000	Statement of profit or loss	16,000
	16,000		**16,000**

Test your understanding 5

Statement of financial position extract below.

	Cost	Accumulated depreciation	Carrying amount
Motor vehicle	12,100	9,075	3,025

Test your understanding 6

Plant and machinery account

Date		£	Date		£
1.1.X6	Balance b/d	5,000	31.12.X6	Balance c/d	5,000
1.1.X7	Balance b/d	5,000			

Office furniture account

Date		£	Date		£
1.1.X6	Balance b/d	800	31.12.X6	Balance c/d	800
1.1.X7	Balance b/d	800			

Depreciation charges account

Date		£	Date		£
31.12.X6	Accumulated dep'n a/c – plant and machinery	640	31.12.X6	SPL	840
31.12.X6	Accumulated dep'n a/c – office furniture	200			
		840			840

Accumulated depreciation account – Plant and machinery

Date		£	Date		£
31.12.X6	Balance c/d	2,440	1.1.X6	Balance b/d	1,800
			31.12.X6	Dep'n charges	640
		2,440			2,440
			1.1.X7	Balance b/d	2,440

Accumulated depreciation account – Office furniture

Date		£	Date		£
31.12.X6	Balance c/d	400	1.1.X6	Balance b/d	200
			31.12.X6	Dep'n expense	200
		___			___
		400			400
		___			___
			1.1.X7	Balance b/d	400

The opening balance on the accumulated depreciation account is calculated as follows:

		Plant and machinery £	Office furniture £
20X4	20% × £5,000	1,000	–
20X5	20% × £(5,000 – 1,000)	800	
	25% × £800		200
		___	___
	Opening balance 1.1.X6	1,800	200
		___	___

The depreciation charge for the year 20X6 is calculated as follows:

	Plant and machinery £	Office furniture £	Total £
20% × (5,000 – 1,800)	640		
25% × £800		200	840
	___	___	

Test your understanding 7

		£
Machine 1	£40,000 × 10%	4,000
Machine 2	£48,000 × 10% × 6/12	2,400
		___
		6,400
		___

Test your understanding 8

Annual depreciation $= \dfrac{£12,640}{5} = £2,528$

CA $= £12,640 - (2 \times £2,528) = £7,584$

This is the cost of the van less the accumulated depreciation to date. It is the amount remaining to be depreciated in the future. It is not a market value.

Test your understanding 9

1. Non-current asset register
2. Any of the following:
   - Asset description
   - Asset identification code
   - Asset location
   - Date of purchase
   - Purchase price
   - Supplier name and address
   - Invoice number
   - Any additional enhancement expenditure
   - Estimated useful life
   - Estimated residual value
   - Accumulated depreciation to date
   - Carrying amount
   - Disposal details
3. It would be easy to locate the machine.

Motor car cost

	£		£
20X3		20X3	
1 Jan Purchase ledger control	12,000	31 Dec Balance c/d	12,000
	———		———
20X4		20X4	
1 Jan Balance b/d	12,000	31 Dec Balance c/d	12,000
	———		———
20X5		20X5	
1 Jan Balance b/d	12,000	31 Dec Balance c/d	12,000
	———		———
20X6			
1 Jan Balance b/d	12,000		

$$\text{Annual depreciation charge} = \frac{12,000 - 2,400}{4}$$

$$= £2,400$$

Motor car – accumulated depreciation account

	£		£
20X3		20X3	
31 Dec Balance c/d	2,400	31 Dec Depreciation charges	2,400
	———		———
20X4		20X4	
31 Dec Balance c/d	4,800	1 Jan Balance b/d	2,400
		31 Jan Depreciation charges	2,400
	———		———
	4,800		4,800
	———		———
20X5		20X5	
31 Dec Balance c/d	7,200	1 Jan Balance b/d	4,800
		31 Dec Depreciation charges	2,400
	———		———
	7,200		7,200
	———		———
		20X6	
		1 Jan Balance b/d	7,200

Depreciation charges account

	£		£
20X3		20X3	
31 Dec Motor car accumulated depreciation	2,400	31 Dec SPL	2,400
20X4		20X4	
31 Dec Motor car accumulated depreciation	2,400	31 Dec SPL	2,400
20X5		20X5	
31 Dec Motor car accumulated depreciation	2,400	31 Dec SPL	2,400

Test your understanding 11

(1) **Straight line method**

Annual depreciation $= \dfrac{\text{Cost} - \text{Scrap value}}{\text{Estimated life}}$

$= \dfrac{£6,000 - £1,000}{8 \text{ years}}$

$= £625$ p.a.

Machine account

	£		£
Year 1: Cost	6,000		

KAPLAN PUBLISHING

Accumulated depreciation

	£		£
Year 1:		Year 1:	
Balance c/d	625	Depreciation charges	625
Year 2:		Year 2:	
Balance c/d	1,250	Balance b/d	625
		Depreciation charges	625
	1,250		1,250
Year 3:		Year 3:	
Balance c/d	1,875	Balance b/d	1,250
		Depreciation charges	625
	1,875		1,875
		Year 4:	
		Balance b/d	1,875

Statement of financial position extract:

		Cost	Accumulated depreciation	Carrying amount
		£	£	£
Non-current asset:				
Year 1	Machine	6,000	625	5,375
Year 2	Machine	6,000	1,250	4,750
Year 3	Machine	6,000	1,875	4,125

(2) Diminishing balance method

		£
Cost		6,000
Year 1	Depreciation 20% × £6,000	1,200
		4,800
Year 2	Depreciation 20% × £4,800	960
		3,840
Year 3	Depreciation 20% × £3,840	768
Carrying amount		3,072

Test your understanding 12

Hilton

(a)

Workings

		Chopper £	Mincer £	Stuffer £	Total £
Cost		4,000	6,000	8,000	18,000
Depreciation	20X6 – 25%	(1,000)			(1,000)
Depreciation	20X7 – 25%	(1,000)	(1,500)		(2,500)
Depreciation	20X8 – 25%	(1,000)	(1,500)	(2,000)	(4,500)
CA at 31 Dec 20X8		1,000	3,000	6,000	10,000

Machinery

	£		£
20X6		**20X6**	
Cash – chopper	4,000	Balance c/d	4,000
20X7		**20X7**	
Balance b/d	4,000		
Cash – mincer	6,000	Balance c/d	10,000
	10,000		10,000
20X8		**20X8**	
Balance b/d	10,000		
Cash – stuffer	8,000	Balance c/d	18,000
	18,000		18,000
20X9			
Balance b/d	18,000		

Accumulated depreciation (machinery)

	£		£
20X6		20X6	
Balance c/d	1,000	Depreciation charges	
		(25% × £4,000)	1,000
	———		———
20X7		20X7	
Balance c/d	3,500	Balance b/d	1,000
		Depreciation charges	
		(25% × £10,000)	2,500
	———		———
	3,500		3,500
	———		———
20X8		20X8	
Balance c/d	8,000	Balance b/d	3,500
		Depreciation charges	
		(25% × £18,000)	4,500
	———		———
	8,000		8,000
	———		———
		20X9	
		Balance b/d	8,000

Depreciation expense (machinery)

	£		£
20X6		20X6	
Accumulated depreciation	1,000	Statement of profit or loss	1,000
	———		———
20X7		20X7	
Accumulated depreciation	2,500	Statement of profit or loss	2,500
	———		———
20X8		20X8	
Accumulated depreciation	4,500	Statement of profit or loss	4,500
	———		———

(b)

Workings

	Metro £	Transit £	Astra £	Total £
Cost	3,200	6,000	4,200	13,400
Depreciation 20X6 – 40%	(1,280)			(1,280)
CA 31.12.X6	1,920			
Depreciation 20X7 – 40%	(768)	(2,400)		(3,168)
CA 31.12.X7	1,152	3,600		
Depreciation 20X8 – 40%	(461)	(1,440)	(1,680)	(3,581)
CA at 31 Dec 20X8	691	2,160	2,520	5,371

Motor vehicles

	£		£
20X6		**20X6**	
Cash – Metro	3,200	Balance c/d	3,200
20X7		**20X7**	
Balance b/d	3,200		
Cash – Transit	6,000	Balance c/d	9,200
	9,200		9,200
20X8		**20X8**	
Balance b/d	9,200		
Cash – Astra	4,200	Balance c/d	13,400
	13,400		13,400
20X9			
Balance b/d	13,400		

Accumulated depreciation (machinery)

	£		£
20X6		20X6	
Balance c/d	1,280	Depreciation charge	1,280
	1,280		1,280
20X7		20X7	
		Balance b/d	1,280
Balance c/d	4,448	Depreciation charge	3,168
	4,448		4,448
20X8		20X8	
		Balance b/d	4,448
Balance c/d	8,029	Depreciation charge	3,581
	8,029		8,029
		Balance b/d	8,029

Depreciation charges (motor vehicles)

	£		£
20X6		20X6	
Accumulated depreciation	1,280	Statement of profit or loss	1,280
20X7		20X7	
Accumulated depreciation	3,168	Statement of profit or loss	3,168
20X8		20X8	
Accumulated depreciation	3,581	Statement of profit or loss	3,581

Test your understanding 13

Depreciation for vehicle sold 1 March 20X3	
(18,000 × 20% × 3/12)	900
Depreciation for vehicle purchased 1 June 20X3	
(10,000 × 20% × 6/12)	1,000
Depreciation for vehicle purchased 1 September 20X3	
(12,000 × 20% × 3/12)	600
Depreciation for other vehicles owned during the year	
((28,400 – 18,000) × 20%)	2,080
	———
Total depreciation for the year ended 30 November 20X3	4,580
	———

Disposal of capital assets

5

Introduction

When a capital asset or non-current asset is disposed of there are a variety of accounting calculations and entries that need to be made.

Firstly, the asset being disposed of must be removed from the accounting records as it is no longer controlled. In most cases the asset will be disposed of for either more or less than its carrying value leading to a profit or a loss on disposal which must be accounted for.

Finally, the fact that the asset has been disposed of must be recorded in the non-current asset register.

In most examinations you will be required to put through the accounting entries for the disposal of a capital asset (i.e. a non-current asset) and to record the disposal in the non-current asset register.

This is a favourite area in examinations and must be fully understood. In particular the method of acquiring a new non-current, with an old asset as a part-exchange is a favourite topic, which will be covered in detail in this chapter.

Finally in this chapter we must consider the purpose of the non-current asset register and how it can be used to regularly check that all of the non-current assets owned by the business are in place.

ASSESSMENT CRITERIA	CONTENTS
Record disposals of non-current assets (2.4)	1 Accounting for the disposal of capital assets 2 Part-exchange of assets 3 Authorising disposals 4 Disposals and the non-current asset register 5 Reconciliation of physical assets to the non-current asset register

1 Accounting for the disposal of capital assets

1.1 Introduction

When a capital or non-current asset is sold then there are two main aspects to the accounting for this disposal:

Firstly the existing entries in the ledger accounts for the asset being disposed of must be removed as the asset is no longer controlled.

Secondly there is likely to be a profit or loss on disposal and this must be calculated and accounted for.

1.2 Removal of existing ledger account balances

When an asset is sold, the balances in the ledger accounts that relate to that asset must be removed. There are two such balances:

(a) the original cost of the asset in the non-current cost account

(b) the depreciation to date on the asset in the accumulated depreciation account.

In order to remove these two balances we must do the following:

Step 1

Open a disposal account.

Step 2

Transfer the two amounts to the disposal account.

Step 3

Enter any proceeds from the sale of the asset in the disposal account.

 Definition – Disposal account

The disposal account is the account which is used to make all of the entries relating to the sale of the asset and also determines the profit or loss on disposal.

1.3 Profit or loss on disposal

The value that the non-current is recorded at in the books of the organisation is the carrying value, i.e. cost less accumulated depreciation. However this is unlikely to be exactly equal to the amount for which the asset is actually sold. The difference between these two is the profit or loss on disposal.

	£
Cost of asset	X
Less: accumulated depreciation	(X)
	—
Carrying value	X
Disposal proceeds	(X)
	—
(Profit)/loss on disposal	X
	—

If the disposal proceeds are greater than the carrying value a profit has been made, if the proceeds are less than the carrying value a loss has been made.

Example 1

A non-current asset cost £14,000

The accumulated depreciation on this asset is £9,600.

This asset has just been sold for £3,800.

(a) What is the profit or loss on disposal?

(b) Write up the relevant ledger accounts to record this disposal.

Solution

(a)

	£
Cost	14,000
Accumulated depreciation	(9,600)
	—
Carrying value	4,400
Proceeds	(3,800)
	—
Loss on disposal	600
	—

(b) **Step 1**

Determine the cost and accumulated depreciation ledger account balances for this asset.

Non-current asset

	£		£
Balance b/d	14,000		

Accumulated depreciation

	£		£
		Balance b/d	9,600

Step 2

Open the disposal account and transfer balances on the above two accounts.

Cost

Debit	Disposal account	£14,000
Credit	Non-current asset account	£14,000

Accumulated depreciation

Debit	Accumulated depreciation	£9,600
Credit	Disposal account	£9,600

Non-current asset

	£		£
Balance b/d	14,000	Disposal	14,000
	———		———
	14,000		14,000
	———		———

Accumulated depreciation

	£		£
Disposal	9,600	Balance b/d	9,600
	———		———
	9,600		9,600
	———		———

Disposal

	£		£
Cost	14,000	Accumulated dep'n	9,600

Step 3

Enter the proceeds in the disposal account and balance the disposal account with the profit/loss on disposal.

Disposal

	£		£
Cost	14,000	Accumulated dep'n	9,600
		Cash	3,800
		Loss – SPL	600
	———		———
	14,000		14,000
	———		———

Note 1: The loss of £600 is credited to the disposal account to balance the account. The corresponding debit is in the statement of profit or loss and represents the loss on the disposal.

Note 2: The profit or loss on disposal can actually be calculated as the balancing figure in the disposal account:

- if there is a debit entry to balance the account then this is a profit on disposal which is credited to the SPL as income

- if there is a credit entry to balance the account then this is a loss on disposal which is debited to the SPL as an additional expense.

Test your understanding 1

A business buys a car for £20,000 on 15 January 20X2 and expects it to have a useful life of five years.

It depreciates the car at 50% reducing balance and sells on 20 December 20X5 for £10,000. The depreciation policy of the business is to charge a full year's depreciation in the year of acquisition and none in the year of disposal.

Record the ledger entries for the four years 20X2 to 20X5. The financial year of the business is 1 January to 31 December.

Clearly show the profit or loss on disposal.

Car account

	£		£

Accumulated depreciation

	£		£

Disposal account

	£		£

1.4 Journal entries

We have already seen that journal entries are an instruction to the bookkeeper to put through double entry in the ledger accounts where the transaction is not necessarily recorded in any of the books of prime entry.

Example 2

Nigel sells his van for £700.

It originally cost £2,000 and so far depreciation has amounted to £1,500.

Record this transaction in the disposals account.

Show the journal entries required to account for this disposal.

Solution

Disposal account

	£		£
Motor van (step 1)	2,000	Accumulated depreciation (step 2)	1,500
SPL – profit on disposal (step 4)	200	Cash (step 3)	700
	_____		_____
	2,200		2,200
	_____		_____

Now for each of the journal entries:

Step 1

To remove the motor van cost from the books of the business.

Dr	Disposals	2,000
Cr	Motor van	2,000

Step 2

To remove the associated depreciation from the books of the business.

Dr   Accumulated depreciation   1,500
Cr   Disposals   1,500

Note: These two entries together effectively remove the carrying value of the van to the disposals account.

Step 3

To record the cash proceeds.

Dr   Cash   700
Cr   Disposals   700

Step 4

Balance the disposal account

The resulting balance is the profit on sale which is transferred to the statement of profit or loss.

Dr   Disposals   200
Cr   Statement of profit or loss   200

1.5   Journal

As with the acquisition of non-current assets, the journal or journal voucher is used as the book of prime entry. The journal voucher for this entire disposal is shown as follows:

Journal entry			No: 234	
Date	4 July 20X8			
Prepared by	J Allen			
Authorised by	A Smith			
Account	**Code**	**Debit** £	**Credit** £	
Disposals	0240	2,000		
Motor vehicles cost	0130		2,000	
Motor vehicles acc. dep'n	0140	1,500		
Disposals	0240		1,500	
Cash at bank (receipts)	0163	700		
Disposals	0240		700	
Totals		4,200	4,200	

Test your understanding 2

Complete the journal voucher below for the following information:

A company buys a car for £20,000.

The depreciation charged to date is £7,500.

The car is sold for £10,000 at the end of three years.

Using the information above and the following account names and codes, complete the journal voucher below:

0130 Motor vehicles at cost

0140 Motor vehicles accumulated depreciation

0163 Cash at bank (receipts)

0240 Disposals

Journal entry No 235

Date	13 June 20X8		
Prepared by	A Tech		
Authorised by	B Jones		
Account	**Code**	**Debit** £	**Credit** £

2 Part-exchange of assets

2.1 Introduction

There is an alternative to selling a non-current asset for cash, particularly if a new asset is to be purchased to replace the one being sold. This is often the case with cars or vans where the old asset may be taken by the seller of the new asset as part of the purchase price of the new asset. This is known as a part-exchange deal.

2.2 Part-exchange deal value

When a part exchange deal takes place the seller of the new asset will place a value on the old asset and this will be its part-exchange value.

Example 3

A new car is being purchased for a list price of £18,000. An old car of the business has been accepted in part-exchange and the payment required for the new car is £14,700.

What is the part-exchange value of the old car?

Solution

	£
List price	18,000
Payment required	14,700
Part-exchange value	3,300

2.3 Accounting for the part-exchange value

The part-exchange value has two effects on the accounting records:

(a)   it is effectively the sale proceeds of the old asset

(b)   it is part of the full cost of the new asset together with the balance paid (whichever method of payment is applicable).

The double entry for the part exchange value is:

•   credit the disposal account as these are the effective proceeds of the old asset

•   debit the new asset cost account as this value is part of the total cost of the new asset.

Example 4

Suppose Nigel had part exchanged his van for a new one.

The old van had cost £2,000 and depreciation amounted to £1,500.

The garage gave him an allowance of £700 against the price of the new van which was £5,000. He paid the balance by cheque.

Show all the accounting entries for the disposal of the old van and the acquisition of the new van.

Solution

Step 1

Transfer balances from van and accumulated depreciation accounts to the disposal account.

Old van

	£		£
Balance b/d	2,000	Disposal	2,000
	2,000		2,000

Accumulated depreciation

	£		£
Disposal	1,500	Balance b/d	1,500
	1,500		1,500

Disposal

	£		£
Old van	2,000	Depreciation	1,500

Note: We have closed off the van and accumulated depreciation account to make the entries clearer.

Step 2

Open a new van account and enter in it:

(a)   the part exchange value (£700) from the disposal account; and

(b)   the balance of the cost of the new van (£4,300).

The £700 part exchange value is also credited to the disposal account as the effective proceeds of the old van.

Disposal

	£		£
Old van	2,000	Depreciation	1,500
		New van	700

New van

	£		£
Disposal	700		
Bank	4,300		

Step 3

Balance the accounts

(a)   Close the disposal account to the statement of profit or loss with a profit of £200 being recorded.

(b)   Bring down the total cost (£5,000) of the new van.

Disposal

	£		£
Old van	2,000	Depreciation	1,500
SPL – profit on disposal – old van	200	New van	700
	2,200		2,200

New van

	£		£
Disposal	700	Balance c/d	5,000
Bank	4,300		
	5,000		5,000
Balance b/d	5,000		

Note 1: You could put all the entries in the one van account. It would look like this.

Motor van

	£		£
Balance b/d	2,000	Disposal	2,000
Disposal	700	Balance c/d	5,000
Bank	4,300		
	————		————
	7,000		7,000
	————		————
Balance b/d	5,000		

Example 5

A business has purchased a new van and the invoice for this van has just been received showing the following details:

	£
Registration number GU44 HFF – list price	18,000.00
VAT at 20%	3,600.00
	————
	21,600.00
Vehicle excise duty	140.00
	————
Total due	21,740.00
Less: part-exchange value Y624 UFD	(4,000.00)
	————
Balance to pay	17,740.00
	————

The old van taken in part exchange originally cost £11,000 and at the time of disposal had accumulated depreciation charged to it of £8,340.

From the invoice you can find the total cost of the new van, £18,000, and the part-exchange value of the old van, £4,000.

Write up the van account, accumulated depreciation on vans account and the disposal account to reflect this transaction.

Solution

Van account

	£		£
Old van – cost	11,000	Disposal account	11,000
New van (18,000-4,000)	14,000		
Disposal account – exchange value	4,000	Balance c/d	18,000
	29,000		29,000
Balance b/d	18,000		

Remember that the vehicle excise duty is revenue expenditure and is therefore not part of the cost of the new van and that VAT on the purchase of vans (rather than cars) is recoverable. Therefore the VAT is debited to the VAT control account rather than the van account. The balance b/d on the van account after all of these transactions is simply the full cost of the van of £18,000.

Accumulated depreciation accounts – van

	£		£
Disposal account	8,340	Balance b/d	8,340

Disposal account

	£		£
Van at cost	11,000	Acc. Depreciation	8,340
Profit on disposal	1,340	Van account – part exchange value	4,000
	12,340		12,340

2.4 Original documentation

In an exam question you will be required to put through the accounting entries for a part-exchange but you may also be required to find some of the information necessary from the sales invoice for the new asset.

Test your understanding 3

On 30 September 20X3 a business part-exchanged a van which it bought on 1 January 20X0 for £6,000 and has depreciated each year at 25% pa by the straight-line method (assuming nil residual value). The business charges a full year's charge in the year of acquisition and none in the year of disposal. The financial year end of the business is 31 December.

It traded this van in for a new one costing £10,000 and pays the supplier £9,200 by cheque.

1   Record the entries in ledger accounts for the disposal of the OLD van.

2   Record the entries in ledger accounts for the addition of the NEW van.

3   Complete the disposal account and calculate the profit/loss on disposal.

3   Authorising disposals

3.1   Introduction

It is important that disposals of non-current assets are properly controlled. For most organisations, this means that there must be some form of written authorisation before a disposal can take place. In some ways, authorisation is even more important for disposals than for additions.

3.2   Importance of authorisation

Disposals can easily be made without the knowledge of management and are difficult to detect from the accounting records alone. Sales of assets are often for relatively small amounts of cash and they may not be supported by an invoice (for example, if they are to an employee of the business). Although the transaction itself may not be significant, failure to detect and record the disposal correctly in the accounting records may result in the overstatement of non-current assets in the accounts.

3.3 Requirements of valid authorisation

Possibilities for written authorisation include board minutes (for material disposals), memos or authorisation forms. The following information is needed:

- date of purchase

- date of disposal

- description of asset

- reason for disposal

- original cost

- accumulated depreciation

- sale proceeds

- authorisation (number of signatures required will depend upon the organisation's procedures).

4 Disposals and the non-current asset register

4.1 Introduction

When a non-current asset is disposed of then this must be recorded not only in the ledger accounts but also in the non-current asset register.

 Example 6

Date of purchase	Invoice number	Serial number	Item	Cost	Accum'd depreciation b/f at 1.1.X8	Date of disposal	Depreciation charge in 20X8	Accum'd depreciation c/f	Disposal proceeds	Loss/ gain on disposal
				£	£		£	£	£	£
3.2.X5	345	3488	Chair	340	102		34	136		
6.4.X6	466	–	Bookcase	258	52		26	78		
10.7.X7	587	278	Chair	160	16	12.7.X8	–			
30.8.X8	634	1228	Table	86			9	9		
				—	—		—	—		
				844	170		69	223		
				—	—		—	—		

Using the non-current asset register example from the previous two chapters (reproduced above) we will now complete the entries for the chair (serial number 278) being disposed of.

The disposal proceeds are £15.

The profit or loss must also be entered into the non-current asset register and the total of all of the profits or losses should equal the amount transferred to the statement of profit or loss for the period.

Solution

(W1)	£
Cost	160
Cumulative dep'n	(16)
CV	144
Proceeds	(15)
Loss	129

Date of purchase	Invoice number	Serial number	Item	Cost	Accum'd depreciation b/d at 1.1.X8	Date of disposal	Depreciation charge in 20X8	Accum'd depreciation c/d	Disposal proceeds	Loss/gain on disposal
				£	£		£	£	£	£
3.2.X5	345	3488	Chair	340	102		34	136		
6.4.X6	466	–	Bookcase	258	52		26	78		
10.7.X7	587	278	Chair	160	16	12.7.X8	–		15	(129)(W1)
30.8.X8	634	1228	Table	86			9	9		
				844	170					
12.7.X8		278	Chair	(160)	(16)					
				684	154		69	223		(129)

The result will be that the disposed assed of will have a zero balance in the non-current asset register at the end of the accounting period.

5 Reconciliation of physical assets to the non-current asset register

5.1 Introduction

One of the purposes of the non-current asset register is to allow control over the non-current assets of a business. Obviously many of the non-current assets are extremely valuable and some are also easily moved, especially assets such as personal computers and cars. Therefore on a regular basis the organisation should carry out random checks to ensure that the non-current assets recorded in the non-current asset register are actually on the premises.

5.2 Details in the non-current asset register

The non-current asset register will show the purchase cost, depreciation and disposal details of the non-current assets that the business owns and have recently disposed of.

The non-current asset register should also normally show the location of the assets. This will either be by an additional column in the non-current asset register or by grouping assets in each department or area of the business together. This enables periodic checks to be carried out to ensure that the physical assets in each department agree to the non-current asset register.

5.3 Discrepancies

A variety of possible discrepancies might appear between the physical assets and the book records.

- An asset recorded in the non-current asset register is not physically present – this might be due to the asset being disposed of but not recorded in the non-current asset register, the asset having been moved to another location or the asset having been stolen or removed without authorisation.

- An asset existing that is not recorded in the non-current asset register – this might be due to the non-current asset register not being up to date or the asset having been moved from another location.

Whatever type of discrepancy is discovered it must be either resolved or reported to the appropriate person in the organisation so that it can be resolved.

5.4 Agreement of accounting records to non-current asset register

The ledger accounts for the non-current assets should also be agreed on a regular basis to the non-current asset register.

The cost total with any disposals deducted should agree to the non-current asset at cost accounts totals.

The accumulated depreciation column total for each class of assets should also agree to the accumulated depreciation account balance for each class of asset.

Any total in the loss or gain on disposals column should also agree to the amount charged or credited to the statement of profit or loss.

On a regular basis the non-current asset register details should be agreed to the physical assets held and to the ledger accounts.

 Test your understanding 4

Spanners Ltd has a car it wishes to dispose of. The car cost £12,000 and has accumulated depreciation of £5,000. The car is sold for £4,000.

Tasks

(a) Clearly state whether there is a profit or a loss on disposal.

(b) Show the entries in the motor car account, accumulated depreciation account and disposal account.

 Test your understanding 5

Baldrick's venture

On 1 April 20X6, Baldrick started a business growing turnips and selling them to wholesalers. On 1 September 20X6 he purchased a turnip-digging machine for £2,700. He sold the machine on 1 March 20X9 for £1,300.

Baldrick's policy for machinery is to charge depreciation on the reducing balance method at 25% per annum. A full year's charge is made in the year of purchase and none in the year of sale.

Required:

For the three years from 1 April 20X6 to 31 March 20X9 prepare the following ledger accounts:

(a)   Machinery account

(b)   Accumulated depreciation account (machinery)

(c)   Depreciation expense account (machinery)

(d)   Disposals account

Bring down the balance on each account at 31 March each year.

 Test your understanding 6

Keith

The following transactions relate to Keith Manufacturing Co Ltd's plant and machinery:

1 January 20X7	Lathe machine purchased for £10,000. It is to be depreciated on a straight line basis with no expected scrap value after four years.
1 April 20X7	Cutting machine purchased for £12,000. It is estimated that after a five-year working life it will have a scrap value of £1,000.
1 June 20X8	Laser machine purchased for £28,000. This is estimated to have a seven year life and a scrap value of £2,800.
1 March 20X9	The cutting machine purchased on 1 April 20X7 was given in part exchange for a new micro-cutter with a purchase price of £20,000. A part-exchange allowance of £3,000 was given and the balance paid by cheque. It is estimated that the new machine will last for five years with a scrap value of £3,000. It will cost £1,500 to install.

The accounting year-end is 31 December. The company depreciates its machines on a straight line basis, charging a full year in the year of purchase and none in the year of sale.

At 31 December 20X6 the plant register had shown the following:

Date of purchase	Machine	Cost	Anticipated residual value	Rate of depreciation
		£	£	
1 June 20X5	Piece machine	10,000	Nil	Straight line over 5 years
1 January 20X6	Acrylic machine	5,000	1,000	Straight line over 5 years
1 June 20X6	Heat seal machine	6,000	Nil	Straight line over 5 years

Required:

Write up the plant and machinery account, the accumulated depreciation account and the disposal accounts for 20X7, 20X8 and 20X9. Show the relevant extracts from the financial statements.

 Test your understanding 7

A motor vehicle which had originally been purchased on 31 October 20X1 for £12,000 was part exchanged for a new vehicle on 31 May 20X3. The new vehicle cost £15,000 and was paid for using the old vehicle and a cheque for £5,000.

Prepare a disposals account for the old vehicle showing clearly the transfer to the statement of profit or loss. (Depreciation for motor vehicles is calculated on a monthly basis at 20% per annum straight line method assuming no residual value.)

Disposals account

Test your understanding 8

A business has purchased a new van for deliveries from Grammoth Garages. The business is not registered for VAT. It received the following invoice from Grammoth Garages:

GRAMMOTH GARAGES
Park Road • Valedon • HE4 8NB
SALES INVOICE

Delivery of Ford Transit Van Registration GS55 OPP

	£
List price	21,000.00
VAT	4,200.00
	25,200.00
Less: part exchange value Ford Transit Van Reg X234 JDF	(5,500.00)
Amount due	19,700.00

The van that was part-exchanged originally cost £16,400 and has been depreciated on a straight-line basis for four years at 15% per annum.

Required:

Write up the motor vans at cost account, accumulated depreciation and the disposal account to reflect the purchase of the new van and the part-exchange of the old van.

6 Summary

The two main aspects to accounting for disposals of non-current assets are to remove all accounting entries for the asset disposed of and to account for any profit or loss on disposal. This can all be done by using a disposal account.

Some assets will not be sold outright but will be transferred as a part-exchange deal when purchasing a new asset. The part-exchange value is not only equivalent to the proceeds of sale but is also part of the cost of the new asset being purchased.

Control over the disposal of non-current assets is extremely important and as such authorisation of a disposal and whether it is as a sale or a part-exchange is key to this. Allied to this is the control feature of the non-current asset register.

All purchases and disposals of non-current assets should be recorded in the non-current asset register and the actual physical presence of the non-current assets should be checked on a regular basis to the non-current asset register details.

Test your understanding answers

Test your understanding 1

	£	Depreciation
Cost	20,000	
20X2 depreciation	(10,000)	10,000
(20,000 × 50%)	———	
	10,000	
20X3 depreciation	(5,000)	5,000
(10,000 × 50%)	———	
	5,000	
20X4 depreciation	(2,500)	2,500
(5,000 × 50%)		———
Total depreciation charged		17,500

(No depreciation is charged in 20X5 as this is the year of disposal)

Car account

	£		£
01/X2 Bank	20,000	12/X2 Balance c/d	20,000
	———		———
	20,000		20,000
	———		
01/X3 Balance b/d	20,000	12/X3 Balance c/d	20,000
	———		———
	20,000		20,000
	———		
01/X4 Balance b/d	20,000	12/X4 Balance c/d	20,000
	———		———
	20,000		20,000
	———		
01/X5 Balance b/d	20,000	12/X5 Disposal a/c	20,000
	———		———
	20,000		20,000

Accumulated depreciation

	£		£
12/X2 Balance c/d	10,000	12/X2 Dep'n charges	10,000
	10,000		10,000
12/X3 Balance c/d	15,000	01/X3 Balance b/d	10,000
		12/X3 Dep'n charges	5,000
	15,000		15,000
12/X4 Balance c/d	17,500	01/X4 Balance b/d	15,000
		12/X4 Dep'n charges	2,500
	17,500		17,500
12/X5 Disposal a/c	17,500	01/X5 Balance b/d	17,500
	17,500		17,500

Disposal account

	£		£
12/X5 Van cost	20,000	12/X5 Accumulated dep'n	17,500
12/X5 Profit on disposal	7,500	12/X5 Proceeds	10,000
	27,500		27,500

Test your understanding 2

Journal entry No 235

Date	13 June 20X8		
Prepared by	A Tech		
Authorised by	B Jones		
Account	**Code**	**Debit** £	**Credit** £
Disposals	0240	20,000	
MV at cost	0130		20,000
MV acc dep'n	0140	7,500	
Disposals	0240		7,500
Cash at bank	0163	10,000	
Disposals	0240		10,000

Test your understanding 3

Van account

	£		£
Cost b/d	6,000	Disposals account	6,000
Disposal account	800		
Bank	9,200	Balance c/d	10,000
	16,000		16,000
Balance b/d	10,000		

Accumulated depreciation

	£		£
Disposal account	4,500	Balance b/d (£6,000 × 25% × 3 years)	4,500
Balance c/d	2,500	Depreciation charge (£10,000 × 25%)	2,500
	7,000		7,000
		Balance b/d	2,500

Disposal account

	£		£
Van	6,000	Accumulated depreciation	4,500
		Part exchange allowance	800
		Loss on disposal	700
	___		___
	6,000		6,000
	___		___

Test your understanding 4

(a) **Profit or loss on disposal**

	£
Cost	12,000
Depreciation	(5,000)
	___
CV	7,000
	___

Comparing the carrying value of £7,000 with the sale proceeds of £4,000, there is a loss of (7,000 – 4,000) = £3,000.

(b) **Ledger account entries**

Disposal of non-current assets account

	£		£
Car cost	12,000	Accumulated depreciation	5,000
		Cash at bank a/c (sales proceeds)	4,000
		Loss on disposal	3,000
	___		___
	12,000		12,000
	___		___

Car account

	£		£
Balance b/d	12,000	Disposal a/c	12,000

Car accumulated depreciation account

	£		£
Disposal a/c	5,000	Balance b/d	5,000

Cash at bank account

	£		£
Disposal a/c	4,000		

Test your understanding 5

Machinery

	£		£
20X7 Cash	2,700	20X7 Balance c/d	2,700
20X8 Balance b/d	2,700	20X8 Balance c/d	2,700
20X9 Balance b/d	2,700	20X9 Disposals account	2,700

Accumulated depreciation (machinery)

	£		£
20X7 Balance c/d	675	20X7 Depreciation expense (25% × £2,700)	675
20X8		20X8 Balance b/d	675
Balance c/d	1,181	Depreciation expense (25% × (£2,700 − £675))	506
20X9 Disposals account	1,181	20X9 Balance b/d	1,181

KAPLAN PUBLISHING

Depreciation expense (machinery)

	£		£
20X7		20X7	
Accumulated depreciation	675	Statement of profit or loss	675
20X8		20X8	
Accumulated depreciation	506	Statement of profit or loss	506

Disposals

	£		£
20X9		20X9	
Machinery – cost	2,700	Accumulated depreciation	1,181
		Cash	1,300
		SPL – loss on disposal	219
	2,700		2,700

Test your understanding 6

Keith

1   Calculate the Balance b/d position at 1 January 20X7:

		Cost	Accumulated depreciation		Accumulated depreciation at 1 Jan 20X7
		£		£	£
Piece machine	(1 June 20X5)	10,000	$\dfrac{£10,000}{5}$	2,000	4,000
Acrylic machine	(1 Jan 20X6)	5,000	$\dfrac{£5,000-£1,000}{5}$	800	800
Heat seal machine	(1 June 20X6)	6,000	$\dfrac{£6,000}{5}$	1,200	1,200
		21,000		4,000	6,000

2   Calculate the annual depreciation on the new assets:

	Cost	Annual depreciation	
	£		£
20X7			
Lathe machine (1 Jan 20X7)	10,000	$\dfrac{£10,000}{4}$	2,500
Cutting machine (1 Apr 20X7)	12,000	$\dfrac{£12,000 - £1,000}{5}$	2,200
Assets b/d at 1 January 20X7	(calc from part 1)		4,000
Charge for the year (20X7)			8,700
20X8			
Lathe machine			2,500
Cutting machine			2,200
Laser machine (1 Jun 20X8)	28,000	$\dfrac{£28,000 - £2,800}{7}$	3,600
Assets b/d at 1 January 20X7			4,000
Charge for the year (20X8)			12,300
20X9			
Lathe machine			2,500
Cutting machine – disposed of			–
Laser machine			3,600
Micro-cutter (1 Apr 20X9)	20,000		
Add: Installation	1,500		
	21,500	$\dfrac{£21,500 - 3,000}{5}$	3,700
Assets b/d at 1 January 20X7			4,000
Charge for the year (20X9)			13,800

3   Show the ledger accounts

Plant and machinery account

	£		£
20X7			
Assets Balance b/d	21,000		
Lathe machine	10,000		
Cutting machine	12,000	Balance c/d 31.12.X7	43,000
	43,000		43,000
20X8			
Assets Balance b/d	43,000		
Laser machine	28,000	Balance c/d 31.12.X8	71,000
	71,000		71,000
20X9			
Assets Balance b/d	71,000	Disposal account	12,000
Micro-cutter			
Disposal 3,000			
Bank account 17,000			
Installation costs 1,500	21,500	Balance c/d 31.12.X9	80,500
	92,500		92,500

Accumulated depreciation

	£		£
20X7		20X7	
		Balance b/d (1)	6,000
Balance c/d	14,700	Depreciation account (2)	8,700
	14,700		14,700
		20X8	
		Balance b/d	14,700
Balance c/d	27,000	Depreciation account	12,300
	27,000		27,000
		20X9	
Disposal account (4)	4,400	Balance b/d	27,000
Balance c/d	36,400	Depreciation account	13,800
	40,800		40,800

4   Calculate the accumulated depreciation on the cutting machine disposed of:

Cutting machine   purchased   1 April 20X7

                         disposed   1 March 20X9

Therefore depreciation should have been charged for 20X7 and 20X8 and none in 20X9, the year of sale.

Accumulated depreciation is £2,200 × 2 = £4,400.

Debit   Accumulated depreciation account   £4,400

Credit Disposal account   £4,400

Depreciation expense

	£		£
20X7		20X7	
Accumulated depreciation	8,700	Statement of profit or loss	8,700
20X8		20X8	
Accumulated depreciation	12,300	Statement of profit or loss	12,300
20X9		20X9	
Accumulated depreciation	13,800	Statement of profit or loss	13,800

Disposals

	£		£
20X9			
Plant and machinery cost	12,000	Accumulated depreciation	4,400
		Part exchange – plant and	
		machinery account	3,000
		Loss on disposal (bal fig)	4,600
	12,000		12,000

5   Disposal journal entries for part exchange:

Debit	Plant and machinery account	£3,000	
Credit	Disposal account		£3,000

Part exchange allowance.

Debit	Statement of profit or loss	£4,600	
Credit	Disposal account		£4,600

Loss on sale

Debit Cost	Plant and machinery (£20,000 – £3,000)	£17,000	
	Installation	£1,500	
		———	£18,500
Credit	Bank account		£18,500

Balance on cost of new machine – micro-cutter

6   Show extracts from financial statements:

Statement of profit or loss extracts

	20X7 £	20X8 £	2009 £
Depreciation	8,700	12,300	13,800
Loss on disposal	–	–	4,600

Statement of financial position extracts

		Cost £	Accumulated depreciation £	Carrying value £
Non-current assets				
20X7	Plant and machinery	43,000	14,700	28,300
20X8	Plant and machinery	71,000	27,000	44,000
20X9	Plant and machinery	80,500	36,400	44,100

Test your understanding 7

Disposals account

	£		£
Motor vehicles	12,000	Accumulated depreciation	3,800
Profit on disposal	1,800	Motor vehicles (part ex)	10,000
	———		———
	13,800		13,800
	———		———

Accumulated depreciation = £12,000 × 20% × 19/12 = 3,800

Test your understanding 8

Motor van account

	£		£
Old van	16,400	Disposal account	16,400
Payables (25,200 – 5,500)	19,700		
Disposal account – trade in value	5,500	Balance c/d	25,200
	———		———
	41,600		41,600
	———		———
Balance b/d	25,200		

Accumulated depreciation

	£		£
Disposal account	9,840	Balance b/d (16,400 × 15% × 4)	9,840

Disposal account

	£		£
Cost	16,400	Accumulated depreciation	9,840
		Trade in value	5,500
		Loss on disposal	1,060
	———		———
	16,400		16,400
	———		———

The extended trial balance – an introduction

Introduction

The examination will contain an exercise involving preparation or completion of an extended trial balance. You need to be familiar with the technique for entering adjustments to the initial trial balance and extending the figures into the statement of financial position and statement of profit or loss columns.

The relevant adjustments you may be required to make are accruals, prepayments, depreciation charges, disposals of non-current assets, irrecoverable and doubtful debts, errors and closing inventory.

In this chapter we introduce the purpose and layout of the extended trial balance. The skills that are detailed below will be achieved once all the adjustments have been reviewed and once the extended trial balance in action has been studied.

ASSESSMENT CRITERIA	CONTENTS
Prepare a trial balance (5.1)	1 From trial balance to extended trial balance
Carry out adjustments to the trial balance (5.2)	
Complete the extended trial balance (5.3)	

1 From trial balance to extended trial balance

1.1 Introduction

In an earlier chapter we have seen how a trial balance is prepared regularly in order to provide a check on the double entry bookkeeping in the accounting system.

The other purpose of the trial balance is as a starting point for the preparation of final accounts. This is often done by using an extended trial balance.

1.2 The purpose of the extended trial balance

 Definition – Extended trial balance

An extended trial balance is a working paper which allows the initial trial balance to be converted into all of the figures required for preparation of the final accounts.

The extended trial balance brings together the balances on all of the general ledger accounts and includes all of the adjustments that are required in order to prepare the final accounts.

1.3 Layout of a typical extended trial balance

A typical extended trial balance (ETB) will have eight columns for each ledger account as follows:

Account name (e.g.)	Trial balance		Adjustments		Statement of profit or loss		Statement of fin. pos.	
	Dr £	Cr £	Dr £	Cr £	Dr £	Cr £	Dr £	Cr £
Sales								
Non-current asset cost								

KAPLAN PUBLISHING

1.4   Procedure for preparing an extended trial balance

Step 1

Each ledger account name and its balance is initially entered in the trial balance columns.

Total the debit and credit columns to ensure they equal i.e. that all balances have been transferred across. Any difference should be put to a suspense account.

Step 2

The adjustments required are then entered into the adjustments column. The typical adjustments required are:

- correction of any errors
- depreciation charges for the period
- write off any irrecoverable debts
- increase or decrease in allowance for doubtful debts
- accruals or prepayments of income and expense
- closing inventory.

Note: it is always important to ensure that all adjustments have an equal and opposite debit and credit. Never enter a one sided journal.

Step 3

Total the adjustments columns to ensure that the double entry has been correctly made in these columns.

Step 4

All the entries on the line of each account are then cross-cast and the total is entered into the correct column in either the statement of profit or loss columns or statement of financial position columns.

Step 5

The statement of profit or loss column totals are totalled in order to determine the profit (or loss) for the period. This profit (or loss) is entered in the statement of profit or loss columns as the balancing figure.

Step 6

The profit (or loss) for the period calculated in step 5 is entered in the statement of financial position columns and the statement of financial position columns are then totalled.

2 Summary

This chapter has introduced the purpose and layout of the extended trial balance. The chapters that follow will review the different accounting adjustments you may need to make. These adjustments will be closing inventory, depreciation, disposals, irrecoverable and doubtful debts, accruals and prepayments. These can all be conveniently put through on the extended trial balance. NB depreciation and disposals were considered in chapters 4 and 5.

Once the adjustments have been reviewed, chapter 14 looks in detail at the extended trial balance in action.

Financial statements and ethical principles

7

Introduction

The preparation of the financial statements – statement of financial position and statement of profit or loss is not required as part of the Advanced Bookkeeping assessment. However this chapter provides an overview of these financial statements as an introduction towards how the knowledge and skills gained in Advanced Bookkeeping will be developed for the Final Accounts Preparation unit.

You should begin to understand how ethical principles apply in the context of work in an accounting environment.

ASSESSMENT CRITERIA
Apply ethical principles when recording transactions (1.4)
Record period end adjustments (4.4)

CONTENTS
1   Financial statements
2   Ethical principles

1 Financial statements

1.1 What are financial statements?

Periodically all types of businesses will produce financial statements in order to show how it has performed and what assets and liabilities it has.

The two principal financial statements are the statement of profit or loss and the statement of financial position.

1.2 Statement of profit or loss

 Definition – Statement of profit or loss

The statement of profit or loss summarises the transactions of a business over an accounting period and determines whether the business has made a profit or a loss for that accounting period of time.

A typical statement of profit or loss is shown below.

Statement of profit or loss of Stanley for the year ended 31 December 20X2

	£	£
Revenue		X
Less: Cost of sales		
Inventory, at cost on 1 January (opening inventory)	X	
Add: Purchases of goods	X	
	―	
	X	
Less: Inventory, at cost on 31 December (closing inventory)	(X)	
	―	
		(X)
		―
Gross profit		X
Sundry income:		
Discounts received	X	
Commission received	X	
Rent received	X	
	―	
		X
		―
		X
Less: Expenses:		
Rent	X	
Rates	X	
Lighting and heating	X	
Telephone	X	
Postage	X	
Insurance	X	
Stationery	X	
Payroll expenses	X	
Depreciation	X	
Accountancy and audit fees	X	
Bank charges and interest	X	
Irrecoverable debts	X	
Allowance for doubtful debts adjustment	X	
Delivery costs	X	
Van running expenses	X	
Selling expenses	X	
Discounts allowed	X	
	―	
		(X)
Net profit		X
		―

The trading account section matches sales to the cost of the goods sold to determine gross profit for the accounting period.

Take careful note of the types of items that appear in the statement of profit or loss. For Final Accounts Preparation you will need to be able to prepare a statement of profit or loss for a sole trader or partnership.

1.3 Statement of financial position

 Definition – Statement of financial position

The statement of financial position is a summary of all of the assets and liabilities of the business on the last day of the accounting period.

An example of a typical sole trader's statement of financial position is given below:

Statement of financial position of Stanley at 31 December 20X2

	Cost	Depreciation	
	£	£	£
Non-current assets			
Freehold factory	X	(X)	X
Machinery	X	(X)	X
Motor vehicles	X	(X)	X
	X	(X)	X
Current assets			
Inventories			X
Receivables	X		
Less: allowance for receivables	(X)		
			X
Other receivables			X
Cash at bank			X
Cash in hand			X
			X

Current liabilities		
Trade payables	X	
Other payables	X	
	——	(X)
Net current assets		X
		——
Total assets less current liabilities		X
Non-current liabilities		
12% loan		(X)
		——
Net assets		X
		——
Capital at 1 January		X
Net profit for the year		X
		——
		X
Less: drawings		(X)
		——
Proprietor's funds		X
		——

📝 Test your understanding 1

Place the following account names under the correct headings and in the correct order they would appear in the statement of financial position.

Receivables	Inventory
Bank overdraft	Payables
VAT payable	Computers
Motor van	Cash
Land	

Non-current assets	Current assets	Current liabilities

Note that the statement of financial position is split into two sections.

(a) The top part of the statement of financial position lists all of the assets and liabilities of the business. This is then totalled by adding together all of the asset values and deducting the liabilities.

The assets are classified as either non-current assets or current assets.

Definition – Non-current assets

Non-current assets are those that will be used within the business over a long period (usually greater than one year), e.g. land and buildings.

Definition – Current assets

Current assets are those that are expected to be realised within the business in the normal course of trading (usually a period less than one year) e.g. inventory.

Current assets are always listed in the reverse order of liquidity, which means how easily they are converted into their liquid or cash form. To this end inventory is shown first, then receivables and then bank and cash balances.

Definition – Current liabilities

Current liabilities are the short term payables of a business. This means payables that are due to be paid within twelve months of the statement of financial position date e.g. trade payables.

Definition – Non-current liabilities

Non-current liabilities are payables that will be paid over a longer period, which is in excess of one year of the statement of financial position date, e.g. loans.

(b)   The bottom part of the statement of financial position shows how the business is funded. For a sole trader this is made up of the capital at the start of the year plus the net profit for the year less any drawings that the owner has taken during the year.

This part of the statement of financial position is also totalled and it should have the same total as the top part of the statement of financial position.

 Definition – The accounting equation

The accounting equation represents the statement of financial position as follows:

ASSETS – LIABILITIES = CAPITAL + PROFIT – DRAWINGS

 Test your understanding 2

1   The final figure calculated in the trading account known as?

Assets   Net profit   Gross profit   Cost of sales

Circle the correct answer

2   State the accounting equation?

Test your understanding 3

Trial balance at 31 December 20X2

	Dr £	Cr £
Capital on 1 January 20X2		106,149
Freehold factory at cost	360,000	
Motor vehicles at cost	126,000	
Inventories at 1 January 20X2	37,500	
Receivables	15,600	
Cash in hand	225	
Bank overdraft		82,386
Payables		78,900
Revenue		307,500
Purchases	158,700	
Wages and salaries	39,060	
Rent and rates	35,400	
Postage	400	
Discounts allowed	6,600	
Insurance	2,850	
Motor expenses	5,500	
Loan from bank		240,000
Sundry expenses	1,000	
Drawings	26,100	
	814,935	814,935

Based upon the trial balance, prepare a statement of profit or loss for the year ended 31 December 20X2 and statement of financial position as at 31 December 20X2.

Test your understanding 4

Lara

The following transactions took place in July 20X6:

1 July	Lara started a business selling cricket boots and put £200 in the bank.
2 July	Marlar lent her £1,000.
3 July	Bought goods from Greig Ltd on credit for £296.
4 July	Bought motor van for £250 cash.
7 July	Made cash sales amounting to £105.
8 July	Paid motor expenses £15.
9 July	Paid wages £18.
10 July	Bought goods on credit from Knott Ltd, £85.
14 July	Paid insurance premium £22.
25 July	Received £15 commission as a result of successful sales promotion of MCC cricket boots.
31 July	Paid electricity bill £17.

Required:

(a) Write up the ledger accounts in the books of Lara.

(b) Extract a trial balance at 31 July 20X6.

Test your understanding 5

Peter

From the following list of balances you are required to draw up a trial balance for Peter at 31 December 20X8:

	£
Fixtures and fittings	6,430
Delivery vans	5,790
Cash at bank (in funds)	3,720
General expenses	1,450
Receivables	2,760
Payables	3,250
Purchases	10,670
Sales revenue	25,340
Wages	4,550
Drawings	5,000
Lighting and heating	1,250
Rent, rates and insurance	2,070
Capital	15,100

 Test your understanding 6

Peter Wall

Peter Wall started business on 1 January 20X8 printing and selling astrology books. He introduced £10,000 capital and was given a loan of £10,000 by Oswald. The following is a list of his transactions for the three months to 31 March 20X8:

1   Purchased printing equipment for £7,000 cash.

2   Purchased a delivery van for £400 on credit from Arnold.

3   Bought paper for £100 on credit from Butcher.

4   Bought ink for £10 cash.

5   Paid £25 for one quarter's rent and rates to 31 March 20X8.

6   Paid £40 for one year's insurance premium.

7   Sold £200 of books for cash and £100 on credit to Constantine.

8   Paid Oswald £450 representing the following:

(i)   Part repayment of principal.

(ii)   Interest calculated at an annual rate of 2% per annum for three months.

9   Received £60 from Constantine.

10   Paid £200 towards the delivery van and £50 towards the paper.

11   Having forgotten his part payment for the paper he then paid Butcher a further £100.

Required:

(a)   Write up all necessary ledger accounts, including cash.

(b)   Extract a trial balance at 31 March 20X8 (before period-end accruals).

2   Ethical principles

2.1   Introduction

Definition – Ethics

Ethics can be defined as the "moral principles that govern a person's behaviour or the conducting of an activity".

The Oxford English Dictionary

Ethics is concerned with how one should act in a certain situation, ensuring the 'right thing' is being done. You are required to understand how to apply ethical principles whilst working in an accounting function.

Business ethics is the application of ethical principles to the problems typically encountered in a business setting. Applying ethics to a business situation is not separate to a consideration of normal moral judgements.

Typical issues that are addressed include:

*   misrepresenting financial performance and position with 'creative accounting' or 'window dressing'

- using legal loopholes to avoid paying tax
- data protection and privacy
- corporate governance
- corporate crime, including insider trading and price fixing
- whistle blowing
- product issues such as patent and copyright infringement, planned obsolescence, product liability and product defects.

2.2 The Code of Ethics for Professional Accountants

The Code of Ethics for Professional Accountants, published by The International Federation of Accountants (IFAC), forms the basis for the ethical codes of many accountancy bodies, including the AAT, ICAEW, ACCA and CIMA.

The Code adopts a principles-based approach. It does not attempt to cover every situation where a member may encounter professional ethical issues, prescribing the way in which he or she should respond. Instead, it adopts a value system, focusing on fundamental professional and ethical principles which are at the heart of proper professional behaviour.

2.3 Five key principles

2.4 Integrity

 Definition – Integrity

Integrity means that a member must be straightforward and honest in all professional and business relationships. Integrity also implies fair dealing and truthfulness.

Accountants are expected to present financial information fully, honestly and professionally and so that it will be properly understood in its context.

 Example 1 – Integrity

A professional accountant should not be associated with reports where the information:

- contains a materially false or misleading statement

- contains statements or information furnished recklessly

- has omissions that make it misleading.

Accountants should abide by relevant law and regulations and remember that, as well as legal documents, letters and verbal agreements may constitute a binding arrangement.

Accountants should strive to be fair and socially responsible and respect cultural differences when dealing with overseas colleagues or contacts. Promises may not be legally binding but repeatedly going back on them can destroy trust, break relationships and lose co-operation.

To maintain integrity, members have the following responsibilities:

2.5 Objectivity

 Definition – Objectivity

Objectivity means that a member must not allow bias, conflict of interest or undue influence of others to override professional or business judgements.

 Example 2 – Objectivity

Suppose that you are part of an audit team at a major client:

*   If you also own shares in the client company, then this could be viewed as a conflict of interest.

*   If you receive excessive hospitality and discounts from the client then this could be seen as an attempt to influence (bribe) you and compromise your objectivity.

Objectivity can also be defined as the state of mind which has regard to all considerations relevant to the task in hand but no other. It is closely linked to the concept of independence:

*   **Independence of mind** is the state of mind that permits the provision of an opinion without being affected by influences that compromise professional judgement, allowing an individual to act with integrity and exercise objectivity and professional scepticism.

*   **Independence of appearance** is the avoidance of facts and circumstances that are so significant that a reasonable and informed third party, having knowledge of all relevant information, would reasonably conclude that a firm's or a member's integrity, objectivity or professional scepticism had been compromised.

Whatever capacity members serve in, they should demonstrate their objectivity in different circumstances.

Objectivity is a distinguishing feature of the profession. Members have a responsibility to:

*   Communicate information fairly and objectively.

*   Disclose fully all relevant information that could reasonably be expected to influence an intended user's understanding of the reports, comments, and recommendations presented.

2.6   The importance of objectivity in accounting

A member must not allow bias, conflict of interest or undue influence of others to override professional or business judgements.

These can include personal self-interest threats and other conflicts of interest.

Personal threats to independence

Self-interest threats to independence can arise when:

- holding a financial interest in a client, such as owning shares

- having undue dependence on total fees from a client

- receiving excessive hospitality and gifts from a client

Similarly familiarity threats to independence can arise when:

- having a close business relationship with a client

- having personal and family relationships with a client.

Threats to independence can also occur due to undue pressures from authority and workload.

Conflict of interest

Threats to objectivity due to a conflict of interest may be created when

- a member in practice competes directly with a client

- a member in practice has a joint venture with a major competitor of a client.

- a member in practice performs services for clients whose interests are in conflict

- a member in practice performs services for clients who are in dispute with each other in relation to the matter or transaction in question.

 Test your understanding 7

Helen, an AAT member working in an accounting practice, has been offered a job by one of her audit clients.

In order to maintain her independence, what course of action should Helen take?

- Resign immediately.

- Inform the partners of her current employer and be removed from the audit of the client.

- Nothing – it is just an offer.

2.7 Professional competence and due care

 Definition – Professional competence

Professional competence means that a member has the knowledge and ability to discharge their responsibilities in accordance with current developments in practice, legislation and technique.

 Definition – Due care

Due care means a member must act diligently and in accordance with applicable technical and professional standards when providing professional services i.e. must not be negligent.

In agreeing to provide professional services, a professional accountant implies that there is a level of competence necessary to perform those services and that his or her knowledge, skill and experience will be applied with reasonable care and diligence.

 Example 3 – Professional competence

Suppose that you are a junior member of the accounts department of a business. Your normal role is to deal with credit control issues. The payroll clerk has been absent for the past few weeks and so the office manager has asked you to process the payroll for the month.

What are the ethical issues associated with this situation?

You may not have the competence to take on this work responsibly. If you are not aware of the bookkeeping requirements associated with accounting for payroll, you may make errors if you do the work without supervision or training. You could suggest to the office manager that you are willing to learn to do this work, but that you would need appropriate training and supervision. In addition, if you were to do this work, and then make errors, it could be suggested that you had fallen short of the standard expected from a person working in an accounting environment, even though you are not yet qualified.

Professional accountants must therefore refrain from performing any services that they are not competent to carry out unless appropriate advice and assistance is obtained to ensure that the services are performed satisfactorily.

Professional competence may be divided into two separate phases:

1   Gaining professional competence – for example, by training to gain the AAT qualification.

2   Maintaining professional competence – accountants need to keep up to date with developments in the accountancy profession including relevant national and international pronouncements on accounting, auditing and other relevant regulations and statutory requirements.

Members have a responsibility to:

*   Maintain an appropriate level of professional competence by ongoing development of their knowledge and skills.

*   Maintain technical and ethical standards in areas relevant to their work through continuing professional development.

*   Perform their professional duties in accordance with relevant laws, regulations, and technical standards.

*   Prepare complete and clear reports and recommendations after appropriate analysis of relevant and reliable information.

Members should adopt review procedures that will ensure the quality of their professional work is consistent with national and international pronouncements that are issued from time to time.

Due professional care applies to the exercise of professional judgement in the conduct of work performed and implies that the professional approaches matters requiring professional judgement with proper diligence.

 Test your understanding 8

Peter, an AAT member, has been asked by a friend to complete his tax self-assessment form for him. Unfortunately, Peter has never completed such a return.

Potentially, which fundamental principle is threatened?

2.8   Confidentiality

 Definition – Confidentiality

A member must, in accordance with the law, respect the confidentiality of information acquired as a result of professional and business relationships and not disclose any such information to third parties without proper and specific authority unless there is a legal or professional right or duty to disclose.

Confidential information acquired as a result of professional and business relationships must not be used for the personal advantage of the member or third parties.

Note that confidentiality is not only a matter of disclosure of information – it also concerns using information for personal advantage or for the advantage of a third party.

 Example 4 – Confidentiality

Suppose that you are an accountant in practice and you discover that the client has just won a major contract. This has yet to be publicised. When a press release is made, the share price is expected to rise significantly.

If you buy the (undervalued) shares, you have breached the principle of confidentiality. You used confidential information with the expectation of making a personal gain.

Members should:

* be prudent in the use and protection of information acquired in the course of their duties. (Please note that the duty of confidentiality continues even after the end of the relationship between the member and the employer or client.)

* not use information for any personal gain or in any manner that would be contrary to the law or detrimental to the legitimate and ethical objectives of the business.

* inform subordinates as appropriate regarding the confidentiality of information acquired in the course of their work and monitor their activities to assure the maintenance of that confidentiality.

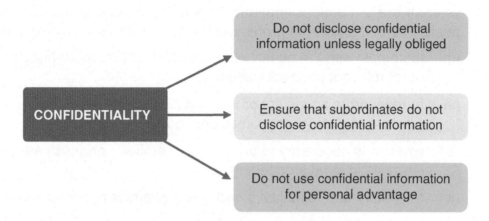

A member must take care to maintain confidentiality even in a social environment. The member should be alert to the possibility of inadvertent disclosure, particularly in circumstances involving close or personal relations, associates and long established business relationships.

The problem with confidentiality is that there are times when disclosure may be permitted or even mandatory.

The following are circumstances where members are or may be required to disclose confidential information or when such disclosure may be appropriate:

(a)   where disclosure is permitted by law and is authorised by the client or the employer

(b)   where disclosure is required by law, for example:

   (i)   production of documents or other provision of evidence in the course of legal proceedings or

   (ii)   disclosure to the appropriate public authorities (for example, HMRC) of infringements of the law that come to light or

   (iii)   disclosure of actual or suspected money laundering or terrorist financing to the member's firm's MLRO (Money Laundering Reporting Officer) or to SOCA (Serious Organised Crime Authority, or

(c) where there is a professional duty or right to disclose, which is in the public interest, and is not prohibited by law. Examples may include:

(i) to comply with the quality review of an IFAC member body or other relevant professional body

(ii) to respond to an inquiry or investigation by the AAT or a relevant regulatory or professional body

(iii) where it is necessary to protect the member's professional interests in legal proceedings or

(iv) to comply with technical standards and ethics requirements.

In deciding whether to disclose confidential information, members should consider the following points:

- whether the interests of all parties, including third parties, could be harmed even though the client or employer (or other person to whom there is a duty of confidentiality) consents to the disclosure of information by the member

- whether all the relevant information is known and substantiated, to the extent that this is practicable. When the situation involves unsubstantiated facts, incomplete information or unsubstantiated conclusions, professional judgement should be used in determining the type of disclosure to be made, if any

- the type of communication or disclosure that may be made and by whom it is to be received; in particular, members should be satisfied that the parties to whom the communication is addressed are appropriate recipients.

 Test your understanding 9

You work in the payroll department of a large business. Your friend Emma has been working in the admin office for the past few months and wants to know what her colleague Alisha earns. Alisha is always buying new clothes and booking holidays to exotic places!

What should you do?

- Provide Emma with the information she wants – she should be able to know whether she's being treated fairly!

- Tell Emma that you are unable to provide her with that information as it is confidential.

2.9   Professional behaviour

 Definition – Professional behaviour

A professional accountant should comply with relevant laws and regulations and should avoid any action that discredits the profession.

Professional behaviour is distinguished by certain characteristics:

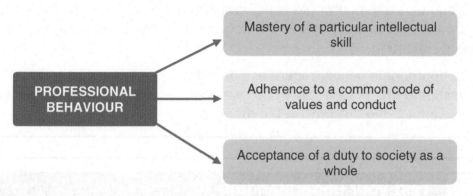

The objectives of the accountancy profession are to work to the highest standards of professionalism, to attain the highest levels of performance and generally to meet the public interest requirement. These objectives require four basic needs to be met:

(i)   **Credibility** – there is a need for credibility in information and information systems.

(ii)   **Professionalism** – there is a need to be clearly identified by employers, clients and other interested parties as a professional person in the accountancy field.

(iii) **Quality of services** – assurance is needed that all services obtained from a professional accountant are carried out to the highest standards of performance.

(iv)   **Confidence** – users of the services of professional accountants should be able to feel confident that there is a framework of professional ethics to govern the provision of services.

Example 5 – Professional behaviour

Suppose that you are working as an accounting technician in practice and your client is very keen for the final accounts to be completed for an upcoming meeting which will discuss the future of the business. Upon review of your work, your manager shows concern about the recoverability of a number of debts, potentially showing an understatement in the irrecoverable debts figure.

Further investigation would cause a delay in the completion of the accounts, which would mean the accounts would not be ready for the client's meeting.

The appropriate action, regardless of pressure from the client, is to investigate the recoverability of these debts as any adjustment required could impact the outcome of the meeting.

 Test your understanding 10

Leo is an AAT student working for an accountancy practice. Leo is currently working on the audit of Robson Ltd and has been told by his senior to 'hurry up and finish the audit as the available budget is almost exceeded'.

Discuss the comment made by the senior.

What is understood by the term 'professionalism' will depend on the context and culture of the business.

It should include:

- **Professional/client relationship:**
    - the client presumes his or her needs will be met without having to direct the process
    - the professional decides which services are actually needed and provides them
    - the professional is trusted not to exploit his or her authority for unreasonable profit or gain.

- **Professional courtesy** – this is a bare minimum requirement of all business communication.

- **Expertise** – professionalism implies a level of competence that justifies financial remuneration.

- **Marketing and promoting services** – accountants should not make exaggerated or defamatory claims in their marketing.

2.10 The importance of transparency and fairness

 Definition – Transparency

Transparency means openness (say, of discussions), clarity, lack of withholding of relevant information unless necessary.

Decisions are made based upon financial accounts and reports. Therefore investors, amongst other stakeholders want transparent information about a business. It is the quality of the financial reports that enables decisions to be made.

 Definition – Fairness

Fairness means a sense of even-handedness and equality. Acting fairly is an ability to reach an equitable judgement in a given ethical situation.

If we act fairly we encourage strong organisational goals and develop strong relationships within a business.

Auditors may refer to financial information as being 'true and fair'. Fair implies that the financial statements present the information faithfully without any element of bias.

Test your understanding 11

You are a trainee accountant in your second year of training within a small practice. A more senior trainee has been on sick leave, and you are due to go on study leave.

You have been told by your manager that, before you go on leave, you must complete a complicated task that the senior trainee was supposed to have done. The deadline suggested appears unrealistic, given the complexity of the work.

You feel that you are not sufficiently experienced to complete the work alone but your manager appears unable to offer the necessary support. You feel slightly intimidated by your manager, and also feel under pressure to be a 'team player' and help out.

However, if you try to complete the work to the required quality but fail, you could face repercussions on your return from study leave.

Required:

Analyse the scenario to determine the following:

(a) Which fundamental principles are involved?

(b) What possible courses of action could be taken?

3 Summary

For Advanced Bookkeeping you need to have a sound knowledge of the items that appear in the financial statements of a sole trader or a partnership in good form. In this chapter we introduced the standard formats of the statement of profit or loss and statement of financial position. However you are not examined on the preparation of the financial statements until Final Accounts Preparation.

You also need to appreciate the importance of ethical behaviour in accounting. This unit introduced ethical principles that need to be applied when working in an accounting environment.

Test your understanding answers

Test your understanding 1

Non-current assets	Current assets	Current liabilities
Land	Inventory	Bank overdraft
Motor van	Receivables	VAT payable
Computers	Cash	Payables

Test your understanding 2

1 Gross profit

2 Assets – Liabilities = Capital + Profit – Drawings

Test your understanding 3

Statement of profit or loss for the year ended 31 December 20X2

	£	£
Revenue		307,500
Less: Cost of sales		
Opening inventory	37,500	
Purchases	158,700	
	196,200	
Less: Closing inventory	0	
		(196,200)
Gross profit		111,300
Less: Expenses		
Rent and rates	35,400	
Insurance	2,850	
Motor expenses	5,500	
Wages and salaries	39,060	
Postage	400	
Sundry expenses	1,000	
Discounts allowed	6,600	
		(90,810)
Profit for the year		20,490

Statement of financial position as at 31 December 20X2

	£	£	£
Non-current assets:			
Freehold factory	360,000	0	360,000
Motor vehicles	126,000	0	126,000
	486,000	0	486,000
Current assets:			
Inventory		0	
Receivables		15,600	
Cash in hand		225	
		15,825	
Current liabilities:			
Payables		78,900	
Bank overdraft		82,386	
		161,286	
Net current assets/(liabilities)			(145,461)
Total assets less current liabilities			340,539
Loan from bank			(240,000)
Net assets			**100,539**
Owner's capital			
Capital at 1.1.X2			106,149
Net profit for the year			20,490
Less: drawings			(26,100)
Proprietors funds			**100,539**

Test your understanding 4

Lara

(a)

Cash

	£		£
Capital	200	Motor van	250
Marlar – loan account	1,000	Motor expenses	15
Revenue	105	Wages	18
Commission	15	Insurance	22
		Electricity	17
		Balance c/d	998
	1,320		1,320
Balance b/d	998		

Purchases

	£		£
Payables	296	Balance c/d	381
Payables	85		
	381		381
Balance b/d	381		

Capital

	£		£
Balance c/d	200	Cash book	200
	200		200
		Balance b/d	200

Marlar – loan

	£		£
Balance c/d	1,000	Cash book	1,000
	1,000		1,000
		Balance b/d	1,000

Motor van

	£			£
Cash book	250	Balance c/d		250
	250			250
Balance b/d	250			

Sales revenue

	£			£
Balance c/d	105	Cash book		105
	105			105
		Balance b/d		105

Motor expenses

	£			£
Cash book	15	Balance c/d		15
	15			15
Balance b/d	15			

Wages

	£			£
Cash book	18	Balance c/d		18
	18			18
Balance b/d	18			

Insurance

	£			£
Cash book	22	Balance c/d		22
	22			22
Balance b/d	22			

Commission received

	£		£
Balance c/d	15	Cash book	15
	15		15
		Balance b/d	15

Electricity

	£		£
Cash book	17	Balance c/d	17
	17		17
Balance b/d	17		

Payables

	£		£
Balance c/d	381	Purchases	296
		Purchases	85
	381		381
		Balance b/d	381

(b)

Lara

Trial balance at 31 July 20X6

	£	£
Cash	998	
Purchases	381	
Capital		200
Loan		1,000
Motor van	250	
Sales revenue		105
Motor expenses	15	
Wages	18	
Insurance	22	
Commission received		15
Electricity	17	
Payables		381
	1,701	1,701

KAPLAN PUBLISHING

Test your understanding 5

Peter

Trial balance at 31 December 20X8

	£	£
Fixtures and fittings	6,430	
Delivery vans	5,790	
Cash at bank	3,720	
General expenses	1,450	
Receivables	2,760	
Payables		3,250
Purchases	10,670	
Revenue		25,340
Wages	4,550	
Drawings	5,000	
Lighting and heating	1,250	
Rent, rates and insurance	2,070	
Capital		15,100
	43,690	43,690

Test your understanding 6

Peter Wall

(a)

Cash

	£		£
Capital	10,000	Equipment	7,000
Loan	10,000	Ink	10
Revenue	200	Rent and rates	25
Receivables	60	Insurance	40
		Loan	400
		Loan interest	50
		Payables	200
		Payables	50
		Payables	100
		Balance c/d	12,385
	20,260		20,260
Balance b/d	12,385		

Payables

	£		£
Cash	200	Van	400
Cash	50	Purchases of paper	100
Cash	100		
Balance c/d	150		
	500		500
		Balance b/d	150

Capital

	£		£
		Cash	10,000

Loan account

	£		£
Cash	400	Cash	10,000
Balance c/d	9,600		
	10,000		10,000
		Balance b/d	9,600

Equipment

	£		£
Cash	7,000		

Van

	£		£
Payables (Arnold)	400		

Purchases of paper

	£		£
Payables (Butcher)	100		

Ink

	£		£
Cash	10		

Rent and rates

	£		£
Cash	25		

Loan interest

	£		£
Cash	50		

Insurance

	£		£
Cash	40		

Revenue

	£		£
Balance c/d	300	Cash	200
		Receivables (Constantine)	100
	300		300
		Balance b/d	300

Receivables

	£		£
Revenue	100	Cash	60
		Balance c/d	40
	100		100
Balance b/d	40		

(b) **Trial balance at 31 March 20X8**

	Debit £	Credit £
Cash	12,385	
Payables		150
Capital		10,000
Loan		9,600
Equipment	7,000	
Van	400	
Purchases of paper	100	
Purchases of ink	10	
Rent and rates	25	
Loan interest	50	
Insurance	40	
Revenue		300
Receivables	40	
	20,050	20,050

Test your understanding 7

Helen should inform her current employers and should be removed from the audit of the client.

 Test your understanding 8

Professional competence and due care.

 Test your understanding 9

Tell Emma that you are unable to provide her with that information as it is confidential. Regardless of Emma being your friend, you have a duty of confidentiality which must not be breached.

 Test your understanding 10

It may be that Leo is working slower than expected, in which case the comment may be simply a harmless attempt at motivation.

However, the comment to hurry up the audit may mean that the job is not done to the correct standard, thus compromising the ethical principle of professional behaviour and due care.

If the senior puts pressure on Leo, then this could be viewed as intimidation which threatens objectivity.

Test your understanding 11

Key fundamental principles affected

(a) **Integrity**: Can you be open and honest about the situation?

(b) **Professional competence and due care**: Would it be right to attempt to complete work that is technically beyond your abilities, without proper supervision? Is it possible to complete the work within the time available and still act diligently to achieve the required quality of output?

(c) **Professional behaviour**: Can you refuse to perform the work without damaging your reputation within the practice? Alternatively, could the reputation of the practice suffer if you attempt the work?

(d) **Objectivity**: Pressure from your manager, combined with the fear of repercussions, gives rise to an intimidation threat to objectivity.

Possible course of action

You should explain to your manager that you do not have sufficient time and experience to complete the work to a satisfactory standard.

However, you should demonstrate a constructive attitude, and suggest how the problem may be resolved. (Your professional body is available to advise you in this respect.) For example, you might suggest the use of a subcontract bookkeeper.

Explore the possibility of assigning another member of staff to supervise your work.

If you feel that your manager is unsympathetic or fails to understand the issue, you should consider how best to raise the matter with the person within the practice responsible for training. It would be diplomatic to suggest to your manager that you raise the matter together, and present your respective views.

It would be unethical to attempt to complete the work if you doubt your competence.

However, simply refusing to, or resigning from your employment, would cause significant problems for both you and the practice. You could consult your professional body. If you seek advice from outside the practice (for example legal advice), then you should be mindful of the need for confidentiality as appropriate.

You should document, in detail, the steps that you take in resolving your dilemma, in case your ethical judgement is challenged in the future.

Accounting for inventory

Introduction

In this chapter we will consider the accounting for opening and closing inventory and the issues that surround valuing and recording closing inventory.

As well as being able to enter a valuation for closing inventory correctly in the extended trial balance and financial statements, candidates can also expect to be assessed on other aspects of inventory valuation from IAS 2.

This will include:

- valuing inventory at the lower of cost and net realisable value

- determining the cost of inventory and its net realisable value

- various methods of costing inventory units and

- a closing inventory reconciliation.

ASSESSMENT CRITERIA	CONTENTS
Record inventory (4.3)	1 Closing inventory in the financial statements 2 Closing inventory reconciliation 3 Valuation of closing inventory 4 Methods of costing 5 Accounting for closing inventory

1 Closing inventory in the financial statements

1.1 Introduction

Most businesses will have a variety of different types of inventory. For a retail business this will be the goods that are in inventory and held for resale. In a manufacturing business there are likely to be raw material inventories (that will be used to make the business's products), partly finished products (known as work in progress) and completed goods ready for sale (known as finished goods).

These inventories are assets of the business and therefore must be included in the financial statements as current assets.

1.2 Counting closing inventory

At the end of the accounting period an inventory count (known as a stock take) will normally take place where the quantity of each line of inventory is counted and recorded. The organisation will then know the number of units of each type of inventory that it has at the year end. The next stage is to value the inventory. Both of these areas will be dealt with in detail later in the chapter.

1.3 Closing inventory and the financial statements

Once the inventory has been counted and valued it must then be included in the financial statements. The detailed accounting for this will be considered later in the chapter.

1.4 Statement of financial position

The closing inventory is an asset of the business and as such will appear on the statement of financial position. It is a current asset and will normally be shown as the first item in the list of current assets, as it is the least liquid of the current assets.

1.5   Statement of profit or loss

The layout of the statement of profit or loss was considered in detail in an earlier chapter. Below is a reminder of how inventory appears as part of the cost of sales in the statement of profit or loss:

	£	£
Revenue		X
Less: cost of sales		
Opening inventory	X	
Plus: purchases	X	
	——	
	X	
Less: closing inventory	(X)	
	——	(X)
		——
Gross profit		X
		——

As you will see the 'cost of sales' figure is made up of the opening inventory, plus the purchases of the business for the period, less the closing inventory.

The opening inventory is the figure included in the accounts as last year's closing inventory.

The purchases figure is the balance on the purchases account.

The closing inventory figure is then deducted in order to determine the cost of the goods actually sold in the period. The items included in the closing inventory have not yet been sold; they cannot be used to determine the cost of the sales within the current year, and so, are deducted. This is an application of the accruals concept – the matching concept; matching the cost of the goods sold with the revenue generated from the sales.

Closing inventory therefore appears in both the statement of financial position and the statement of profit or loss.

2 Closing inventory reconciliation

2.1 Introduction

Before the inventory of a business can be valued, the physical amount of inventory held must be counted and the amounts physically on hand checked to the stores records. Any discrepancies must be investigated. This is known as a closing inventory reconciliation.

2.2 Stores records

For each line of inventory the stores department should keep a 'bin card' or 'inventory card' which shows the following:

* the quantity of inventory received from suppliers (sourced from delivery notes or goods received notes). This should be netted off by any goods returned to the suppliers (sourced from credit notes or despatch notes)

* the quantity issued for sale or use in manufacture (sourced from store requisitions)

* any amounts returned to the stores department (sourced from goods returned notes), and

* the amount/balance of units that should be on hand at that time.

At any point in time the balance on the stores record should agree with the number of items of that line of inventory physically held by the stores department.

2.3 Possible reasons for differences

If there is a difference between the quantity physically counted and the stores records this could be for a variety of reasons:

* Goods may have been delivered and therefore have been physically counted but the stores records have not yet been updated to reflect the delivery.

* Goods may have been returned to suppliers and therefore will not have been counted but again the stores records have not yet been updated.

- Goods may have been issued for sales or for use in manufacturing, therefore they are not in the stores department but the stores records do not yet reflect this issue.

- Some items may have been stolen so are no longer physically in inventory.

- Errors may have been made, either in counting the number of items held, or in writing up the stores records.

 Example 1

At 30 June 20X4 a sole trader carried out an inventory count and compared the quantity of each line of inventory to the inventory records. In most cases the actual inventory quantity counted agreed with the stores records but, for three lines of inventory, the sole trader found differences.

	Inventory code		
	FR153	JE363	PT321
Quantity counted	116	210	94
Inventory record quantity	144	150	80

The inventory records and documentation were thoroughly checked for these inventory lines and the following was discovered:

- On 28 June, 28 units of FR153 had been returned to the supplier as they were damaged. A credit note has not yet been received and the despatch note had not been recorded in the inventory records.

- On 29 June, a goods received note showed that 100 units of JE363 had arrived from a supplier but this had not yet been entered in the inventory records.

- Also on 29 June, 14 units of PT321 had been recorded as an issue to sales, however they were not physically dispatched to the customer until after the inventory was counted.

- On 28 June, the sole trader had taken 40 units of JE363 out of inventory in order to process a rush order for a customer and had forgotten to update the inventory record.

The closing inventory reconciliation must now be performed and the actual quantities for each line of inventory that are to be valued must be determined.

Solution

Closing inventory reconciliation – 30 June 20X4

FR153	*Quantity*
Inventory record	144
Less: Returned to supplier	(28)
Counted	116

When valuing the FR153 inventory line, the actual quantity counted of 116 should be used. There should also be a journal entry to reflect the purchase return:

Debit   Purchases ledger control account

Credit   Purchases returns

JE363	*Quantity*
Inventory record	150
Add: GRN not recorded	100
Less: Sales requisition	(40)
Counted	210

The quantity to be valued should be the quantity counted of 210 units. If the sale has not been recorded then an adjustment will be required for the value of the sales invoice:

Debit   Sales ledger control account

Credit   Sales account

In addition, if the purchase has not been recorded then an adjustment will be required for the value of the purchase invoice:

Debit   Purchases

Credit   Purchase ledger control account

PT321	*Quantity*
Inventory record	80
Add: Subsequent sale	14
Counted	94

KAPLAN PUBLISHING

In this case the amount to be valued is the inventory record amount of 80 units and if the sale has not been recorded then an adjustment must be made at the selling price of the 14 units, (note that this is done as the inventory was sold on 30th June, pre period end, but after the inventory count):

Debit   Sales ledger control account

Credit   Sales account

3 Valuation of closing inventory

3.1 Introduction

Now that we know how many units of inventory we have from the inventory count, we will consider how the units of inventory are valued.

3.2 IAS 2

IAS 2 *Inventory* deals with the way in which inventories should be valued for inclusion in the financial statements. The basic rule from IAS 2 is that inventories should be valued at: 'the lower of cost and net realisable value'.

Definition – Cost of inventory

Cost is defined in IAS 2 as 'that expenditure which has been incurred in the normal course of business in bringing the product or service to its present location and condition.

This expenditure should include, in addition to cost of purchase, such costs of conversion as are appropriate to that location and condition'.

3.3 Cost

Purchase cost is defined as:

'including import duties, transport and handling costs and any other directly attributable costs, less trade discounts, rebates and subsidies'.

Costs of conversion includes:

- direct production costs

- production overheads, and

- other overheads attributable to bringing the product to its present location and condition.

This means the following:

- Only **production overheads** – not those for marketing, selling and distribution – should be included in cost.

- Exceptional spoilage, idle capacity and other abnormal costs are not part of the cost of inventories.

- General management and non-production related administration costs should not be included in inventory cost.

So far, then, we can summarise that the **cost of inventory** is:

- the purchase price from the supplier, less any trade discounts

- any delivery costs to get it to its current location, and

- the production cost of any work performed on it since it was purchased.

This means that different items of the same inventory in different locations may have different costs.

🖉 Test your understanding 1

A company had to pay a special delivery charge of £84 on a delivery of urgently required games software it had purchased for resale. This amount had been debited to office expenses account.

(a) This treatment is incorrect. Which account should have been debited? (Tick)

> Purchases account ☐
>
> Inventory account ☐
>
> Returns Inwards account ☐

(b) Give the journal entry to correct the error.

3.4 Net realisable value

Definition – Net realisable value

IAS 2 defines net realisable value (NRV) as 'the actual or estimated selling price (net of trade but before settlement discounts) less all further costs to completion and all costs to be incurred in marketing, selling and distributing'.

NRV can be summarised as the actual or estimated selling price less any future costs that will be incurred before the product can be sold.

Example 2

Jenny manufactures widgets. Details of the basic version are given below:

	Cost	Selling price	Selling cost
	£	£	£
Basic widgets	5	10	2

What value should be attributed to each widget in inventory?

Solution

Inventory valuation	£
Cost	5
Net realisable value (£10 – £2)	8

Therefore inventory should be valued at £5 per widget, the lower of cost and NRV.

It is wrong to add the selling cost of £2 to the production cost of £5 and value the inventory at £7 because it is not a production cost.

3.5 Justification of the IAS 2 rule

The valuation rule from IAS 2 that inventory must be valued at the lower of cost and net realisable value is an example of an old accounting concept known as 'prudence.' It is still relevant with regards to inventory today but it is now seen as a simple application of the accruals concept and revenue recognition rules.

Normally inventories are likely to sell for a high enough price that NRV is higher than cost (i.e. they are sold for a profit). If inventories were valued at NRV then the accounts would include the profit before they were sold. This is not allowed and so the inventory should be valued at cost.

In some circumstances it is possible that the selling price of the goods has fallen so that NRV is now lower than the original cost of the goods (i.e. they will be sold at a loss). In these circumstances the business should take a prudent approach and record the loss immediately. Therefore these goods should be valued at net realisable value.

3.6 Separate items or groups of inventory

IAS 2 also makes it quite clear that when determining whether the inventory should be valued at cost or net realisable value EACH item of inventory or groups of similar items should be considered separately.

Example 3

A business has three lines of inventory A, B and C. The details of cost and NRV for each line is given below:

	Cost £	NRV £
A	1,200	2,000
B	1,000	800
C	1,500	2,500
	3,700	5,300

What is the value of the closing inventory of the business?

Solution

It is incorrect to value the inventory at £3,700, the total cost, although it is clearly lower than the total NRV. Each line of inventory must be considered separately.

	Cost £	NRV £	Inventory value £
A	1,200	2,000	1,200
B	1,000	800	800
C	1,500	2,500	1,500
	3,700	5,300	3,500

You will see that the NRV of B is lower than its cost and therefore the NRV is the value that must be included for B.

Make sure that you look at each inventory line separately and do not just take the total cost of £3,700 as the inventory value.

 Test your understanding 2

Karen sells three products: A, B and C. At the company's year-end, the inventories held are as follows:

	Cost £	Selling price £
A	1,200	1,500
B	6,200	6,100
C	920	930

At sale a 5% commission is payable by the company to its agent.

What is the total value of these inventories in the company's accounts?

(Complete the following table)

	Cost £	Selling price £	NRV £
A			
B			
C			

Total inventory valuation =

3.7　Adjustment to closing inventory value

If closing inventory has been valued at cost and it is subsequently determined that some items of have a net realisable value which is lower than cost, then the valuation of the closing inventory must be reduced.

4 Methods of costing

4.1　Introduction

In order to determine the valuation of closing inventory the cost must be compared to the net realisable value. We have seen how cost is defined and the major element of cost will be the purchase price of the goods.

In many cases organisations buy goods at different times and at different prices, as such it is difficult to determine the exact purchase price of the goods that are left in inventory at the end of the accounting period. Therefore assumptions have to be made about the movement of inventory in and out of the warehouse.

You need to be aware of two methods of determining the purchase price of the goods – first in first out and weighted average cost. The last-in-first-out method, which used to be common, is not permitted by IAS 2.

4.2　First in, first out

The first in, first out (FIFO) method of costing inventory makes the assumption that the goods going out of the warehouse are the earliest purchases. Therefore the inventory items left are the most recent purchases.

4.3　Weighted average cost

The weighted average cost method values inventory at the weighted average of the purchase prices each time inventory is issued. This means that the total purchase price of the inventory is divided by the number of units of inventory, but this calculation must be carried out before every issue out of the warehouse.

5 Accounting for closing inventory

5.1 Introduction

You will need to be able to enter closing inventory in the statement of profit or loss and statement of financial position; and to correctly enter the figure for closing inventory in the extended trial balance. Therefore in this section accounting entries for inventory will be considered.

5.2 Opening inventory

In some of the trial balances that you have come across in this text you may have noticed a figure for opening inventory. This is the balance on the inventory account that appeared in last year's statement of financial position as the closing inventory figure. This inventory account then has no further entries put through it until the year end which is why it still appears in the trial balance.

Remember that all purchases of goods are accounted for in the purchases account, they should never be entered directly into the inventory account.

5.3 Year end procedure

At the year-end a set of adjustments must be made in order to correctly account for inventories in the statement of profit or loss and the statement of financial position.

Step 1

The opening inventory balance in the inventory account (debit balance as this was a current asset at the end of last year) is transferred to the statement of profit or loss as part of cost of sales.

The double entry for this is:

Dr   Statement of profit or loss (opening inventory in cost of sales)

Cr   Inventory account

This opening inventory balance has now been removed.

Step 2

The closing inventory, at its agreed valuation, is entered into the ledger accounts with the following double entry:

Dr   Closing inventory (asset on the statement of financial position)

Cr   Closing inventory (in cost of sales)

We will study this double entry with an example.

Example 4

John prepares accounts to 31 December 20X4.

His opening inventory on 1 January 20X4 is £20,000. During the year he purchases goods which cost £200,000. At 31 December 20X4 his closing inventory is valued at £30,000.

You are required to enter these amounts into the ledger accounts and transfer the amounts as appropriate to the statement of profit or loss.

(You should open a statement of profit or loss account in the ledger and treat it as part of the double entry as this will help you to understand the double entry).

Solution

Step 1

Open the required accounts and enter the opening inventory and purchases into the accounts.

Opening inventory

		£		£
1.1.X4	Balance b/d	20,000		

Purchases

		£		£
1.1.X4	PDB	200,000		

Statement of profit or loss

	£		£

Step 2

Write off the opening inventory and purchases to the statement of profit or loss.

Opening inventory

	£		£
1.1.X4 Balance b/d	20,000	31.12.X4 SPL	20,000

Purchases

	£		£
PDB	200,000	31.12.X4 SPL	200,000
	———		———
	200,000		200,000
	———		———

Statement of profit or loss

	£		£
31.12.X4 Opening inventory	20,000		
31.12.X4 Purchases	200,000		

Note

(a)   The opening inventory of £20,000 was brought down as an asset at the end of December 20X3, and has remained in the ledger account for the whole year without being touched.

At 31 December 20X4 it is finally written off to the debit of the statement of profit or loss as part of the cost of sales.

(b)   Purchases of goods made during the year are accumulated in the purchases account. At the end of the year (31 December 20X4) the entire year's purchases are written off to the debit of the statement of profit or loss as the next element of cost of sales. The purchases account now balances and we have closed it off. Next year will start with a nil balance on the purchases account.

Step 3

Enter the closing inventory £30,000 into the inventory account.

Closing inventory statement of profit or loss

	£		£
		31.12.X4 Closing inventory	30,000

Closing inventory statement of financial position

	£		
31.12.X4 Closing inventory	30,000		

Note

The double entry for closing inventory is therefore:

Debit   Closing inventory statement of financial position

Credit Closing inventory statement of profit or loss

(a) On the closing inventory statement of financial position account, we are just left with a debit entry of £30,000. This is the closing inventory at 31 December 20X4 and is the opening inventory at 1 January 20X5. This £30,000 will be entered on the statement of financial position and it will remain untouched in the inventory account until 31 December 20X5.

(b) The statement of profit or loss has a balance of £190,000. This is the cost of sales for the year. If we write this out in its normal form, you will see what we have done.

Step 4

Transfer the credit entry for closing inventory to the statement of profit or loss and bring down the balances on the inventory and the statement of profit or loss.

Closing inventory statement of profit or loss

	£		£
31.12.X4 SPL	30,000	31.12.X4 Closing inventory	30,000
	30,000		30,000

Statement of profit or loss

	£		£
31.12.X4 Op. inventory	20,000	31.12.X4 Closing inventory	30,000
31.12.X4 Purchases	200,000	31.12.X4 Balance c/d	190,000
	220,000		220,000
31.12.X4 Balance b/d (Cost of sales)	190,000		

Statement of profit or loss at 31.12.X4

	£	£
Revenue (not known)		X
Cost of sales		
Opening inventory (1.1.X4)	20,000	
Add: purchases	200,000	
	————	
	220,000	
Less: closing inventory (31.12.X4)	(30,000)	
	————	190,000

For the purposes of the exam you need to remember the following:

Opening inventory is recorded as part of **cost of sales** (as above) in the **statement of profit or loss.**

Closing inventory is recorded as part of **cost of sales** (as above) and as **current assets** in the **statement of financial position**.

Example 5

A business has a figure for opening inventory in its trial balance of £10,000. The closing inventory has been counted and valued at £12,000.

Show the entries in the ledger accounts to record this.

Solution

Opening inventory statement of profit or loss

	£		£
Balance b/d – opening inventory	10,000	SPL	10,000
	————		————
	10,000		10,000

Closing inventory statement of profit or loss

	£		£
SPL	12,000	Closing inventory (SFP)	12,000
	————		————
	12,000		12,000

Closing inventory statement of financial position			
	£		£
Closing inventory (SPL)	12,000	Balance c/d	12,000
	12,000		12,000
Balance b/d	12,000		

Statement of profit or loss			
	£		£
Opening inventory	10,000	Closing inventory	12,000

Test your understanding 3

1   Where will the closing inventory appear in the statement of financial position? (Tick)

Non-current assets ☐

Current assets   ☐

2   Where will the closing inventory appear in the statement of profit or loss? (Tick)

Expenses   ☐

Cost of sales   ☐

3   A line of inventory has been counted and the inventory count shows that there are 50 units more in the inventory room than is recorded on the inventory card. What possible reasons might there be for this difference?

_____

_____

_____

_____

4   Complete the following sentence.

Inventory should be valued at the _____ of_____ and _____

5   The closing inventory of a sole trader has been valued at cost of £5,800 and recorded in the trial balance. However, one item of inventory which cost £680 has a net realisable value of £580. What is the journal entry required for this adjustment? (Tick)

Debit   **Credit**

Closing inventory SoFP   Closing inventory SPL   ☐

Closing inventory SPL   Closing inventory SoFP ☐

 Test your understanding 4

Phil Townsend is the proprietor of Infortec and he sends you the following note:

'I have been looking at the inventory valuation for the year end and I have some concerns about the Mica40z PCs.

We have ten of these in inventory, each of which cost £500 and are priced to sell to customers at £580. Unfortunately they all have faulty hard drives which will need to be replaced before they can be sold. The cost is £100 for each machine.

However, as you know, the Mica40z is now out of date and having spoken to some computer retailers I am fairly certain that we are going to have to scrap them or give them away for spares. Perhaps for now we should include them in the closing inventory figure at cost. Can you please let me have your views.'

Required:

Write a memo in reply to Phil Townsend's note. Your memo should refer to alternative inventory valuations and to appropriate accounting standards.

Test your understanding 5

Melanie Langton trades as 'Explosives'.

You have received the following note from Melanie Langton:

'I have been looking at the draft financial statements you have produced. In the valuation of the closing inventory you have included some of the jeans at less than cost price. The figure you used is net realisable value and this has effectively reduced the profit for the period.

The closing inventory will be sold in the next financial period and my understanding of the accruals concept is that the revenue from selling the inventory should be matched against the cost of that inventory.

This is not now possible since part of the cost of the inventory has been written off in reducing the closing inventory valuation from cost price to net realisable value.'

Required:

Write a suitable response to Melanie Langton in the form of a memorandum.

Your answer should include references to relevant accounting concepts and to IAS 2.

6 Summary

In this chapter we have considered inventory valuation and how to record opening and closing inventory adjustments, in accordance with accounting standard IAS 2.

Test your understanding answers

 Test your understanding 1

(a)   Purchases account

			£	£
(b)	Dr	Purchases a/c	84	
	Cr	Office expenses a/c		84

 Test your understanding 2

Inventory is valued at the lower of cost and net realisable value (costs to be incurred 5% in selling inventory are deducted from selling price in computing NRV).

	Cost	Selling price	NRV
	£	£	£
A	1,200	1,500	1,425
B	6,200	6,100	5,795
C	920	930	884

Total inventory values (1,200 + 5,795 + 884) = **£7,879**

Test your understanding 3

1   As a current asset.

2   As a reduction to cost of sales.

3   •   A delivery has not yet been recorded on the inventory card.

     •   A return of goods from a customer has not yet been recorded on the inventory card.

     •   An issue to sales has been recorded on the inventory card but not yet despatched.

     •   A return to a supplier has been recorded on the inventory card but not yet despatched.

4   Inventory should be valued at the lower of cost and NRV (net realisable value).

5   Debit   Closing inventory – SPL   £100

     Credit   Closing inventory – SoFP   £100

 Test your understanding 4

M E M O

To:	Phil Townsend	**Ref:**	Valuation of inventory
From:	Accounting Technician	**Date:**	29 November 20XX

I note your observations concerning the inventory valuation and the issue of the Mica 40z PCs.

IAS 2 Inventory, states that inventory should be valued at the lower of cost and net realisable value. The NRV of a Mica 40z is £480.

If we were confident that we could sell them at that price then that would be the value for inventory purposes as this is lower than their cost of £500.

However, as you feel we are likely to scrap these computers, then I recommend we write them off to a zero inventory valuation immediately as the net realisable value is, in effect, zero.

Test your understanding 5

M E M O

To: Melanie Langton **Ref:** Closing inventory valuation

From: Accounting Technician **Date:** X-X-20XX

I refer to your recent note concerning the valuation of the closing inventory. As far as the accounting concepts are concerned, the cost of inventory would normally be matched against income in compliance with the accruals concept (i.e. purchase costs of inventory are recognised in the same period as the revenue from selling those items). Most of your inventory will be valued at cost rather than net realisable value, as the latter is usually higher than cost due to the need to achieve profit margins, and IAS 2 requires inventory to be valued at the lower of cost and net realisable value. If, however, the estimated selling price were to fall below cost (for example if market conditions changed or if the goods became damaged) then the IAS 2 principle just identified would require you to impair the value of inventory down to the estimated NRV.

I hope this fully explains the points raised in your note.

Irrecoverable and doubtful debts

Introduction

When producing a trial balance or extended trial balance, and eventually a set of final accounts, a number of adjustments are often required to the initial trial balance figures.

One of these adjustments may be to the receivables balance in order to either write off any irrecoverable debts or to provide for any allowance for doubtful debts.

ASSESSMENT CRITERIA
Record irrecoverable debts and allowances for doubtful debts (4.2)

CONTENTS
1 Problems with receivable accounts
2 Irrecoverable debts
3 Doubtful debts
4 Types of allowances for doubtful debts
5 Writing off a debt already provided for
6 Money received from irrecoverable and doubtful debts

1 Problems with receivable accounts

1.1 Introduction

When sales are made to credit customers the double entry is to debit the receivables account (sales ledger control account) and credit the sales account. Therefore the sale is recorded in the accounts as soon as the invoice is sent out to the customer on the basis that the customer will pay for these goods.

1.2 Conditions of uncertainty

In conditions of uncertainty more evidence is needed of the existence of an asset than is needed for the existence of a liability.

This has been known in the past as the **concept of prudence**. Therefore if there is any evidence of significant uncertainty about the receipt of cash from a receivable then it may be that this asset, the receivable, should not be recognised.

1.3 Aged receivable analysis

 Definition – Aged receivable analysis

An aged receivable analysis shows when the elements of the total debt owed by each customer were incurred.

An aged receivable analysis should be produced on a regular basis and studied with care. If a customer has old outstanding debts or if the customer has stopped paying the debts owed regularly then there may be a problem with this receivable.

1.4 Other information about receivables

It is not uncommon for businesses to go into liquidation or receivership in which case it is often likely that any outstanding credit supplier will not receive payment. This will often be reported in the local or national newspapers or the information could be discovered informally from conversation with other parties in the same line of business.

If information is gathered about a receivable with potential problems which may mean that your organisation will not receive full payment of the amounts due then this must be investigated.

However care should be taken as customers are very important to a business and any discussion or correspondence with the customer must be carried out with tact and courtesy.

2 Irrecoverable debts

2.1 Information

If information is reliably gathered that a credit customer is having problems paying the amounts due from them then a decision has to be made about how to account for this uncertainty. This will normally take the form of deciding whether the debt is an irrecoverable debt or a doubtful debt.

2.2 What is an irrecoverable debt?

 Definition – Irrecoverable debt

An irrecoverable debt is a debt that is not going to be received from the credit customer (receivable).

Therefore an irrecoverable debt is one that the organisation is reasonably certain will not be received at all from the credit customer. This may be decided after discussions with the credit customer (receivable), after legal advice if the customer has gone into liquidation or simply because the credit customer has disappeared.

2.3 Accounting treatment of an irrecoverable debt

An irrecoverable debt is one where it has been determined that the debt will never be recovered and therefore the receivable amount must not be recognised.

The double entry reflects the fact that:

(a) the business no longer has the debt, so this asset must be removed from the books

(b) the business must put an expense equal to the debt as a charge to its statement of profit or loss because it has 'lost' this money. It does this by putting the expense initially through an 'irrecoverable debt expense' account.

The double entry for the irrecoverable debt is:

Dr Irrecoverable debts expense account

Cr Sales ledger control account (SLCA)

There is also a credit entry in the individual receivable's account in the subsidiary sales ledger to match the entry in the SLCA.

Example 1

Lewis reviews his receivables (which total £10,000) and notices an amount due from John of £500. He knows that this will never be recovered so he wants to write it off.

Solution

Sales ledger control account

	£		£
Balance b/d	10,000	Irrecoverable debts expense	500
		Balance c/d	9,500
	10,000		10,000
Balance b/d	9,500		

Irrecoverable debts expense

	£		£
SLCA	500	SPL	500

In the subsidiary sales ledger there will also be an entry in John's account:

John's account

	£		£
Balance b/d	500	Irrecoverable debts written off	500

Test your understanding 1

A business has total receivables of £117,489. One of these debts from J Casy totalling £2,448 is now considered to be irrecoverable and must be accounted for.

Record the accounting entries in the general ledger for the irrecoverable debt.

Sales ledger control account

	£		£

Irrecoverable debts expense

	£		£

The accounting treatment of irrecoverable debts means that the debt is not recognised as a receivable in the accounting records and the statement of profit or loss is charged with an expense.

3 Doubtful debts

3.1 Introduction

In the previous section we considered debts that we were reasonably certain would not be recovered. The recoverability position with some receivables is not so clear cut. The organisation may have doubts about whether the debt will be received but may not be certain that it will not.

3.2   Doubtful debts

 Definition – Doubtful debt

Doubtful debts are receivables about which there is some question as to whether or not the debt will be received.

The situation here is not as clear cut as when a debt is determined to be irrecoverable and the accounting treatment is therefore different. If there is doubt about the recoverability of this debt then according to the prudence concept this must be recognised in the accounting records but not to the extreme of writing the debt off.

Recording an allowance for doubtful debts is an example of the application of the accruals concept; it is estimating future irrecoverable debts and therefore improves the accuracy of the financial statements.

3.3   Accounting treatment of doubtful debts

As the debt is only doubtful rather than irrecoverable we do not need to write it off but the doubt has to be reflected another way. This is done by setting up an allowance for doubtful debts.

 Definition – Allowance for doubtful debt

An allowance for doubtful debts is an amount that is netted off against the receivables balance in the statement of financial position to show that there is some doubt about the recoverability of those amounts.

An allowance for doubtful debts account is credited in order to net this off against the receivables balance and the debit entry is made to an allowance for doubtful debts adjustment expense account recognised in the statement of profit or loss.

The double entry therefore is:

Dr Allowance for doubtful debts adjustment account (SPL)

Cr Allowance for doubtful debts account (SFP)

Example 2

At the end of his first year of trading Roger has receivables of £120,000 and has decided that of these there is some doubt as to the recoverability of £5,000 of this balance.

Set up the allowance for doubtful debts in the ledger accounts and show how the net receivables would appear in the statement of financial position at the end of the year.

Solution

Allowance for doubtful debts account

	£		£
		Allowance for doubtful debts adjustments	5,000

Allowance for doubtful debt adjustment account

	£		£
Allowance for doubtful debts	5,000		

Statement of financial position extract

	£
Receivables	120,000
Less: Allowance for doubtful debts	(5,000)
	————
Net receivables	115,000
	————

The accounting treatment of doubtful debts ensures that the statement of financial position clearly shows that there is some doubt about the collectability of some of the debts and the statement of profit or loss is charged with the possible loss from not collecting these debts.

3.4 Changes in the allowance

As the allowance for doubtful debts account is a statement of financial position balance, the balance on that account will remain in the ledger accounts until it is changed. When the allowance is altered, **only the increase or the decrease** is charged or credited to the allowance for doubtful debt adjustment.

Increase in allowance:

    Dr Allowance for doubtful debt **adjustment** account (SPL)

    Cr Allowance for doubtful debts account (SoFP)

Decrease in allowance:

    Dr Allowance for doubtful debts account (SoFP)

    Cr Allowance for doubtful debt **adjustment** account (SPL)

 Example 3

At the end of the second year of trading Roger feels that the allowance should be increased to £7,000. At the end of the third year of trading Roger wishes to decrease the allowance to £4,000.

Show the entries in the ledger accounts required at the end of year 2 and year 3 of trading.

Solution

Allowance for doubtful debts account

	£		£
		Balance b/d	5,000
End of year 2 balance c/d	7,000	Year 2 – Allowance for doubtful debts adjustment account	2,000
	———		———
	7,000		7,000
	———		———
Year 3 – Allowance for doubtful debts adjustment account	3,000	Balance b/d	7,000
End of year 3 balance c/d	4,000		
	———		———
	7,000		7,000
	———		———
		Balance b/d	4,000

Allowance for doubtful debts adjustment account

	£		£
Year 2 Allowance for doubtful debt account	2,000	Statement of profit or loss year 2	2,000
	2,000		2,000
Statement of profit or loss year 3	3,000	Year 3 Allowance for doubtful debt account	3,000
	3,000		3,000

Take care that the statement of profit or loss is only debited or credited with the increase or decrease in the allowance each year.

4 Types of allowances for doubtful debts

4.1 Introduction

There are two main types of allowances for doubtful debts:

* specific allowances
* general allowances.

This does not affect the accounting for allowance for doubtful debts but it does affect the calculation of the allowance.

4.2 Specific allowances

Definition – Specific allowance

A specific allowance is an allowance against identified specific debts.

This will normally be determined by close scrutiny of the aged receivable analysis in order to determine whether there are specific debts that the organisation feels may not be paid.

4.3 General allowance

 Definition – General allowance

A general allowance is an allowance against receivables as a whole normally expressed as a percentage of the receivable balance.

Most businesses will find that not all of their receivables pay their debts. Experience may indicate that generally a percentage of debts, say 3%, will not be paid.

The organisation may not know which debts these are going to be but they will maintain an allowance for 3% of the receivable balance at the year end.

Care should be taken with the calculation of this allowance as the percentage should be of the receivable balance after deducting any specific allowances as well as any irrecoverable debts written off.

Order of dealing with irrecoverable debts and doubtful debts:

1   Write off irrecoverable debts

2   Create specific allowances

3   Calculate the net receivables figures after both irrecoverable debts and specific allowances

4   Calculate the general provision using the net receivables figure from point 3.

 Example 4

A business has receivables of £356,000 of which £16,000 are to be written off as irrecoverable debts.

Of the remainder a specific allowance is to be made against a debt of £2,000 and a general allowance of 4% is required against the remaining receivables.

The opening balance on the allowance for doubtful debts account is £12,000.

Show the entries in the allowance for doubtful debts account, the allowance for doubtful debts adjustment account and the irrecoverable debts expense account.

Solution

Calculation of allowance required:

		£
	Receivables	356,000
1	Less: irrecoverable debt to be written off	(16,000)
2	Less: specific allowances	(2,000)
3	Remaining receivables	338,000
4	General allowance 4% × £338,000	13,520
	Specific allowance	2,000
	Allowance at year end	15,520

Allowance for doubtful debts (note 1)

	£		£
		Balance b/d	12,000
Balance c/d	15,520	Allowance for doubtful debts adjustment – increase in allowance	3,520
	15,520		15,520
		Balance b/d	15,520

Sales ledger control account (note 2)

	£		£
Balance b/d	356,000	Irrecoverable debt expense – written off	16,000
		Balance c/d	340,000
	356,000		356,000
Balance b/d	340,000		

Irrecoverable debt expense account

	£		£
Receivables (Note 2)	16,000	Statement of profit or loss	16,000
	16,000		16,000

Allowance for doubtful debts adjustment account

	£		£
Allowance for doubtful debts account (Note 1)	3,520	Statement of profit or loss	3,520
	———		———
	3,520		3,520
	———		———

Note 1

The balance on the allowance account is simply 'topped-up' (or down) at each year end. In this case the required allowance has been calculated to be £15,520. The existing allowance is £12,000 so the increase is calculated as:

	£
Allowance at start of year b/f	12,000
Allowance required at year end	15,520
	———
Increase in allowance	3,520
	———

This is credited to the allowance account and debited to the allowance for doubtful debt adjustment account.

Note 2

The £16,000 irrecoverable debt is written out of the books. The double entry for this is to credit the SLCA and debit the irrecoverable debt expense.

Note that the allowance does not affect the SLCA.

Any specific allowance must be deducted from the receivables balance before the general allowance percentage is applied.

 Test your understanding 2

DD makes an allowance for doubtful debts of 5% of receivables.

On 1 January 20X5 the balance on the allowance for doubtful debts account was £1,680.

During the year the business incurred irrecoverable debts amounting to £1,950. On 31 December 20X5 receivables amounted to £32,000 after writing off the irrecoverable debts of £1,950.

Required:

Write up the relevant accounts for the year ended 31 December 20X5.

Test your understanding 3

Peter had the following balances in his trial balance at 31 March 20X4:

	£
Total receivables	61,000
Allowance for doubtful debts at 1 April 20X3	1,490

After the trial balance had been prepared it was decided to carry forward at 31 March 20X4 a specific allowance of £800 and a general allowance equal to 1% of remaining receivables. It was also decided to write off debts amounting to £1,000.

What is the total charge for irrecoverable and doubtful debts which should appear in the company's statement of profit or loss for the year ended 31 March 20X4?

5 Writing off a debt already provided for

5.1 Introduction

It may happen that a doubtful debt allowance is made at a year end, and then it is decided in a later year to write the debt off completely as an irrecoverable debt as it will not be received.

 Example 5

At 31 December 20X2, John has a balance on the SLCA of £20,000 and a specific allowance for doubtful debts of £1,000 which was created in 20X1.

This £1,000 relates to A whose debt was thought to be doubtful. There is no general allowance.

At 31 December 20X2, A has still not paid and John has decided to write the debt off as irrecoverable.

Make the related entries in the books.

Solution

Step 1

Open the SLCA and the allowance account.

SLCA

	£		£
Balance b/d	20,000		

Allowance for doubtful debts

	£		£
		Balance b/d	1,000

Step 2

Remove A's debt from the accounts.

A's £1,000 is included in the £20,000 balance on the SLCA, and this has to be removed. Similarly, the £1,000 in the allowance account related to A.

The double entry is simply to:

Debit   Allowance account with £1,000

Credit   SLCA with £1,000

SLCA

	£		£
Balance b/d	20,000	Allowance	1,000

Allowance for doubtful debts

	£		£
SLCA	1,000	Balance b/d	1,000

Note that there is no impact on the statement of profit or loss. The profits were charged with £1,000 when an allowance was made for A's debt, and there is no need to charge profits with another £1,000.

6 Money received from irrecoverable and doubtful debts

6.1 Receipt of a debt previously written off as irrecoverable

Occasionally money may be received from a receivable whose balance has already been written off as an irrecoverable debt.

The full double entry for this receipt has two elements:

Dr   Sales ledger control account

Cr   Irrecoverable debt expense account

In order to reinstate the receivable that has been previously written off.

Dr   Bank account

Cr   Sales ledger control account

To account for the cash received from this receivable.

However this double entry can be simplified to:

Dr   Bank account

Cr   Irrecoverable debts expense account (or a separate irrecoverable debts recovered account)

Note that the receivable is not reinstated as there is both a debit and credit to the sales ledger control account which cancel each other out.

6.2   Receipt of a debt previously provided against

On occasion money may be received from a receivable for whose balance a specific allowance was previously made.

The double entry for this receipt is:

Dr   Bank account

Cr   Sales ledger control account

This is accounted for as a normal receipt from a receivable and at the year end, the requirement for an allowance against this debt will no longer be necessary.

🔆 Example 6

At the end of 20X6 Bjorn had made an allowance of £500 against doubtful receivables. This was made up as follows:

		£
Specific allowance	A	300
Specific allowance	50% × B	200
		–––––
		500
		–––––

At the end of 20X7 Bjorn's receivables total £18,450. After reviewing each debt he discovers the following, none of which have been entered in the books: (1) A has paid £50 of the debt outstanding at the beginning of the year. (2) B has paid his debt in full.

Show the ledger entries required to record the above.

Step 1

Calculate the new allowance required at the year end.

	£
A	250
B	Nil
	250

Step 2

Enter the cash on the SLCA.

Sales ledger control account

	£		£
Balance b/d	18,450	Cash – A	50
		Cash – B	400
		Balance c/d	18,000
	18,450		18,450
Balance b/d	18,000		

Step 3

Bring down the new allowance required in the allowance account.

Allowance for doubtful debts adjustment account

	£		£
		Allowance for doubtful debts	250

Allowance for doubtful debts account

	£		£
Allowance for doubtful debt adjustment	250	Balance b/d	500
Balance c/d	250		
	500		500
		Balance b/d	250

Note: Because the allowance has been reduced from £500 to £250, there is a credit entry in the allowance for doubtful debt adjustment account which will be taken to the statement of profit or loss.

6.3 Journal entries

As with the depreciation charge for the year and any accrual or prepayment adjustments at the year end, any irrecoverable debts or doubtful debt allowances are transactions that will not appear in any of the books of prime entry.

Therefore, the source document for any irrecoverable debt write offs or increases or decreases in doubtful debt allowances must be the transfer journal. The necessary journals must be written up and then posted to the relevant ledger accounts at the year end.

Test your understanding 4

Record the following journal entries needed in the general ledger to deal with the items below.

(a) Entries need to be made for an irrecoverable debt of £240.

Journal	Dr £	Cr £

(b) Entries need to be made for a doubtful debt allowance. The receivable's balance at the year end is £18,000 and an allowance is to be made against 2% of these.

Journal	Dr £	Cr £

(c) A sole trader has an opening balance on his allowance for doubtful debts account of £2,500. At his year end he wishes to make an allowance for 2% of his year end receivables of £100,000.

Journal	Dr £	Cr £

(d) Entries need to be made for an amount of £200 that has been recovered, it was previously written off in the last accounting period.

Journal	Dr £	Cr £

Test your understanding 5

John Stamp has opening balances at 1 January 20X6 on his receivables account and allowance for doubtful debts account of £68,000 and £3,400 respectively.

During the year to 31 December 20X6 John Stamp makes credit sales of £354,000 and receives cash from his receivables of £340,000.

At 31 December 20X6 John Stamp reviews his receivables listing and acknowledges that he is unlikely ever to receive debts totalling £2,000. These are to be written off as irrecoverable.

John also wishes to provide an allowance against 5% of his remaining receivables after writing off the irrecoverable debts.

You are required to write up the:

- Receivables account

- Allowance for doubtful debts account and the irrecoverable debts expense account for the year to 31 December 20X6

- Show the receivables and allowance for doubtful debts extract from the statement of financial position at that date.

 Test your understanding 6

Angola

Angola started a business on 1 January 20X7 and during the first year of business it was necessary to write off the following debts as irrecoverable:

		£
10 April	Cuba	46
4 October	Kenya	29
6 November	Peru	106

On 31 December 20X7, after examination of the sales ledger, it was decided to provide an allowance against two specific debts of £110 and £240 from Chad and Chile respectively and to make a general allowance of 4% against the remaining debts.

On 31 December 20X7, the total of the receivables balances stood at £5,031; Angola had not yet adjusted this total for the irrecoverable debts written off.

Required:

Show the accounts for irrecoverable debts expense and allowance for doubtful debts.

 Test your understanding 7

Zambia

On 1 January 20X8 Angola sold his business, including the receivables, to Zambia. During the year ended 31 December 20X8 Zambia found it necessary to write off the following debts as irrecoverable:

		£
26 February	Fiji	125
8 August	Mexico	362

He also received on 7 July an amount of £54 as a final dividend against the debt of Peru which had been written off during 20X7.

No specific allowance were required at 31 December 20X8 but it was decided to make a general allowance of 5% against outstanding receivables.

On 31 December 20X8 the total of the receivables balances stood at £12,500 (before making any adjustments for irrecoverable debts written off during the year) and the balance b/d on the allowance for doubtful debts account stood at £530.

Required:

Show the accounts for irrecoverable debt expense and allowance for doubtful debts, bringing forward any adjustments for Angola.

7 Summary

When sales are made on credit they are recognised as income when the invoice is sent out on the assumption that the money due will eventually be received from the receivable.

However according to the prudence concept if there is any doubt about the recoverability of any of the debts this must be recognised in the accounting records.

The accounting treatment will depend upon whether the debt is considered to be an irrecoverable debt or a doubtful debt.

Irrecoverable debts are written out of the sales ledger control account.

However, for doubtful debts an allowance is set up which is netted off against the receivables figure in the statement of financial position. The charge or credit to the statement of profit or loss each year for doubtful debts is either the increase or decrease in the allowance for doubtful debts required at the end of the each year.

Test your understanding answers

Test your understanding 1

Sales ledger control account

	£		£
Balance b/d	117,489	Irrecoverable debts expense	2,448
		Balance c/d	115,041
	117,489		117,489
Balance b/d	115,041		

Irrecoverable debts expense account

	£		£
Sales ledger control account	2,448	SPL	2,448

Test your understanding 2

Allowance for doubtful debts accounts

	£		£
Irrecoverable debts exps	80	Balance b/d	1,680
Balance c/d	1,600		
	1,680		1,680
		Balance b/d	1,600

Note: the allowance required at 31 December 20X5 is calculated by taking 5% of the total receivables at 31 December 20X5 (i.e. 5% × £32,000 = £1,600). As there is already an allowance of £1,680, there will be a release of the allowance (decrease) of £80.

Irrecoverable debts expense

	£		£
Irrecoverable debts written off	1,950		
		Statement of profit or loss	1,950
	1,950		1,950

Allowance for doubtful debts adjustment

	£		£
		Allowance for doubtful debts	80
Statement of profit or loss	80		
	80		80

Test your understanding 3

Allowance for doubtful debts accounts

	£		£
Allowance for doubtful debts adjustment	98	Balance b/d	1,490
Balance c/d	1,392		
	1,490		1,490
		Balance b/d (800 + 592)	1,392

Required allowance of £1,392 is made up of the specific allowance of £800 and a general allowance calculated as £592 ((£61,000 − £1,000 − £800) × 1%)

Irrecoverable debts expense

	£		£
Irrecoverable debts written off	1,000		
		Statement of profit or loss	1,000
	1,000		1,000

Allowance for doubtful debts adjustment

	£		£
		Allowance for doubtful debts	98
Statement of profit or loss	98		
	98		98

Test your understanding 4

(a) Entries need to be made for an irrecoverable debt of £240; main ledger accounts therefore will be as below.

Journal	Dr £	Cr £
Irrecoverable debts expense account	240	
Sales ledger control account		240

(b) Allowance is calculated as £18,000 × 2%.

Journal	Dr £	Cr £
Allowance for doubtful debt adjustment account	360	
Allowance for doubtful debts account		360

(c)   Allowance for doubtful debts are ((100,000 × 2%) – 2,500)

Journal	Dr £	Cr £
Allowance for doubtful debts	500	
Allowance for doubtful debt adjustment account		500

(d)   Entries need to be made for an amount of £200 in the bank and irrecoverable debt expense account.

Journal	Dr £	Cr £
Bank account	200	
Irrecoverable debt expense account		200

Test your understanding 5

Step 1

Write up the receivables account showing the opening balance, the credit sales for the year and the cash received.

Receivables

20X6	£	20X6	£
1 Jan Bal b/d	68,000	31 Dec Cash	340,000
31 Dec Revenue	354,000		

Step 2

Write off the irrecoverable debts for the period:

Dr   Irrecoverable debts expense account

Cr   Receivables account

Irrecoverable debts expense

20X6	£	20X6	£
31 Dec Receivables	2,000		

Receivables

20X6	£	20X6	£
1 Jan Balance b/d	68,000	31 Dec Cash	340,000
		31 Dec Irrecoverable	
31 Dec Revenue	354,000	debts expense	2,000

Step 3

Balance off the receivables account to find the closing balance against which the allowance is required.

Receivables

20X6		£	20X6		£
1 Jan	Balance b/d	68,000	31 Dec	Cash	340,000
31 Dec	Revenue	354,000	31 Dec	Irrecoverable debts expense	2,000
			31 Dec	Balance c/d	80,000
		422,000			422,000
20X7					
1 Jan	Balance b/d	80,000			

Step 4

Set up the allowance required of 5% of £80,000 = £4,000. Remember that there is already an opening balance on the allowance for doubtful debts account of £3,400 therefore only the increase in allowance required of £600 is credited to the allowance account and debited to the allowance for doubtful debt adjustment account.

Allowance for doubtful debt adjustment

20X6	£	20X6	£
Allowance for doubtful debts	600	31 Dec SPL	600
	600		600

Allowance for doubtful debts

20X6	£	20X6	£
		1 Jan Balance b/d	3,400
31 Dec Balance c/d		31 Dec Allowance for	
	4,000	doubtful debt adjustment	600
	———		———
	4,000		4,000
	———		———
		20X7	
		1 Jan Balance b/d	4,000

Step 5

The relevant extract from the statement of financial position at 31 December 20X6 would be as follows:

	£	£
Current assets		
Receivables	80,000	
Less: Allowance for doubtful debts	(4,000)	
	———	76,000

Test your understanding 6

Angola

Allowance doubtful debts

	£		£
		Irrecoverable debts	
Balance c/d	530	expense account	530
	———		———
	530		530
	———		———
		Balance b/d	530

Irrecoverable debts expense

	£		£
Receivables written off			
Cuba	46	Statement of profit or loss	711
Kenya	29		
Peru	106		
Allowance account	530		
	———		———
	711		711
	———		———

Working – Allowance carried down

Specific:	£110 + £240	£350
General:	4% × (£5,031 – £46 – £29 – £106 – £350)	£180
		____
		530
		____

Note:

Only one account is being used for allowance for doubtful debt adjustment and irrecoverable debt expense. This is because the entries in the allowance for doubtful debt adjustment account and the irrecoverable debt expense account affect the statement of profit or loss.

Test your understanding 7

Zambia

Allowance for doubtful debts

	£		£
		Balance b/d	530
Balance c/d (W1)		Irrecoverable debts expense account	
	601	extra charge required (W2)	71
	____		____
	601		601
	____		____
		Balance b/d	601

Working

1 **Allowance carried down**

		£
Specific:		
General:	5% × (£12,500 – £125 – £362)	601
		____
		601
		____

2   **Extra charge required**

	£
Allowance required at end of year	601
Allowance brought down and available	530
Increase required in allowance	71

Irrecoverable debts expense

	£		£
Receivables written off			
Fiji	125	Cash	54
Mexico	362	Statement of profit or loss	504
Allowance account	71		
	558		558

Control account reconciliations

Introduction

Before the preparation of a trial balance or extended trial balance, we should consider reconciling the sales ledger control account and the purchases ledger control account.

The purpose is to detect any errors made in accounting for sales and purchases and to ensure that the correct figure is used for receivables and payables in the statement of financial position.

ASSESSMENT CRITERIA	CONTENTS
Carry out financial period end routines (1.5)	1 Subsidiary ledgers 2 Contra entries 3 Sales and purchases ledger control accounts 4 Control account reconciliations

1 Subsidiary ledgers

1.1 Introduction

As you have seen in your earlier studies double entry bookkeeping is performed in the ledger accounts in the general ledger. This means that when double entry is performed with regard to credit sales and purchases this takes place in the sales ledger control account and purchases ledger control account.

The details of each transaction with each customer and supplier are also recorded in the subsidiary ledgers. There will be a subsidiary ledger for receivables (called the sales ledger) and a subsidiary ledger for payables (called the purchases ledger).

Note: The sales ledger control account can also be called the receivables ledger control account, while the purchases ledger control account can also be called the payables ledger control account.

1.2 Sales ledger

 Definition – Sales ledger

The sales ledger is a collection of records for each individual receivable of the organisation. It may alternatively be called the receivables ledger.

The record for each receivable is normally in the form of a ledger account and each individual sales invoice, credit note and receipt from the receivable is recorded in the account. These accounts are known as subsidiary (memorandum) accounts as they are not part of the double entry system.

This means that at any time it is possible to access the details of all the transactions with a particular receivable and the balance on that receivable's account.

1.3 Purchases ledger

 Definition – Purchases ledger

The purchases ledger is a collection of records for each individual payable of the organisation. It may alternatively be called the payables ledger.

The record for each payable is normally in the form of a ledger account and each individual purchase invoice, credit note and payment to the payable is recorded in the account. These accounts are again known as subsidiary (memorandum) accounts as they are not part of the double entry system.

This means that at any time it is possible to access the details of all of the transactions with a particular payable and the balance on that payable's account.

1.4 Credit sales

In the general ledger the double entry for credit sales (with VAT) is:

Dr   Sales ledger control account (gross amount)

Cr   VAT (VAT amount)

Cr   Sales account (net amount)

The figures that are used in the double entry are the totals taken from the sales day book for the period.

Each individual invoice (including VAT) from the sales day book is then debited to the individual receivable accounts in the sales ledger to increase the amount owed by the receivable.

Example 1

Celia started business on 1 January 20X5 and made all of her sales on credit terms. No discount was offered for prompt payment. VAT should be ignored. During January 20X5, Celia made the following credit sales:

	£
To Shelagh	50
To John	30
To Shelagh	25
To Godfrey	40
To Shelagh	15
To Godfrey	10

Solution

By the end of January 20X5 the **sales day book (SDB)** will appear as follows:

Customer	Invoice no.	£
Shelagh	1	50
John	2	30
Shelagh	3	25
Godfrey	4	40
Shelagh	5	15
Godfrey	6	10
		___
		170
		___

At the end of the month, the following **double-entry in the general ledger** will be made:

		£	£
Debit	Sales ledger control account	170	
Credit	Sales account		170

Also the following postings will be made to the **memorandum accounts in the sales ledger:**

		£
Debit	Shelagh	50
Debit	John	30
Debit	Shelagh	25
Debit	Godfrey	40
Debit	Shelagh	15
Debit	Godfrey	10

The **sales ledger** will now show:

John

	£		£
SDB	30		

Shelagh

	£		£
SDB	50		
SDB	25		
SDB	15		

Godfrey

	£		£
SDB	40		
SDB	10		

The **general ledger** will include:

Sales ledger control account

	£		£
SDB	170		

Sales

	£		£
		SDB	170

1.5   Cash receipts from receivables

The cash receipts from receivables are initially recorded in the cash receipts book. The double entry in the general ledger is:

Dr   Bank account

Cr   Sales ledger control account

The figure used for the posting is the total from the cash receipts book.

Each individual receipt is then credited to the individual receivable accounts in the sales ledger to reduce the amount owed by the receivable.

Example 2

Continuing with Celia's business. During January 20X5, the following amounts of cash were received:

	£
From John	30
From Godfrey	10
From Shelagh	50

Solution

By the end of the month the analysed cash book will show:

Debit side

Date	Narrative	Total £	Sales ledger £	Cash sales £	Other £
1/X5	John	30	30		
1/X5	Godfrey	10	10		
1/X5	Shelagh	50	50		
		90	90		

Now for the double-entry. At the end of the month, the bank account in the general ledger will be debited and the sales ledger control account in the general ledger will be credited with £90.

Memorandum entries will be made to the individual accounts in the sales ledger as follows:

		£
Credit	John	30
Credit	Godfrey	10
Credit	Shelagh	50

The sales ledger will now show:

John

	£		£
SDB	30	Analysed cash book	30

Shelagh

	£		£
SDB	50	Analysed cash book	50
SDB	25	Balance c/d	40
SDB	15		
	——		——
	90		90
	——		——
Balance b/d	40		

Godfrey

	£		£
SDB	40	Analysed cash book	10
SDB	10	Balance c/d	40
	——		——
	50		50
	——		——
Balance b/d	40		

The general ledger will include:

Sales ledger control account

	£		£
SDB	170	Analysed cash book	90
		Balance c/d	80
	——		——
	170		170
	——		——
Balance b/d	80		

Sales account

	£		£
		SDB	170

Cash account

	£		£
Analysed cash book	90		

The trial balance will show:

	Dr £	Cr £
Sales ledger control account	80	
Sales		170
Cash	90	
	170	170

Notes

- As the individual accounts in the sales ledger are not part of the double-entry, they will not appear in the trial balance.

- The total of the individual balances in the sales ledger should agree to the balance on the sales ledger control account. Normally before the trial balance is prepared a reconciliation will be performed between the individual accounts and the sales ledger control account:

	£
John	–
Shelagh	40
Godfrey	40
Total per individual accounts	80
Balance per sales ledger control account	80

This reconciliation will help to ensure the accuracy of our postings. We shall look at this in more detail later in this chapter.

If all of the entries in the control account and the sales ledger have been made correctly then the total of the individual balances in the sales ledger should equal the balance on the sales ledger control account in the general ledger.

1.6 Sales returns

The double entry for sales returns (with VAT) is:

Dr   Sales returns account (net amount)

Dr   VAT (VAT amount)

Cr   Sales ledger control account (gross amount)

Each return (including VAT) is also credited to the individual receivable's account in the sales ledger to reduce the amount owed by the receivable.

1.7 Discounts allowed

Discounts allowed to receivables are recorded in the discounts allowed book if a receivable takes advantage of a prompt payment discount. The double entry for these discounts (with VAT if VAT registered) is:

Dr   Discounts allowed account (net amount)

Dr   VAT (VAT amount)

Cr   Sales ledger control account (gross amount)

The discount (including VAT) is also credited to the individual receivable's account in the sales ledger to show a reduction to the amount owed by the receivable.

1.8 Accounting for purchases on credit

The accounting system for purchases on credit works in the same manner as for sales on credit and is summarised as follows.

The total of the purchases day book is used for the double entry in the general ledger:

Dr   Purchases account (net amount)

Dr   VAT (VAT amount)

Cr   Purchases ledger control account (gross amount)

Each individual invoice (including VAT) is also credited to the individual payable accounts in the purchases ledger to increase the amount owed to the payable.

The total of the cash payments book is used for the double entry in the general ledger:

Dr   Purchases ledger control account

Cr   Bank account

Each individual payment is then debited to the payable's individual account in the purchases ledger to decrease the amount owed to the payable.

1.9 Purchases returns

The double entry for purchases returns is:

Dr   Purchases ledger control account (gross amount)

Cr   VAT (VAT amount)

Cr   Purchases returns account (net amount)

Each purchase return is also debited to the individual payable's account in the purchases ledger to decrease the amount owed to the payable.

1.10   Discounts received

Discounts received from suppliers are recorded in the discounts received book when they are deducted from payments made to the supplier due to taking up an offer of a prompt payment discount. They are then posted in the general ledger as:

Dr   Purchases ledger control account (gross amount)

Cr   VAT (VAT amount)

Cr   Discounts received account (net amount)

Each discount (including VAT) is also debited to the individual payable's account in the purchases ledger to show a reduction to the amount owed.

2   Contra entries

2.1   Introduction

A business sometimes sells goods to, and purchases goods from, the same person, i.e. one of the receivables is also a payable. As it would seem pointless to pay the payable and then receive payment for the debt, a business will often offset as much as is possible of the receivable and the payable balances. The entry that results is called a contra entry and the double entry for this is:

Dr   Purchases ledger control account

Cr   Sales ledger control account

Example 3

Celia sells goods to Godfrey but also purchases some supplies from him. At the end of the period, Godfrey owes Celia £40 but Celia also owes Godfrey £50. The balances on the accounts in the subsidiary sales and purchases ledgers in Celia's books will be:

Sales ledger

Godfrey

	£		£
Balance b/d	40		

Purchases ledger

Godfrey

	£		£
		Balance b/d	50

The maximum amount which can be offset is £40 and after recording the contra entries the accounts will show:

Sales ledger

Godfrey

	£		£
Balance b/d	40	Contra with purchase ledger	40
	___		___

Purchases ledger

Godfrey

	£		£
Contra with sales ledger	40	Balance b/d	50
Balance c/d	10		
	___		___
	50		50
	___		___
		Balance b/d	10

I.e. Celia still owes Godfrey £10.

We have so far considered only the individual receivables' and payables' accounts but we know that every entry which is put through an individual account must also be recorded in the control accounts in the general ledger. Assuming that the balances before the contras on the sales ledger control account (SLCA) and the purchases ledger control account (PLCA) were £15,460 and £12,575 respectively, they will now show:

SLCA

	£		£
Balance b/d	15,460	Contra with PLCA	40
		Balance c/d	15,420
	_____		_____
	15,460		15,460
	_____		_____
Balance b/d	15,420		

PLCA

	£		£
Contra with SLCA	40	Balance b/d	12,575
Balance c/d	12,535		
	12,575		12,575
		Balance b/d	12,535

i.e. receivables and payables have both been reduced by £40.

3 Sales and purchases ledger control accounts

3.1 Introduction

Now that we have reminded you of the entries to the sales ledger and purchases ledger control accounts we will summarise the typical entries in these accounts.

3.2 Proforma sales ledger control account

Sales ledger control account			
	£		£
Balance b/d	X	Returns per returns day book	X
Sales per sales day book	X	Cash from receivables *	X
		Discounts allowed *	X
		Irrecoverable debts written off	X
		Contra with purchases ledger control a/c	X
		Balance c/d	X
	X		X
Balance b/d	X		

3.3 Proforma purchases ledger control account

Purchases ledger control account

	£		£
		Balance b/d	X
Cash to suppliers *	X	Purchases per purchase day	X
Discounts received *	X	book	
Returns per returns day book	X		
Contra with sales ledger control a/c	X		
Balance c/d	X		
	X		X
		Balance b/d	X

* Per cash book, discounts allowed and received books.

Test your understanding 1

The following information is available concerning Meads' sales ledger:

	£
Receivables 1.1.X7	3,752
Returns inwards	449
Cheques received from customers, subsequently dishonoured	25
Credit sales in year to 31.12.X7	24,918
Cheques from receivables	21,037
Cash from receivables	561
Purchases ledger contra	126
Cash sales	3,009

Required:

Write up the sales ledger control account for the year ended 31 December 20X7.

Sales ledger control account

	£		£

4 Control account reconciliations

4.1 Introduction

As we have seen earlier in the chapter the totals of the balances on the sales or purchases ledgers should agree with the balance on the sales ledger control account and purchases ledger control account respectively.

If the balances do not agree then there has been an error in the accounting which must be investigated and corrected.

Therefore this reconciliation of the total of the subsidiary ledger balances to the control account total should take place on a regular basis, usually monthly, and certainly should take place before the preparation of a trial balance.

4.2 Procedure

The steps involved in performing a control account reconciliation are as follows:

Step 1

Determine the balance on the control account.

Step 2

Total the individual balances in the subsidiary ledger.

Step 3

Compare the two totals as they should agree.

Step 4

If the totals do not agree then the difference must be investigated and corrected.

4.3 Possible reasons for differences

Errors could have taken place in the accounting in the control account or in the individual customer or supplier accounts in the subsidiary ledgers. Possible errors include:

- Errors in casting (i.e. adding up) of the day books – this means that the totals posted to the control accounts are incorrect but the individual entries to the subsidiary ledgers are correct.

- A transposition error made in posting to either the control account or the individual accounts in the subsidiary ledger.

- A contra entry has not been recorded in all of the relevant accounts i.e. the control accounts and the subsidiary ledger accounts.

- A balance has been omitted from the list of subsidiary ledger balances.

- A balance in the subsidiary ledger has been included in the list of balances as a debit when it was a credit, or vice versa.

4.4 Treatment of the differences in the control account reconciliation

When the reasons for the difference have been discovered the following procedure takes place:

- the control account balance is adjusted for any errors affecting the control account

- the list of subsidiary ledger balances is adjusted for any errors that affect the list of individual balances

- after these adjustments the balance on the control account should agree to the total of the list of individual balances.

The key to these reconciliations is to be able to determine which types of error affect the control account and which affect the list of balances.

 Example 4

The balance on Diana's sales ledger control account at 31 December 20X6 was £15,450. The balances on the individual accounts in the sales ledger have been extracted and total £15,705. Diana is not VAT registered. On investigation the following errors are discovered:

(1) a debit balance of £65 has been omitted from the list of balances

(2) a contra between the subsidiary purchases and sales ledgers of £40 has not been recorded in the control accounts

(3) discounts allowed totalling £70 have been recorded in the individual accounts but not in the control account

(4) the sales day book was 'overcast' by £200 (this means the total was added up as £200 too high), and

(5) an invoice for £180 was recorded correctly in the sales day book but was posted to the receivables' individual account as £810.

Solution

Step 1

We must first look for those errors which will mean that the control account is incorrectly stated: they will be points 2, 3 and 4 above.

The control account is then adjusted as follows.

Sales ledger control account

	£		£
Balance b/d	15,450	Contra	40
		Discounts allowed	70
		Overcast of SDB	200
		Adjusted balance c/d	15,140
	------		------
	15,450		15,450
	------		------
Balance b/d	15,140		

Step 2

There will be errors in the total of the individual balances per the sales ledger as a result of points 1 and 5. The extracted list of balances must be adjusted as follows:

	£
Original total of list of balances	15,705
Debit balance omitted	65
Transposition error (810 – 180)	(630)

	15,140

Step 3

As can be seen, the adjusted total of the list of balances now agrees with the adjusted balance per the sales ledger control account.

Test your understanding 2

The balance on Mead's sales ledger control account is £6,522.

Mead extracts his list of receivables' balances at 31 December 20X7 and they total £6,617.

He discovers the following:

(1)   The sales day book has been under cast by £100.

(2)   A contra with the purchase ledger of £20 with the account of Going has not been entered in the control account.

(3)   The account of Murdoch in the sales ledger which shows a credit balance of £65 has been shown as a debit balance in the list of balances.

(4)   McCormack's account with a debit balance of £80 has been omitted from the list of balances.

(5)   Discounts allowed of £35 recorded in the sales ledger were not shown in the sales ledger control account.

Mead is not VAT registered.

Required:

Show the necessary adjustment to the sales ledger control account and prepare a statement reconciling the list of balances with the balance on the sales ledger control account.

Sales ledger control account

	£		£
	___		___
	___		___

List of balances per sales ledger

	£
Total per draft list	
Less:	
	___
Add:	
	___
Total per receivables' control account	___

4.5 Purchases ledger control account reconciliation

The procedure for a purchases ledger control account reconciliation is just the same as for the sales ledger control account reconciliation however you must remember that the entries are all the other way around.

Example 5

The balance on John's purchases ledger control account at 31 May 20X5 was £14,667. However the total of the list of balances from the purchases ledger totalled £14,512.

Upon investigation the following errors were noted:

(1)   an invoice from J Kilpin was credited to his account in the purchases ledger as £210 whereas it was correctly entered into the purchases day book as £120.

(2)   the cash payments book was under cast by £100.

(3)   a transfer of £50 from a receivables' account in the sales ledger to their account in the purchases ledger has been correctly made in the subsidiary ledgers but not in the control accounts (a contra entry).

(4)   a debit balance of £40 on a payable's account in the subsidiary ledger was included in the list of balances as a credit balance.

(5)   the discounts received total of £175 was not posted to the control account in the general ledger.

John is not VAT registered.

Required:

Reconcile the corrected balance on the purchases ledger control account with the correct total of the list of payables' balances from the subsidiary ledger.

Solution

Purchases ledger control account

	£		£
Under cast of CPB (2)	100	Balance b/d	14,667
Contra (3)	50		
Discounts received (5)	175		
Adjusted balance c/d	14,342		
	_____		_____
	14,667		14,667
	_____		_____
		Balance b/d	14,342

List of balances per purchase ledger

	£
Total per draft list	14,512
Transposition error (210 – 210) (1)	(90)
Debit balance included as a credit balance (2 × 40) (4)	(80)
	_____
	14,342
	_____

 Test your understanding 3

The total of the list of balances extracted from Morphy's purchases ledger on 30 September 20X1 amounted to £5,676 which did not agree with the balance on the purchases ledger control account of £6,124.

(1) An item of £20 being purchases from R Fischer had been posted from the purchases day book to the credit of Lasker's account.

(2) On 30 June 20X1 Spasskey had been debited for goods returned to him, £85, and no other entry had been made.

(3) Credit balances in the purchases ledger amounting to £562 and debit balances amounting to £12 (Golombek, £7, Alexander £5) had been omitted from the list of balances.

(4) Morphy had correctly recorded returns outwards of £60. However, these returns were later disallowed. No record was made when the returns were disallowed.

(5) A contra of £90 with the sales ledger had been recorded twice in the control account.

(6) The purchases day book has been undercast by £100.

(7) A payment to Steinitz of £3 for a cash purchase of goods had been recorded in the petty cash book and posted to his account in the purchases ledger, no other entry having been made.

Morphy is not VAT registered.

Required:

(a) Prepare the purchases ledger control account showing the necessary adjustments.

(b) Prepare a statement reconciling the original balances extracted from the purchases ledger with the corrected balance on the purchases ledger control account.

Purchases ledger control account

	£		£

List of balances per purchases ledger

	£
Total per draft list	

Test your understanding 4

1   What is the double entry in the general ledger for sales returns?

2   What is the double entry in the general ledger for discounts received (ignore VAT)?

3   When preparing the sales ledger control account reconciliation it was discovered that discounts allowed had been under cast in the discounts allowed book by £100. You should ignore VAT. What is the double entry required to correct this?

4   A credit note sent to a credit customer for £340 had been entered in the customer's account in the sales ledger at £430. How would this be adjusted for in the sales ledger control account reconciliation?

5   When preparing the purchases ledger control account reconciliation it was discovered that the total of the purchases returns day book had been posted as £1,300 rather than £300. What is the double entry required to correct this?

6   A payment to a credit supplier was correctly recorded in the cash payments book at £185 but was posted to the payable's individual account in the purchase ledger as £158. How would this be adjusted for in the purchases ledger control account reconciliation?

7   A contra entry for £100 had only been entered in the general ledger accounts and not in the subsidiary ledger accounts. How would this be adjusted for in the purchases ledger control account reconciliation?

Test your understanding 5

Mortimer Wheeler

Mortimer Wheeler is a general dealer and is not VAT registered. The following is an extract from the opening trial balance of his business at 1 January 20X6:

		Dr £	Cr £
Cash		1,066	
Trade receivables		5,783	
Trade payables			5,531
Allowance for doubtful debts			950

Receivables and payables are listed below:		£
Receivables	Pitt-Rivers	1,900
	Evans	1,941
	Petrie	1,942
		5,783
Payables	Cunliffe	1,827
	Atkinson	1,851
	Piggott	1,853
		5,531

In January the following purchases, sales and cash transactions were made:

		£			£
Purchases	Cunliffe	950	Payments	Cuncliffe	900
	Atkinson	685		Atkinson	50
	Piggott	1,120		Piggott	823
		2,755			1,773

		£			£
Sales	Pitt-Rivers	50	Receipts	Pitt-Rivers	–
	Evans	1,760		Evans	1,900
	Petrie	1,665		Petrie	1,942
		3,475			3,842

The £950 allowance was against 50% of Pitt-Rivers' debt. Pitt-Rivers was declared bankrupt half way through the year.

Evans denied knowledge of £41 of the balance outstanding at 1 January 20X6 and Mortimer felt that this amount should be provided for as a doubtful debt.

Mortimer received £15 discount from Cunliffe for prompt payment.

Required:

Write up:

(a) Sales and purchases accounts, sales and purchases ledger control accounts, the allowance for doubtful debts account and the irrecoverable debts expense account, the sales and purchases ledgers.

(b) Lists of receivables and payables balances at the end of January.

Test your understanding 6

Data

The individual balances of the accounts in the sales ledger of a business were listed, totalled and compared with the £73,450 balance of the sales ledger control account.

The total of the list came to £76,780 and after investigation the following errors were found:

(a) A customer account with a balance of £400 was omitted from the list.

(b) A £50 discount allowed had been debited to a customer's account.

(c) A customer's account with a balance of £2,410 was included twice in the list.

(d) A customer's balance of £320 was entered in the list as £230.

(e) A customer with a balance of £540 had been written off as an irrecoverable debt during the year but the balance was still included in the list.

(f) Sales returns totalling £770 (including VAT) had been omitted from the relevant customer accounts.

Task

Make appropriate adjustments to the total of the list using the table below. For each adjustment show clearly the amount involved and whether the amount is to be added or subtracted.

	£
Total from listing of balances	76,780
Adjustment for (a) add/(subtract)	....
Adjustment for (b) add/(subtract)	....
Adjustment for (c) add/(subtract)	....
Adjustment for (d) add/(subtract)	....
Adjustment for (e) add/(subtract)	....
Adjustment for (f) add/(subtract)	....
Revised total to agree with sales ledger control account	....

Test your understanding 7

On 30 November 20X3 the balances of the accounts in the purchases ledger of a business were listed, totalled and then compared with the updated balance of the purchases ledger control account. The total of the list of balances amounted to £76,670. After investigation the following errors were found:

(a)   A credit purchase of £235 (inclusive of VAT) had been omitted from a supplier's account in the purchases ledger.

(b)   A payment of £1,600 to a supplier had been credited to the supplier's account in the purchases ledger.

(c)   A supplier's balance of £1,194 had been listed as £1,914.

Enter the appropriate adjustments in the table shown below. For each adjustment show clearly the amount involved and whether the amount is to be added or subtracted.

	£
Total from listing of balances	76,670
Adjustment for (a) add/subtract*	....
Adjustment for (b) add/subtract*	....
Adjustment for (c) add/subtract*	....
Revised total to agree with purchases ledger control account	....

 Test your understanding 8

A credit sale, made by The Pine Warehouse, was correctly entered into the general ledger but was then credited to the customer's memorandum account in the sales ledger.

(a)   Would the error be detected by drawing up a trial balance?

Yes / No

(b)   Briefly explain the reason for your answer to (a).

5 Summary

The chapter began with a revision of the entries from the books of prime entry to the sales ledger and purchases ledger control accounts and to the sales ledger and purchases ledger.

If the entries are all correctly made the balance on the control account should agree to the total of the list of balances in the appropriate subsidiary ledger. This must however be checked on a regular basis by carrying out a reconciliation of the control account and the total of the list of balances.

The process of carrying out a control account reconciliation is to consider each error and determine whether it affects the control account, the individual receivable/payable accounts in the subsidiary ledger or both. The control account will then be adjusted to find a corrected balance and this should agree to the corrected total of the individual accounts from the subsidiary ledger.

KAPLAN PUBLISHING

Test your understanding answers

Test your understanding 1

Sales ledger control account

	£		£
Balance b/d	3,752	Returns inwards	449
Cheques dishonoured	25	Cheques	21,037
Credit sales	24,918	Cash	561
		Contra with purchases ledger	126
		Balance c/d	6,522
	28,695		28,695
Balance b/d	6,522		

NB: cash sales do not affect the SLCA

Test your understanding 2

Sales ledger control account

	£		£
Balance b/d	6,522	Contra with purchases ledger (2)	20
Sales day book (1)	100	Discounts (5)	35
		Balance c/d	6,567
	6,622		6,622
Balance b/d	6,567		

List of balances per sales ledger

	£
Total per draft list	6,617
Less: Murdoch's balance included as a credit (3) (£65 × 2)	(130)
	6,487
Add: McCormack's balance (4)	80
Total per receivables' control account	6,567

Test your understanding 3

Purchases ledger control account

	£		£
Returns allowed (2)	85	Balance b/d	6,124
Balance c/d	6,289	Returns disallowed (4)	60
		Correction of contra recorded twice (5)	90
		Under cast of purchases day book (6)	100
	6,374		6,374
		Balance b/d	6,289

List of balances per purchases ledger

	£
Total per draft list	5,676
Credit balances omitted (3)	562
Debit balances omitted (3)	(12)
Returns disallowed (4)	60
Petty cash purchase (7) (used incorrectly to reduce amount owing for credit purchases)	3
	6,289

(**Note** point (1) in the question does not affect the overall balance of the accounts. It has been treated correctly but posted to the wrong suppliers account)

Test your understanding 4

1 Debit   Sales returns account

   Credit   Sales ledger control account

2 Debit   Purchases ledger control account

   Credit   Discounts received account

3	Debit	Discounts allowed account	£100
	Credit	Sales ledger control account	£100

4 The total of the list of receivable balances would be increased by £90 (£430 – £340).

5	Debit	Purchases returns account	£1,000
	Credit	Purchases ledger control account	£1,000

6 The total of the list of payable balances would be reduced by £27 (£185 – £158).

7 The total of the list of payable balances would be reduced by £100.

Test your understanding 5

Mortimer Wheeler

(a)

Revenue

	£		£
SPL	3,475	Sales ledger control a/c	3,475

Purchases

	£		£
Purchases ledger control a/c	2,755	SPL	2,755

Sales ledger control account

	£		£
Balance b/d	5,783	Cash	3,842
Revenue	3,475	Irrecoverable debts – expense	1,950
		Balance c/d	3,466
	9,258		9,258
Balance b/d	3,466		

Purchases ledger control account

	£		£
Cash	1,773	Balance b/d	5,531
Discount	15	Purchases	2,755
Balance c/d	6,498		
	8,286		8,286
		Balance b/d	6,498

Allowance for doubtful debts

	£		£
Irrecoverable debt expense (bal figure)	909	Balance b/d	950
Balance c/d	41		
	950		950
		Balance b/d	41

Irrecoverable debt expense

	£		£
Sales ledger control account (Pitt-Rivers)	1,950	Allowance for doubtful debts	909
		SPL	1,041
	1,950		1,950

Sales ledger

Pitt-Rivers

	£		£
Balance b/d	1,900	Irrecoverable debt	1,950
Revenue	50		
	——		——
	1,950		1,950
	——		——

Evans

	£		£
Balance b/d	1,941	Cash	1,900
Revenue	1,760	Balance c/d	1,801
	——		——
	3,701		3,701
	——		——
Balance b/d	1,801		

Petrie

	£		£
Balance b/d	1,942	Cash	1,942
Revenue	1,665	Balance c/d	1,665
	——		——
	3,607		3,607
	——		——
Balance b/d	1,665		

Purchase ledger

Cunliffe

	£		£
Cash	900	Balance b/d	1,827
Discount	15	Purchases	950
Balance c/d	1,862		
	——		——
	2,777		2,777
	——		——
		Balance b/d	1,862

Atkinson

	£		£
Cash	50	Balance b/d	1,851
Balance c/d	2,486	Purchases	685
	2,536		2,536
		Balance b/d	2,486

Piggott

	£		£
Cash	823	Balance b/d	1,853
Balance c/d	2,150	Purchases	1,120
	2,973		2,973
		Balance b/d	2,150

(b) **List of receivables**

	£
Evans	1,801
Petrie	1,665
	3,466

List of payables

	£
Cunliffe	1,862
Atkinson	2,486
Piggott	2,150
	6,498

Test your understanding 6

		£
Total from listing of balances		76,780
Adjustment for (a)	~~add~~/subtract*	400
Adjustment for (b)	add/~~subtract*~~	(100)
Adjustment for (c)	add/~~subtract*~~	(2,410)
Adjustment for (d)	~~add~~/subtract*	90
Adjustment for (e)	add/~~subtract*~~	(540)
Adjustment for (f)	add/~~subtract*~~	(770)
Revised total		73,450

Test your understanding 7

	£
Total from listing of balances	76,670
Adjustment for (a) add/~~subtract~~	235
Adjustment for (b) ~~add~~/subtract	(3,200)
Adjustment for (c) ~~add~~/subtract	(720)
Revised total to agree with purchases ledger control account	72,985

Test your understanding 8

(a) No

(b) The trial balance is constructed by extracting the various balances from the general ledger. If no errors have been made then the total of the debit balances should be equal to the total of the credit balances. In this case the error was made in the sales ledger and since the balances of the accounts in the sales ledger are not included in the trial balance, the error would not be detected.

Bank reconciliations

Introduction

In addition to reconciling the sales and purchases ledger control accounts, before the preparation of a trial balance or extended trial balance, we must also perform a bank reconciliation. A bank reconciliation compares the bank statement (external document) and the cash book (internal document).

ASSESSMENT CRITERIA
Carry out financial period end routines (1.5)

CONTENTS
1   Bank reconciliations

1 Bank reconciliations

1.1 Introduction

At regular intervals the cashier must check that the cash book is correct by comparing the cash book with the bank statement.

Why might they not agree?

Uncleared lodgements

*   Cheques we have paid into the bank have not yet cleared.
*   The cash book is up to date.

Unpresented cheques

*   Cheques we have written have not yet been taken to the bank or have not yet cleared.
*   The cash book is up to date.

Unrecorded transactions

*   The cash book may not be up to date if not all transactions have been recorded.
*   Examples include direct credits into the bank account or transactions made using the direct payment facility commonly known as BACS.
*   Other examples of where there may be unrecorded transactions in the cash book include bank charges, standing orders or direct debits that appear in the bank statement which have not yet been updated in the cash book.

1.2 Bank reconciliation process

(1)   Tick off outstanding items from previous reconciliation and agree the opening balance between the cash book and bank statement.

(2)   Tick off items in the debit side of the cash book (cash received) to the bank statement.

(3) Tick off items in the credit side of the cash book (cash payments) to the bank statement.

(4) Update the cash book with any items not ticked in the bank statement – i.e. unrecorded transactions.

(5) Any items that now remain unticked in the cash book should be included in the reconciliation – i.e. as uncleared lodgements or unpresented cheques.

1.3 Bank reconciliation proforma

	£	£
Balance per bank statement		X
Add: uncleared lodgements		
Details		X
Less: unpresented cheques		
Details	X	
Details	X	(X)
Balance per cash book		X

Example 1

The balance showing on Pinkie's bank statement is a credit of £19,774 (in funds) and the balance on the cash book is a debit balance of £7,396.

The bank statement is compared to the cash book and the following differences were identified:

(1) Bank charges paid of £52 were not entered in the cash book.

(2) A cheque payment for £650 has been incorrectly recorded in the cash book as £560.

(3) Cheque payments to suppliers totalling an amount of £7,400 have been written but are not yet showing in the bank statement.

(4) A BACS receipt of £5,120 from a customer has not been entered in the cash book.

Required:

Identify the THREE adjustments you need to make to the cash book and record these adjustments in the cash book ledger. Reconcile the bank statement to the cash book.

The three adjustments to the cash book are:

(1) Bank charges of £52 should be entered into the cash book on the credit side.

(2) The cheque payment that was incorrectly recorded in the cash book should be corrected. The payment was understated by £90, this will be entered on the credit side of the cash book.

(4) The BACS receipt of £5,120 should be entered into the cash book on the debit side.

Solution

Cash book

	£		£
Balance b/d	7,396	Bank charges (1)	52
BACS receipt (4)	5,120	Cheque (650 – 560) (2)	90
		Balance c/d	12,374
	12,516		12,516
Balance b/d	12,374		

Bank reconciliation

	£
Balance per bank statement	19,774
Less unpresented cheques (3)	(7,400)
Balance per cash book	12,374

Test your understanding 1

Given below is the cash book of a business and the bank statement for the week ending 20 April 20X1.

Required:

Compare the cash book to the bank statement and note any differences that you find.

Cash book

		£			£
16/4	Donald & Co	225.47	16/4	Balance b/d	310.45
17/4	Harper Ltd	305.68	17/4	Cheque 03621	204.56
	Fisler Partners	104.67	18/4	Cheque 03622	150.46
18/4	Denver Ltd	279.57	19/4	Cheque 03623	100.80
19/4	Gerald Bros	310.45		Cheque 03624	158.67
20/4	Johnson & Co	97.68	20/4	Cheque 03625	224.67
			20/4	Balance c/d	173.91
		1,323.52			1,323.52

EXPRESS BANK   CONFIDENTIAL

High Street   Account   CURRENT   Sheet no. 0213
Fenbury
TL4 6JY   Account name P L DERBY LTD
Telephone: 0169 422130

Statement date 20 April 20X1   *Account Number* 40429107

Date	Details	Withdrawals (£)	Deposits (£)	Balance (£)
16/4	Balance from sheet 0212			310.45 OD
17/4	DD – District Council	183.60		494.05 OD
18/4	Credit		225.47	
19/4	Credit		104.67	
	Cheque 03621	240.56		
	Bank interest	3.64		408.11 OD
20/4	Credit		305.68	
	Credit		279.57	
	Cheque 03622	150.46		
	Cheque 03624	158.67		131.99 OD

DD	Standing order	DD	Direct debit	CP	Card purchase
AC	Automated cash	OD	Overdrawn	TR	Transfer

Test your understanding 2

Graham

The cash account of Graham showed a debit balance of £204 on 31 March 20X3. A comparison with the bank statements revealed the following:

			£
1	Cheques drawn but not presented		3,168
2	Amounts paid into the bank but not credited		723
3	Entries in the bank statements not recorded in the cash account		
	(i)	Standing orders	35
	(ii)	Interest on bank deposit account	18
	(iii)	Bank charges	14
4	Balance on the bank statement at 31 March		2,618

Tasks

(a) Show the appropriate adjustments required in the cash account of Graham bringing down the correct balance at 31 March 20X3.

(b) Prepare a bank reconciliation statement at that date.

 Test your understanding 3

The following are the cash book and bank statements of KT Ltd.

Receipts June 20X1

CASH BOOK – JUNE 20X1				
Date	Details	Total	Sales ledger control	Other
1 June	Balance b/d	7,100.45		
8 June	Cash and cheques	3,200.25	3,200.25	–
15 June	Cash and cheques	4,100.75	4,100.75	–
23 June	Cash and cheques	2,900.30	2,900.30	–
30 June	Cash and cheques	6,910.25	6,910.25	–
		£24,212.00	£17,111.55	

Payments June 20X1

Date	Payee	Cheque no	Total £	Purchase ledger control £	Operating overhead £	Admin overhead £	Other £
1 June	Hawsker Chemical	116	6,212.00	6,212.00			
7 June	Wales Supplies	117	3,100.00	3,100.00			
15 June	Wages and salaries	118	2,500.00		1,250.00	1,250.00	
16 June	Drawings	119	1,500.00				1,500.00
18 June	Blyth Chemical	120	5,150.00	5,150.00			
25 June	Whitby Cleaning Machines	121	538.00	538.00			
28 June	York Chemicals	122	212.00	212.00			
			19,212.00	15,212.00	1,250.00	1,250.00	1,500.00

Bank statement

Crescent Bank plc
High Street
Sheffield
Account: Alison Robb t/a KT Ltd
Account no: 57246661

Statement no: 721

Page 1

Date	Details	Payments £	Receipts £	Balance £
20X1				
1 June	Balance b/d			8,456.45
1 June	113	115.00		8,341.45
1 June	114	591.00		7,750.45
1 June	115	650.00		7,100.45
4 June	116	6,212.00		888.45
8 June	CC		3,200.25	4,088.70
11 June	117	3,100.00		988.70
15 June	CC		4,100.75	5,089.45
15 June	118	2,500.00		2,589.45
16 June	119	1,500.00		1,089.45
23 June	120	5,150.00		4,060.55 O/D
23 June	CC		2,900.30	1,160.25 O/D

Key:	S/O	Standing Order	DD	Direct debit
	CC	Cash and cheques	CHGS	Charges
	BACS	Bankers automated clearing	O/D	Overdrawn

Task

Examine the business cash book and the business bank statement shown in the data provided above. Prepare a bank reconciliation statement as at 30 June 20X1. Set out your reconciliation in the proforma below.

Proforma

BANK RECONCILIATION STATEMENT AS AT 30 JUNE 20X1

£

Balance per bank statement
Add: Uncleared lodgements:

Less: Unpresented cheques:

Balance per cash book   £

2 Summary

The final bank reconciliation needs to be prepared prior to the final financial statements being drawn up. This is a comparison between the bank statement (external document) and the cash book (internal document). It is necessary to complete the reconciliation on a regular basis to ensure that the cash book is updated and any errors are identified.

Test your understanding answers

Test your understanding 1

Cash book

		£			£
16/4	Donald & Co	225.47✓	16/4	Balance b/d	310.45✓
17/4	Harper Ltd	305.68✓	17/4	Cheque 03621	204.56
	Fisler Partners	104.67✓	18/4	Cheque 03622	150.46✓
18/4	Denver Ltd	279.57✓	19/4	Cheque 03623	100.80
19/4	Gerald Bros	310.45		Cheque 03624	158.67✓
20/4	Johnson & Co	97.68	20/4	Cheque 03625	224.67
			20/4	Balance c/d	173.91
		1,323.52			1,323.52

There are three unticked items on the bank statement:

- direct debit £183.60 to the District Council

- cheque number 03621 £240.56 – this has been entered into the cash book as £204.56

- bank interest £3.64.

The unticked items on the bank statement would be updated to the cash book.

Cheques 03623 and 03625 are unticked items in the cash book but these are payments that have not yet cleared through the banking system. Also the receipts from Gerald Bros and Johnson & Co have not yet cleared the banking system.

The payments of cheques 03623 and 03625 are known as unpresented cheques and would form part of the reconciliation between the bank statement balance and the cash book balance.

The receipts from Gerald Bros and Johnson & Co are known as uncleared lodgements and would form part of the reconciliation between the bank statement balance and the cash book balance.

EXPRESS BANK			CONFIDENTIAL

High Street   Account   CURRENT   Sheet no. 0213
Fenbury
TL4 6JY   Account name P L DERBY LTD
Telephone: 0169 422130

Statement date 20 April 20X1   *Account Number* 40429107

Date	Details	Withdrawals (£)	Deposits (£)	Balance (£)
16/4	Balance from sheet 0212			310.45 OD
17/4	DD – District Council	183.60		494.05 OD
18/4	Credit		225.47✓	
19/4	Credit		104.67✓	
	Cheque 03621	240.56		
	Bank interest	3.64		408.11 OD
20/4	Credit		305.68✓	
	Credit		279.57✓	
	Cheque 03622	150.46✓		
	Cheque 03624	158.67✓		131.99 OD

DD	Standing order	DD	Direct debit	CP	Card purchase
AC	Automated cash	OD	Overdrawn	TR	Transfer

Test your understanding 2

Graham

(a)

Cash account

	£		£
Balance b/d	204		
Interest on deposit account (ii)	18	Standing orders (i)	35
		Bank charges (iii)	14
		Balance c/d	173
	222		222
Balance b/d	173		

(b)

BANK RECONCILIATION STATEMENT AT 31 MARCH 20X3

	£
Balance per bank statement	2,618
Add Uncleared lodgements	723
	3,341
Less Unpresented cheques	(3,168)
Balance per cash account	173

📝 Test your understanding 3

BANK RECONCILIATION STATEMENT AS AT 30 JUNE 20X1

	£	£
Balance per bank statement		(1,160.25) O/D
Uncleared lodgements:		
Cash & cheques (cashbook 30 June)		6,910.25
		5,750.00
Unpresented cheques:		
121 Whitby Cleaning Machines	538.00	
122 York Chemicals	212.00	
		(750.00)
Balance per cash book (W1)		£5,000.00

(W1)

Balance as per cash book:	
Total receipts (incl. op. bal)	£24,212.00
Total payments	(£19,212.00)
	£5,000.00

Accruals and prepayments

12

Introduction

In this chapter we review the need to account for accruals and prepayments of income and expenses.

ASSESSMENT CRITERIA
Record accruals and prepayments in income and expense accounts (4.1)

CONTENTS

1 Recording income and expenditure
2 Accruals
3 Prepayments
4 Income accounts
5 Journal entries

1 Recording income and expenditure

1.1 The accruals concept

 Definition – The accruals concept

The accruals basis of accounting requires that transactions should be reflected in the financial statements for the period in which they occur. This means that the amount of income should be recognised as it is earned and expenses when they are incurred. This is not necessarily when cash is received or paid.

For example, consider credit sales and credit purchases. When a sale is made on credit it is still recorded even though it may be a considerable time before the cash is actually received from the customer.

1.2 Recording sales and purchases on credit

Sales on credit are recorded in the ledger accounts from the sales day book. The double entry is to credit sales and debit the sales ledger control account (receivables account).

Therefore all sales made in the period are accounted for in that accounting period whether or not the money has yet been received from the customer.

Purchases on credit are recorded in ledger accounts from the purchases day book. The double entry is to debit purchases and credit the purchases ledger control account (payables account).

Again this means that the purchases are recorded at the date of the purchase whether or not the supplier has yet been paid.

1.3 Recording expenses of the business

Most business expenses such as rent, rates, telephone, power costs etc tend to be entered into the ledger accounts from the cash payments book. This means that the amount recorded in the ledger accounts is only the cash payment.

In order to accord with the accruals concept the amount of the expense to be recognised in the statement of profit or loss may be different to the cash payments made during the accounting period.

Expenses should be charged to the statement of profit or loss at the amount incurred in the accounting period rather than the amount of cash that has been paid during the period.

2 Accruals

2.1 Introduction

If an expense is to be adjusted then the adjustment may be an accrual or a prepayment. Note, that even if the business does not know the exact amount, they must make a prudent estimate of accrued cost.

 Definition – Accrual of expense

An accrual is an expense that has been incurred during the accounting period but has not been paid by the period end, i.e. a liability.

 Example 1

A business has a year end of 31 December. During the year 20X1 the following electricity bills were paid:

		£
15 May	4 months to 30 April	400
18 July	2 months to 30 June	180
14 Sept	2 months to 30 August	150
15 Nov	2 months to 31 October	210

The business estimated that the average monthly electricity bill is £100.

What was the total charge for electricity for the year ended 31 December 20X1?

Solution

	£
Jan to April	400
May to June	180
July to August	150
Sept to Oct	210
Accrual for Nov/Dec (2 × 100)	200
	———
Total charge	1,140
	———

Test your understanding 1

Olwen commenced business on 1 May 20X0 and is charged rent at the rate of £6,000 per annum. During the period to 31 December 20X0, he paid rent of £3,400.

What should his charge in the statement of profit or loss for the period to 31 December 20X0 be in respect of rent?

2.2 Accounting for accruals

The method of accounting for an accrual is to:

(a) **debit the expense account**

to increase the expense to reflect the fact that an expense has been incurred; and

(b) **credit an accruals account** (or the same expense account)

to reflect the fact that there is a liability for the expense.

Note that the credit entry can be made in one of two ways:

Method 1:   credit a separate accruals account; or

Method 2:   carry down a credit balance on the expense account.

 Example 2

Using the electricity example from above, the accounting entries will now be made in the ledger accounts.

Solution

Method 1 – separate accruals account

Electricity account

	£		£
15 May CPB	400		
18 July CPB	180		
14 Sept CPB	150		
15 Nov CPB	210		
31 Dec Accrual a/c	200	SPL	1,140
	_____		_____
	1,140		1,140
	_____		_____

Accruals account

	£		£
		Electricity account	200

Using this method the statement of profit or loss is charged with the full amount of electricity used in the period and there is an accrual or payable to be shown in the statement of financial position of £200 in the accruals account. Any other accruals such as telephone, rent, etc would also appear in the accruals account as a credit balance. The total of the accruals would appear in the statement of financial position as a payable.

Method 2 – using the expense account

Electricity account

	£		£
15 May CPB	400		
18 July CPB	180		
14 Sept CPB	150		
15 Nov CPB	210		
31 Dec Accrual c/d	200	SPL	1,140
	———		———
	1,140		1,140
	———		———
		Balance b/d	200

Again with this method the statement of profit or loss charge is the amount of electricity used in the period and the credit balance on the expense account is shown as an accrual or payable in the statement of financial position.

 Test your understanding 2

Olwen commenced business on 1 May 20X0 and is charged rent at the rate of £6,000 per annum. During the period to 31 December 20X0, he actually paid £3,400.

Write up the ledger account for rent for the period to 31 December 20X0 using method 2 (as explained above).Clearly state whether the year-end adjustment is an accrual or prepayment.

Rent account

	£		£

2.3 Opening and closing balances

When the accrual is accounted for in the expense account then care has to be taken to ensure that the accrual brought down is included as the opening balance on the expense account at the start of the following year.

Example 3

Continuing with our earlier electricity expense example the closing accrual at the end of 20X0 was £200. During 20X1 £950 of electricity bills were paid and a further accrual of £220 was estimated at the end of 20X1.

Write up the ledger account for electricity for 20X1 clearly showing the charge to the statement of profit or loss and any accrual balance.

Solution

Electricity account

	£		£
Cash paid during the year	950	Balance b/d – opening accrual	200
Balance c/d – closing accrual	220	SPL	970
	1,170		1,170
		Balance b/d	220

The opening balance b/d of £200 relates to expenses incurred in the prior year. Therefore of the £950 cash paid, £200 relates to the prior year and £750 to the current year. In addition the business owes a further £220 for the current year that it has not yet paid.

 Test your understanding 3

The insurance account of a business had an opening accrual of £340 at 1 July 20X0. During the year insurance payments of £3,700 were made and it has been calculated that a closing accrual of £400 was required.

Prepare the insurance expense account for the year ended 30th June 20X1 and close it off by showing the transfer to the statement of profit or loss.

Insurance expenses

	£		£
	___		___
	___		___

---

3 Prepayments

3.1 Introduction

Another type of adjustment that might need to be made to an expense account is to adjust for a prepayment.

 Definition – Prepayment of expense

A prepayment is a payment made during the accounting period (and therefore debited to the expense account) for an expense that relates to the following accounting period.

Example 4

The rent of a business is £3,000 per quarter payable in advance. During 20X0 the rent ledger account shows that £15,000 of rent was paid during the year.

What was the correct charge to the statement of profit or loss for the year and what was the amount of any prepayment at 31st December 20X0?

Solution

The statement of profit or loss charge should be £12,000 for the year, four quarterly charges of £3,000 each. The prepayment is £3,000 (£15,000 – £12,000), rent paid in advance for next year.

 Test your understanding 4

Julie paid £1,300 insurance during the year to 31 March 20X6. The charge in the statement of profit or loss for the year to 31 March 20X6 was £1,200.

What was the amount of the prepayment at 31 March 20X6?

3.2 Accounting for prepayments

Accounting for prepayments is the mirror image of accounting for accruals.

(a) **credit the expense account**

to reduce the expense by the amount of the prepayment; and

(b) **debit a prepayment account**

to show that the business has an asset (the prepayment) at the period end.

The debit entry can appear in one of two places:

Method 1: a debit to a separate prepayments account; or

Method 2: a debit balance carried down on the expense account.

Example 5

A business paid rent of £3,000 per quarter payable in advance. During 20X0 the rent ledger account shows that £15,000 of rent has been paid during the year.

Show how these entries would be made in the ledger accounts.

Solution

Method one – separate prepayments account and rent account

Rent account

	£		£
Cash payments	15,000	Prepayments account	3,000
		SPL	12,000
	———		———
	15,000		15,000
	———		———

Prepayments account

	£		£
Rent account	3,000		

The charge to the statement of profit or loss is now the correct figure of £12,000 and there is a debit balance on the prepayments account.

This balance on the prepayments account will appear as a prepayment within current assets in the statement of financial position at the period end date.

Method two – balance shown on the expense account.

Rent account

	£		£
Cash payments	15,000	SPL	12,000
		Balance c/d – prepayment	3,000
	———		———
	15,000		15,000
	———		———
Balance b/d – prepayment	3,000		

The expense to the statement of profit or loss is again £12,000 and the debit balance on the account would appear as a prepayment within current assets in the statement of financial position.

3.3 Opening and closing balances

As with accounting for accruals, care must be taken with opening prepayment balances on the expense account. If there is a closing prepayment balance on an expense account then this must be included as an opening balance at the start of the following year.

 Example 6

Continuing with the previous rent example the prepayment at the end of 20X0 was £3,000. The payments for rent during 20X1 were £15,000 and the charge for the year was £14,000.

Write up the ledger account for rent clearly showing the charge to the statement of profit or loss and the closing prepayment at 31 December 20X1.

Solution

Rent account

	£		£
Balance b/d – opening prepayment	3,000	SPL charge	14,000
Cash payments	15,000	Balance c/d – prepayment (bal fig)	4,000
	―――――		―――――
	18,000		18,000
	―――――		―――――
Balance b/d – prepayment	4,000		

Note that you were given the charge for the year in the question and therefore the prepayment figure is the missing or balancing amount.

The opening balance b/d relates to £3,000 of cash paid in the prior year. This relates to this year's rent and is therefore added to the current year rent expense (i.e. the year the cost was incurred).

Test your understanding 5

The following information relates to the rent and rates account of a business:

Balances as at:	1 April 20X0 £	31 March 20X1 £
Prepayment for rates expenses	20	30
Accrual for rent expense	100	120

The bank summary for the year shows payments for rent and rates of £840.

Prepare the rent and rates account for the year ended 31st March 20X1 and close it off by showing the transfer to the statement of profit or loss.

Rent and rates expense account

£		£
——		——
——		——

3.4 Approach to accruals and prepayments

There are two approaches to writing up expenses accounts with accruals or prepayments. This will depend upon whether the charge to the statement of profit or loss is the balancing figure or whether the accrual or prepayment is the balancing figure.

Approach 1 – enter any opening accrual /prepayment

– enter the cash paid during the period

– enter the closing accrual/prepayment that has been given or calculated

– enter the charge to the statement of profit or loss as a balancing figure

Approach 2 – enter any opening accrual/prepayment

– enter the cash paid during the period

– enter the statement of profit or loss charge for the period

– enter the closing accrual/prepayment as the balancing figure

4 Income accounts

4.1 Introduction

As well as having expenses some businesses will also have sundry forms of income. The cash received may not always be the same as the income earned in the accounting period and therefore similar adjustments to those for accruals and prepayments in the expense accounts will be required.

4.2 Accruals of income

 Definition – Accrual of income

An accrual of income is income that has been earned but has not yet been received. It may be referred to as 'accrued income'.

If the amount of income received in cash is less than the income earned for the period then this additional income must be accrued for. This is done by:

- **credit the income account**

    to increase income and

- **debit accrued income** (within current assets in the statement of financial position)

    to recognise the asset of the cash due.

4.3 Income prepaid

 Definition – Prepayment of income

A prepayment of income is payment received in advance of it being earned. It may also be referred to as 'prepaid income' or 'deferred income'.

If the amount of cash received is greater than the income earned in the accounting period then this income has been prepaid by the payer. The accounting entries required here are:

- **debit the income account**

  to reduce income and

- **credit prepaid income** (within current liabilities in the statement of financial position)

  to recognise the liability for the amount of income that has been prepaid and not yet earned.

 Example 7

Minnie's business has two properties, A and B, that are rented out to other parties. The rental on property A for the year is £12,000 but only £10,000 has been received. The rental on property B is £15,000 and the client has paid £16,000 this year.

Write up separate rent accounts for properties A and B showing the income credited to the statement of profit or loss and any closing balances on the income accounts.

Explain what each balance means.

Solution

Rent account – A

	£		£
SPL	12,000	Cash received	10,000
		Balance c/d – income accrued	2,000
	___		___
	12,000		12,000
	___		___
Balance b/d income accrued	2,000		

This would be a receivable balance in the statement of financial position showing that Minnie is owed £2,000 for rent on this property.

Rent account – B			
	£		£
SPL	15,000	Cash received	16,000
Balance c/d – income prepaid	1,000		
	16,000		16,000
		Balance b/d – income prepaid	1,000

This would be a payable balance in the statement of financial position indicating that too much cash has been received for this rental.

 Test your understanding 6

Hyde wishes to use your shop to display and sell framed photographs. He will pay £40 per month for this service in cash.

(a) How would you account for this transaction each month?

(b) If, at the end of the year, Hyde owed one month's rental, how would this be treated in the accounts?

(c) Which accounting concept is being applied?

5 Journal entries

5.1 Introduction

As with accounting for depreciation expense, accruals and prepayments are adjustments to the accounts which do not appear in the accounting records from the primary records. Therefore, adjustments for accruals and prepayments must be entered into the accounting records by means of a journal entry.

Example 8

An accrual for electricity is to be made at the year-end of £200. Show the journal entry required for this adjustment.

Solution

Journal entry			No:
Date			
Prepared by			
Authorised by			
Account	**Code**	**Debit £**	**Credit £**
Electricity account	0442	200	
Accruals	1155		200
Totals		200	200

 Test your understanding 7

A prepayment adjustment is to be made at the year end of £1,250 for insurance expense.

Record the journal entry required for this adjustment.

The following account codes and account names should be used.

0445 Insurance

1000 Prepayment

Journal entry			No:
Date			
Prepared by			
Authorised by			
Account	**Code**	**Debit £**	**Credit £**
Totals			

Test your understanding 8

Siobhan

Siobhan, the proprietor of a sweet shop, provides you with the following information relating to sundry expenditure and income of her business for the year ended 31 December 20X4:

1   **Rent payable**

    £15,000 was paid during 20X4 to cover the 15 months ending 31 March 20X5.

2   **Gas**

    £840 was paid during 20X4 to cover gas charges from 1 January 20X4 to 31 July 20X4. Gas charges can be assumed to accrue evenly over the year. There was no outstanding balance at 1 January 20X4.

3   **Advertising**

    Included in the payments totalling £3,850 made during 20X4 was an amount of £500 payable in respect of a planned advertising campaign for 20X5.

4   **Bank interest**

    The bank statements of the business show that the following interest was charged to the account.

For period up to 31 May 20X4	Nil (no overdraft)
For 1 June – 31 August 20X4	£28
1 September – 30 November 20X4	£45

    The bank statements for 20X5 show that £69 was charged to the account on 28 February 20X5.

5   **Rates**

    Towards the end of 20X3 £4,800 was paid to cover the six months ended 31 March 20X4.

    In May 20X4 £5,600 was paid to cover the six months ended 30 September 20X4.

    In early 20X5 £6,600 was paid for the six months ending 31 March 20X5.

6   **Rent receivable**

During 20X4, Siobhan received £250 rent from Joe Soap for the use of a lock-up garage attached to the shop, for the six months ended 31 March 20X4.

She increased the rent to £600 pa from 1 April 20X4, and during 20X4 Joe Soap paid her rent for the full year ending 31 March 20X5.

Required:

Write up ledger accounts for each of the above items, showing:

(a)   the opening balance at 1 January 20X4, if any

(b)   any cash paid or received

(c)   the closing balance at 31 December 20X4

(d)   the charge or credit for the year to the statement of profit or loss.

 Test your understanding 9

A Crew

The following is an extract from the trial balance of A Crew at 31 December 20X1:

	Dr
	£
Stationery	560
Rent	900
Rates	380
Lighting and heating	590
Insurance	260
Wages and salaries	2,970

Stationery which had cost £15 was still in hand at 31 December 20X1.

Rent of £300 for the last three months of 20X1 had not been paid and no entry has been made in the books for it.

Of the account balance for rates, £280 was for the 12 months ended 31 March 20X2. The remaining balance was for the 3 months ended 31 March 20X1.

Fuel had been delivered on 18 December 20X1 at a cost of £15 and had been consumed by 31 December 20X1. No invoice had been received for the £15 fuel in 20X1 and no entry has been made in the records of the business.

£70 of the insurance paid was insurance cover for the year ending 31 December 20X2. Nothing was owing to employees for wages and salaries at the close of 20X1.

Required:

Record the above information in the relevant accounts, showing the transfers to the statement of profit or loss for the year ended 31 December 20X1.

 Test your understanding 10

A Metro

A Metro owns a number of antique shops and, in connection with this business, he runs a small fleet of motor vans. He prepares his accounts to 31 December each year.

On 1 January 20X0 the amount prepaid for motor tax and insurance was £570.

On 1 April 20X0 he paid £420 which represented motor tax on six of the vans for the year ended 31 March 20X1.

On 1 May 20X0 he paid £1,770 insurance for all ten vans for the year ended 30 April 20X1.

On 1 July 20X0 he paid £280 which represented motor tax for the other four vans for the year ended 30 June 20X1.

Required:

Write up the account for 'motor tax and insurance' for the year ended 31 December 20X0.

6 Summary

In order for the final accounts to accord with the accruals concept, the cash receipts and payments for income and expenses must be adjusted to ensure that they include all of the income earned during the year and expenses incurred during the year.

The sales and purchases are automatically dealt with through the sales ledger control account and purchases ledger control account.

However the expenses and sundry income of a business are recorded in the ledger accounts on a cash paid and received basis and therefore adjustments for accruals and prepayments must be made by journal entries.

Test your understanding answers

Test your understanding 1

$(\frac{8}{12} \times £6,000) = £4,000$ — The expense should reflect the proportion of the year's £6,000 charge consumed, not what has been paid.

Test your understanding 2

Rent account

	£		£
Cash payments	3,400	Statement of profit or loss $(6,000 \times \frac{8}{12})$	4,000
Balance c/d – accrual	600		
	———		———
	4,000		4,000
	———		———
		Balance b/d – accrual	600

Test your understanding 3

Insurance expenses

	£		£
Cash payments	3,700	Balance b/d – opening accrual	340
Balance c/d – closing accrual	400	SPL charge (bal fig)	3,760
	———		———
	4,100		4,100
	———		———
		Balance b/d – accrual	400

Test your understanding 4

The prepayment was £1,300 – 1,200 = £100

Test your understanding 5

Rent and rates expenses

	£		£
Balance b/d	20	Balance b/d	100
Cash	840	Statement of profit or loss	850
Balance c/d	120	(bal fig)	
		Balance c/d	30
	980		980
Balance b/d	30	Balance b/d	120

Test your understanding 6

(a) Dr   Cash account

     Cr   Sundry Income a/c (or any other sensible account name)

(b) A sundry receivable

     Dr   sundry receivable (SoFP)

     Cr   sundry income (SPL)

(c) Accruals concept

Test your understanding 7

Journal entry			No:
Date			
Prepared by			
Authorised by			
Account	**Code**	**Debit** £	**Credit** £
Prepayment	1000	1,250	
Insurance	0445		1,250
Totals		1,250	1,250

Test your understanding 8

Rent payable

	£		£
Cash paid	15,000	Statement of profit or loss	12,000
		Balance c/d (prepayment)	3,000
	———		———
	15,000		15,000
	———		———
Balance b/d (prepayment)	3,000		

Gas

	£		£
Cash paid	840	Statement of profit or loss	1,440
Balance c/d (840 × 5/7) (accrual)	600		
	———		———
	1,440		1,440
	———		———
		Balance b/d (accrual)	600

Advertising

	£		£
Cash	3,850	Statement of profit or loss	3,350
		Balance c/d (prepayment)	500
	———		———
	3,850		3,850
	———		———
Balance b/d (prepayment)	500		

Bank interest

	£		£
Cash	28	Statement of profit or loss	96
Cash	45		
Balance c/d ($\frac{1}{3} \times 69$)			
(accrual)	23		
	——		——
	96		96
	——		——
		Balance b/d (accrual)	23

Rates

	£		£
Balance b/d			
(prepayment $\frac{3}{6} \times 4{,}800$)	2,400	SPL	11,300
Cash	5,600		
Balance c/d ($\frac{3}{6} \times 6{,}600$)	3,300		
(accrual)			
	——		——
	11,300		11,300
	——		——
		Balance b/d (accrual)	3,300

Rent receivable

	£		£
Balance b/d ($250 \times 3/6$)			
(receivable = accrued			
income)	125	Cash	250
Statement of profit or loss			
(W)	575	Cash	600
Balance c/d ($3/12 \times 600$)			
(deferred income)	150		
	——		——
	850		850
	——		——
		Balance b/d (payable =	
		deferred income)	150

Working – Statement of profit or loss credit for rent receivable

	£
1 January 20X4 – 31 March 20X4 ($\frac{3}{6} \times 250$)	125
1 April 20X4 – 31 December 20X4 ($\frac{9}{12} \times 600$)	450
	——
	575
	——

Test your understanding 9

A Crew

Stationery

	£		£
31 Dec Balance per trial balance	560	31 Dec SPL	545
		31 Dec Balance c/d (prepayment)	15
	560		560
1 Jan Balance b/d (prepayment)	15		

Rent

	£		£
31 Dec Balance per trial balance	900	31 Dec SPL	1,200
31 Dec Balance c/d (accrual)	300		
	1,200		1,200
		1 Jan Balance b/d (accrual)	300

Rates

	£		£
31 Dec Balance per trial balance	380	31 Dec SPL	310
		31 Dec Balance c/d (prepayment (280 × 3/12)	70
	380		380
1 Jan Balance b/d (prepayment)	70		

Lighting and heating

	£		£
31 Dec Balance per trial balance	590	31 Dec SPL	605
31 Dec Balance c/d (accrual)	15		
	605		605
		1 Jan Balance b/d (accrual)	15

Insurance

	£		£
31 Dec Balance per trial balance	260	31 Dec SPL	190
		31 Dec Balance c/d (prepayment)	70
	260		260
1 Jan Balance b/d (prepayment)	70		

Wages and salaries

	£		£
31 Dec Balance per trial balance	2,970	31 Dec SPL	2,970

📝 **Test your understanding 10**

A Metro

Motor tax and insurance

	£		£
Balance b/d (prepayment)	570	SPL (W2)	2,205
Cash		Balance c/d (W1)	
		(prepayment)	835
1 April	420		
1 May	1,770		
1 July	280		
	3,040		3,040
Balance b/d (prepayment)	835		

Workings

1 **Prepayment at the end of the year** £

Motor tax on six vans paid 1 April 20X0 ($\frac{3}{12} \times 420$)   105

Insurance on ten vans paid 1 May 20X0 ($\frac{4}{12} \times 1{,}770$)   590

Motor tax on four vans paid 1 July 20X0 ($\frac{6}{12} \times 280$)   140

Total prepayment   835

2 **SPL charge for the year**

There is no need to calculate this as it is the balancing figure, but it could be calculated as follows.

   £

Prepayment b/d   570

Motor tax ($\frac{9}{12} \times 420$)   315

Insurance ($\frac{8}{12} \times 1{,}770$)   1,180

Motor tax ($\frac{6}{12} \times 280$)   140

SPL charge   2,205

Suspense accounts and errors

Introduction

When preparing a trial balance or an extended trial balance it is likely that a suspense account will have to be opened and then any errors and omissions adjusted for and the suspense account cleared.

There are a variety of different types of errors that candidates need to be aware of. Some of the errors are detected by a trial balance and some are not.

Before the final accounts are prepared the suspense account must be cleared by correcting each of the errors that have caused the trial balance not to balance.

ASSESSMENT CRITERIA	CONTENTS
Prepare a trial balance (5.1) Carry out adjustments to the trial balance (5.2)	1 The trial balance 2 Opening a suspense account 3 Clearing the suspense account

1 The trial balance

1.1 Introduction

We saw in an earlier chapter that one of the purposes of the trial balance is to provide a check on the accuracy of the double entry bookkeeping and it is important that this is done regularly. Once all ledger balances have been extracted and the trial balance has been prepared, it might be that the trial balance does not balance – i.e. total debits do not equal total credits. If the trial balance does not balance then an error or a number of errors have occurred and this must be investigated and the errors corrected.

However if the trial balance does balance this does not necessarily mean that all of the entries are correct as there are some types of errors that are not detected by the trial balance.

1.2 Errors where the trial balance does not balance

The following types of error will cause a difference in the trial balance and therefore will be detected by the trial balance and can be investigated and corrected:

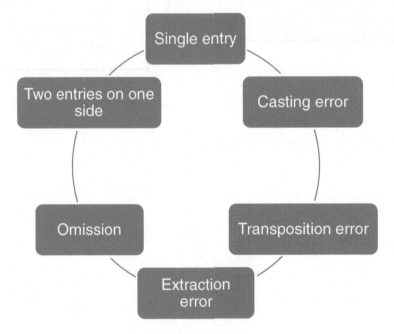

Definition – Single entry error

If only one side of a double entry has been made then this means that the trial balance will not balance e.g. if only the debit entry for receipts from receivables has been made then the debit total on the trial balance will exceed the credit balance.

Definition – Casting error

If a ledger account has not been balanced correctly due to a casting error then this will mean that the trial balance will not balance.

Definition – Transposition error

If an amount in a ledger account or a balance on a ledger account has been transposed and incorrectly recorded then the trial balance will not balance e.g. a debit entry was recorded correctly as £5,276, but the related credit entry was entered as £5,726.

Definition – Extraction error

If a ledger account balance is incorrectly recorded on the trial balance, either by recording the wrong figure or putting the balance on the wrong side of the trial balance, then the trial balance will not balance.

Definition – Omission error

If a ledger account balance is inadvertently omitted from the trial balance then the trial balance will not balance.

Definition – Two entries on one side

If a transaction is entered as a debit in two accounts, or as a credit in two accounts, instead of the normal debit and credit entry, then the trial balance will not balance.

1.3 Errors where the trial balance still balances

Certain other errors cannot be detected by preparing a trial balance, as these errors will not cause a difference between the total debits and total credits in that trial balance.

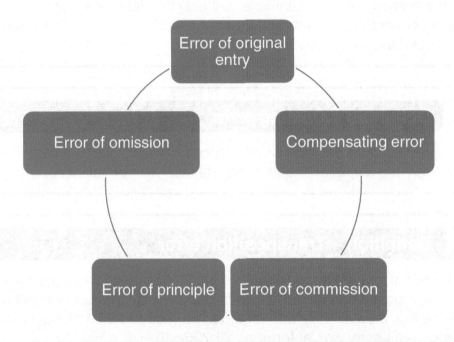

Definition – Error of original entry

This is where the wrong figure is entered as both the debit and credit entry e.g. a payment of the electricity expense was correctly recorded as a debit in the electricity account and a credit to the bank account but it was recorded as £300 instead of £330.

Definition – Compensating error

This is where two separate errors are made, one on the debit side of a particular ledger account and the other on the credit side of a different ledger account. By coincidence the two errors are of the same amount and therefore cancel each other out when the trial balance is prepared.

Definition – Error of commission

With this type of error a debit entry and an equal credit entry have been made. However one of the entries has been to the wrong account e.g. if the electricity expense was debited to the rent account but the credit entry was correctly made in the bank account – here both the electricity account and rent account will be incorrect but the trial balance will still balance.

 Definition – Error of principle

This is similar to an error of commission in that part of an entry has been posted to the wrong account. However, the error is one of principle. For example, instead of capitalising the cost of a non-current asset on the statement of financial position (by debiting non-current assets) the cost has been debited to a statement of profit or loss expense account. This is fundamentally incorrect but the trial balance will still balance.

 Definition – Error of omission

This is where an entire double entry is omitted from the ledger accounts. As both the debit and credit have been omitted the trial balance will still balance.

1.4 Correction of errors

Whatever type of error is discovered, either by producing the trial balance or by other checks on the ledger accounts, it will need to be corrected. Errors will normally be corrected by putting through a double entry journal for the correction.

The procedure for identifying what journal is required to correct those errors is as follows:

| Step 1
What did you do? | • Determine the precise nature of the incorrect double entry that has been made. |

| Step 2
What should you have done? | • Determine the correct entries that should have been made. |

| Step 3
What is the correction? | • Produce a journal entry that cancels the incorrect part and puts through the correct entries. |

 Example 1

The electricity expense of £450 has been correctly credited to the bank account but has been debited to the rent account.

Step 1 – What did they do?

| Dr | Rent account | £450 |
| Cr | Bank account | £450 |

Step 2 – What should they have done?

| Dr | Electricity account | £450 |
| Cr | Bank account | £450 |

Step 3 – What is the correction?

The journal entry required is:

| Dr | Electricity account | £450 |
| Cr | Rent account | £450 |

Note that this removes the incorrect debit from the rent account and puts the correct debit into the electricity account.

Test your understanding 1

Colin returned some goods to a supplier because they were faulty. The original purchase price of these goods was £8,260.

The ledger clerk has correctly accounted for the transaction but has used the figure £8,620 in error.

Required:

What is the correcting entry which needs to be made?

2 Opening a suspense account

2.1 Introduction

A suspense account is a temporary account that can be created to deal with any errors or omissions arising in our general ledger accounting. It means that it is possible to continue with the production of financial accounts whilst the reasons for any errors are investigated and then corrected.

2.2 Reasons for opening a suspense account

A suspense account will be opened in two main circumstances:

(a) an unknown entry – i.e. the bookkeeper does not know how to deal with one side of a transaction

(b) the trial balance does not balance.

2.3 Unknown entry

In some circumstances the bookkeeper may come across a transaction for which there is some uncertainty of the correct double entry and therefore, rather than making an error, one side of the entry will be posted to a suspense account until the correct entry can be determined.

Example 2

A new bookkeeper is dealing with a cheque received from a garage for £800 for the sale of an old car. He correctly debits the bank account with the amount of the cheque but does not know what to do with the credit entry.

Solution

He will enter it in the suspense account:

Suspense account

	£		£
		Bank account – receipt from sale of car	800

2.4 Trial balance does not balance

If the total of the debits on the trial balance does not equal the total of the credits, then an error or a number of errors have been made. These must be investigated, identified and eventually corrected.

In the meantime, the difference between the debit total and the credit total is inserted as a suspense account balance in order to make the two totals agree.

 Example 3

The totals of the trial balance are as follows:

	Debits £	Credits £
Totals as initially extracted	108,367	109,444
Suspense account, to make the TB balance	1,077	
	109,444	109,444

Suspense account

	£		£
Opening balance	1,077		

Test your understanding 2

The debit balances on a trial balance exceed the credit balances by £2,600.

Required:

Open up a suspense account to record this difference.

3 Clearing the suspense account

3.1 Introduction

Whatever the reason for the suspense account being opened, it is only ever a temporary account. The reasons for the difference must be identified and then correcting entries should be put through the ledger accounts, via the journal, in order to correct the accounts and clear the suspense account balance to zero.

3.2 Procedure for clearing the suspense account

Step 1

Determine the incorrect entry that has been made or the omission from the ledger accounts – i.e. the reason for the creation of the suspense account balance.

Step 2

Determine the double entry journal required to correct the error or omission – this will not always require an entry to the suspense account e.g. when the electricity expense was debited to the rent account the journal entry did not require any entry to be made in the suspense account.

Step 3

Post the correcting journals through the ledger accounts and calculate any revised balances carried down. When all the corrections have been made the suspense account should normally have no remaining balance on it.

Example 4

Some purchases for cash of £100 have been correctly entered into the cash account but no entry has been made in the purchases account. An entry of £100 was debited to the suspense account.

Draft a journal entry to correct this error.

Solution

Step 1 – Reason for suspense account

The cash account has been credited with £100 but no other entry was made. In this case the Dr would have been posted to the suspense account.

Did do:

Dr	Suspense	£100
Cr	Cash account	£100

Should have done:

Dr	Purchases	£100
Cr	Cash account	£100

Step 2 – Correction journal

A debit entry is required in the purchases account and the credit is to the suspense account to cancel the original debit and to clear the balance to nil.

		£	£
Dr	Purchases account	100	
Cr	Suspense account		100

Being correction of double entry for cash purchases.

Remember that normally a journal entry needs a narrative to explain what it is for – however in most examinations you are told not to provide the narratives so always read the requirements carefully.

Example 5

On 31 December 20X0 the trial balance of John Jones, a small manufacturer who is not VAT registered, failed to agree and the difference of £967 was entered as a debit balance on a suspense account. After the final accounts had been prepared, the following errors were discovered and the balance on the suspense account was eliminated.

(1)   A purchase of goods from A Smith for £170 had been credited in error to the account of H Smith.

(2)   The purchase day book was under cast by £200.

(3)   Machinery purchased for £150 had been debited to the purchases account.

(4)   Discounts received of £130 had been debited to the discounts received account.

(5)   Rates paid by a cheque for £46 had been debited to the rates account as £64.

(6)   Cash drawings by the owner of £45 had been posted to the cash account correctly but not posted to the drawings account.

(7)   A non-current asset balance of £1,200 had been omitted from the trial balance.

Note: The control accounts are part of the double-entry.

Required:

(a)   Show the journal entries necessary to correct the above errors.

(b)   Show the entries in the suspense account to eliminate the differences entered in the suspense account.

Solution

Tuition note: Not all the errors relate to the suspense account. Part of the way of dealing with these questions is to identify which entries do not relate to the suspense account. Do not assume that they all do just because this is a question about suspense accounts.

(a)   **Journal – John Jones**

		Dr £	Cr £
31 December 20X0			
1	H Smith	170	
	A Smith		170

Being adjustment of incorrect entry for purchases from A Smith – this correction takes place in the purchases ledger (no effect on suspense account).

2	Purchases		200	
	Purchases ledger control account			200

Being the correction of undercast purchases day book (no effect on suspense account as control account is the double entry, however the error should have been found during the reconciliation of the control account).

3	Machinery		150	
	Purchases			150

Being adjustment for wrong entry for machinery purchased (no effect on suspense account).

4	Suspense account		260	
	Discount received			260

Being correction of discounts received entered on wrong side of account.

5	Suspense account		18	
	Rates			18

Being correction of transposition error to rates account.

6	Drawings		45	
	Suspense account			45

Being completion of double entry for drawings.

7	Non-current asset		1,200	
	Suspense account			1,200

Being inclusion of non-current asset balance. There is no double entry for this error in the ledger as the mistake was to omit the item from the trial balance.

(b)

Suspense account

	£		£
Difference in trial balance	967	Drawings	45
Discounts received	260	Non-current asset per trial balance	1,200
Rates	18		
	1,245		1,245

Test your understanding 3

GA (not VAT registered) extracted the following trial balance from his ledgers at 31 May 20X4.

	£	£
Petty cash	20	
Capital		1,596
Drawings	1,400	
Sales		20,607
Purchases	15,486	
Purchases returns		210
Inventory (1 January 20X4)	2,107	
Fixtures and fittings	710	
Sales ledger control	1,819	
Purchases ledger control		2,078
Carriage on purchases	109	
Carriage on sales	184	
Rent and rates	460	
Light and heat	75	
Postage and telephone	91	
Sundry expenses	190	
Cash at bank	1,804	
	24,455	24,491

The trial balance did not agree. On investigation, GA discovered the following errors which had occurred during the month of May.

(a) **Record the journal entries to correct the errors below**.

(1) In extracting the receivables balance the credit side of the sales ledger control account had been overcast by £10.

Journal	Dr £	Cr £

(2) An amount of £4 for carriage on sales had been posted in error to the carriage on purchases account.

Journal	Dr £	Cr £

(3) A credit note for £17 received from a payable had been entered in the purchase returns account but no entry had been made in the purchase ledger control account.

Journal	Dr £	Cr £

(4) £35 charged by Builders Ltd for repairs to GA's private residence had been charged, in error, to the sundry expenses account.

Journal	Dr £	Cr £

(5) A payment of a telephone bill of £21 had been entered correctly in the cash book but had been posted, in error, to the postage and telephone account as £12.

Journal	Dr £	Cr £

(b) **Show how the suspense account is cleared**

Suspense account

(c)   **Re-write the trial balance as it would appear after all the above corrections have been made.**

Trial balance for GA at 31 May 20X4

	£	£
Petty cash		
Capital		
Drawings		
Sales		
Purchases		
Purchases returns		
Inventory (1 January 20X4)		
Fixtures and fittings		
Sales ledger control		
Purchases ledger control		
Carriage on purchases		
Carriage on sales		
Rent and rates		
Light and heat		
Postage and telephone		
Sundry expenses		
Cash at bank		
	_____	_____
	_____	_____

Test your understanding 4

The following questions are about errors and suspense accounts.

1   A telephone expense is debited to the rent expense account. This is an example of (tick the correct answer):

A casting error ☐

An error of commission ☐

A compensating error ☐

A single entry ☐

2   A repair expense is debited to a non-current asset account. This is an example of (tick the correct answer):

A casting error ☐

An error of commission ☐

A compensating error ☐

An error of principle ☐

3   Discounts received of £400 have been entered as a credit into the discount allowed account. What is the journal entry required to correct this?

Debit	**Credit**	
Discounts received	Discounts allowed	☐
Discounts allowed	Discounts received	☐

4   The total of the debit balances on a trial balance are £312,563 whilst the credit balances total to £313,682. Will the suspense account balance be a debit or a credit balance?

Debit of £1,119 ☐

Credit of £1,119 ☐

5   Purchases returns of £210 had been correctly posted to the
    purchases ledger control account but had been debited to the
    purchases returns account. What is the journal entry required to
    correct this?

Debit	**Credit**	
Purchase returns account	Purchase ledger control account	☐
Suspense account	Purchase returns account	☐

6   An invoice from a supplier for £485 had been entered in the
    purchases day book as £458. What journal entry is required to
    correct this?

Debit	**Credit**	
Purchase account	Purchase ledger control account	☐
Purchases account	Suspense account	☐

7   When producing the trial balance the telephone account expense
    of £300 was omitted from the trial balance. What journal entry is
    required to correct this?

Debit	**Credit**	
Suspense account	Telephone account	☐
Telephone account	Suspense account	☐

8   Motor expenses of £500 were correctly dealt with in the bank
    account but were debited to the motor vehicles non-current asset
    account. What journal entry is required to correct this?

Debit	**Credit**	
Bank account	Motor vehicles at cost account	☐
Motor expenses account	Motor vehicles at cost account	☐

Test your understanding 5

On extracting a trial balance the accountant of ETT discovered a suspense account with a debit balance of £1,075 included; he also found that the debits (including the suspense account) exceeded the credits by £957.

He posted this difference to the suspense account and then investigated the situation.

He discovered:

(a)   A debit balance of £75 on the postages account had been incorrectly extracted on the trial balance as £750 debit.

(b)   A payment of £500 to a payable, X, had been correctly entered in the bank account, but no entry had been made in the payables control account.

(c)   When a motor vehicle had been purchased during the year the bookkeeper did not know what to do with the debit entry so he made the entry Dr Suspense, Cr bank £1,575.

(d)   A credit balance of £81 in the sundry income account had been incorrectly extracted on the trial balance as a debit balance.

(e)   A receipt of £5 from a receivable had been correctly posted to the receivables control account but had been entered in the cash account as £625.

(f)   The bookkeeper was not able to deal with the receipt of £500 from the proprietor of ETT's own bank account, and he made the entry Dr Bank and Cr Suspense.

(g)   No entry has been made for a cheque of £120 received from a receivable.

(h)   A receipt of £50 from a receivable had been entered into the receivables control account as £5 and into the cash at bank account as £5.

Task

Show how the suspense account balance is cleared by means of a ledger account.

Test your understanding 6

Julia

The difference on the trial balance of Julia's business whereby the credit column exceeded the debit by £144 has been transferred to a suspense account.

The following errors had been made:

1   Purchase of goods from A Myers for £120 had been credited to the account of H Myers.

2   A total from the sales day book of £27 had been credited to the control account.

3   Sale of plant for £190 had been credited to sales.

4   One total of £120 from the sales day book had been debited to the sales ledger control account as £12.

5   Sales day book undercast by £200.

6   Rent payable accrued as £30 in the previous period had not been entered as an opening balance in the current period.

7   Petty cash balance of £12 omitted from the trial balance.

Required:

Prepare the necessary journal entries, and the entries in the suspense account to clear it.

4 Summary

Preparation of the trial balance is an important element of control over the double entry system but it will not detect all errors.

The trial balance will still balance if a number of types of error are made. If the trial balance does not balance then a suspense account will be opened temporarily to make the debits equal the credits in the trial balance.

The errors or omissions that have caused the difference on the trial balance must be discovered and then corrected using journal entries.

Not all errors will require an entry to the suspense account. However, any that do should be put through the suspense account in order to try to eliminate the balance on the account.

Test your understanding answers

Test your understanding 1

Step 1 – What did they do?

The purchases ledger control account has been debited and the purchases returns account credited but with £8,620 rather than £8,260.

Dr	Purchases ledger control account	£8,620
Cr	Purchases returns account	£8,620

Step 2 – What should they have done?

Dr	Purchases ledger control account	£8,260
Cr	Purchases returns account	£8,260

Step 3 – What is the correction?

Both of the entries need to be reduced by the difference between the amount used and the correct amount (8,620 – 8,260) = £360

Journal entry:		£	£
Dr	Purchases returns account	360	
Cr	Purchases ledger control account		360

Being correction of misposting of purchase returns

Test your understanding 2

As the debit balances exceed the credit balances the balance needed is a credit balance to make the two totals equal.

Suspense account

	£		£
		Opening balance	2,600

Test your understanding 3

			Dr £	Cr £
1	Debit	Sales ledger control account	10	
	Credit	Suspense account		10

being correction of overcast in receivables' control account

			Dr £	Cr £
2	Debit	Carriage on sales	4	
	Credit	Carriage on purchases		4

being correction of posting to the wrong account

			Dr £	Cr £
3	Debit	Purchases ledger control account	17	
	Credit	Suspense account		17

being correction of omitted credit note entry

			Dr £	Cr £
4	Debit	Drawings	35	
	Credit	Sundry expenses		35

being correction to posting of payment for private expenses

			Dr £	Cr £
5	Debit	Postage and telephone	9	
	Credit	Suspense account		9

being correction of transposition error

Suspense account

	£		£
Difference per trial balance (24,455 – 24,491)	36	SLCA	10
		PLCA	17
		Postage and telephone	9
	36		36

Trial balance after adjustments

	Dr £	Cr £
Petty cash	20	
Capital		1,596
Drawings	1,435	
Sales		20,607
Purchases	15,486	
Purchases returns		210
Inventory (1 January 20X4)	2,107	
Fixtures and fittings	710	
Sales ledger control	1,829	
Purchases ledger control		2,061
Carriage on purchases	105	
Carriage on sales	188	
Rent and rates	460	
Light and heat	75	
Postage and telephone	100	
Sundry expenses	155	
Cash at bank	1,804	
	24,474	24,474

Test your understanding 4

1   An error of commission.

2   An error of principle.

3   Debit   Discount allowed account   £400
     Credit   Discount received account   £400

4   £1,119 debit balance

5   Debit   Suspense account   £420
     Credit   Purchases returns account   £420

6	Debit	Purchases account	£27
	Credit	Purchases ledger control account	£27
7	Debit	Telephone account (TB)	£300
	Credit	Suspense account	£300
8	Debit	Motor expenses account	£500
	Credit	Motor vehicles at cost account	£500

📝 Test your understanding 5

Suspense account

	£		£
Balance b/d	1,075	Trial balance – difference	957
Postage (trial balance only) (a)	675	Payables control (b)	500
Sundry income (trial balance only) (d)	162	Non-current asset – cost (c)	1,575
Cash (e)	620		
Capital account – ETT (f)	500		
	———		———
	3,032		3,032
	———		———

Explanatory notes:

The £1,075 debit balance is already included in the books, whilst the £957 is entered on the credit side of the suspense account because the trial balance, as extracted, shows debits exceeding credits by £957. Although the two amounts arose in different ways they are both removed from suspense by the application of double entry.

(a) The incorrect extraction is corrected by amending the balance on the trial balance and debiting the suspense account with £675. In this case the 'credit' entry is only on the trial balance, as the postages account itself shows the correct balance, the error coming in putting that balance on the trial balance.

(b) The non-entry of the £500 to the debit of X's account causes the account to be incorrectly stated and the trial balance to be unbalanced. To correct matters Dr Payables control Cr Suspense.

(c) The suspense entry here arose from adherence to double entry procedures, rather than a numerical error. In this case the bookkeeper should have Dr Non-current asset – cost, Cr Bank instead of Dr Suspense, Cr Bank, so to correct matters the entry Dr Non-current asset – cost, Cr Suspense is made.

(d) Is similar to (a), but note that the incorrect extraction of a credit balance as a debit balance means that twice the amount involved has to be amended on the trial balance and debited to suspense account.

(e) Is similar to (b) – on this occasion Dr Suspense, Cr Cash, and amend the cash account balance on the trial balance.

(f) Is similar to (c). The bookkeeper should have Dr Bank, Cr ETT – capital, but has instead Dr Bank, Cr Suspense, so to correct matters Dr Suspense, Cr Capital.

(g) Item (g) does not appear in the suspense account as the error does not affect the imbalance of the trial balance. As no entry has been made for the cheque, the correcting entry is

	£	£
Dr Cash at bank account	120	
Cr Receivables control account		120

(h) item (h) also does not appear in the suspense account. Although an entry has been made in the books which was wrong, the entry was incorrect for both the debit and credit entry. The correcting entry is

	£	£
Dr Cash at bank account	45	
Cr Receivables control account		45

Test your understanding 6

Julia

Suspense account

	£		£
Difference on trial balance	144	SLCA (£27 × 2) (2)	54
Rent payable account (6)	30	SLCA (120 – 12) (4)	108
		Petty cash account (7)	12
	174		174

Journal entries

		£	£
Dr	H Myers' account	120	
	Cr A Myers' account		120

Correction of posting to incorrect personal account (1).

		£	£
Dr	Sales ledger control account	54	
	Cr Suspense account		54

Correction of posting to wrong side of SLCA (2).

		£	£
Dr	Revenue account	190	
	Cr Disposal account		190

Correction of error of principle – sales proceeds of plant previously posted to revenue account (3).

		£	£
Dr	SLCA	108	
	Cr Suspense account		108

Correction of posting £12 rather than £120 (4).

		£	£
Dr	Sales ledger control account	200	
	Cr Revenue account		200

Correction of undercasting of sales day book (5).

		£	£
Dr	Suspense account	30	
	Cr Rent payable account		30

Amount of accrual not Balance b/d on the account (6).

		£	£
Dr	Petty cash account (not posted)	12	
	Cr Suspense account		12

Balance omitted from trial balance (7).

The extended trial balance – in action

Introduction

As discussed in chapter 6 'The extended trial balance – an introduction', the examination will contain an exercise involving preparation or completion of an extended trial balance. You need to be familiar with the technique for entering adjustments to the initial trial balance and extending the figures into the statement of financial position and statement of profit or loss columns.

The relevant adjustments (accruals, prepayments, depreciation charges, irrecoverable and doubtful debts, errors and closing inventory), have all been covered in previous chapters.

In this chapter we will bring all of this knowledge together in preparation of an extended trial balance.

ASSESSMENT CRITERIA	CONTENTS
Prepare a trial balance (5.1)	1 Procedure for preparing an extended trial balance
Carry out adjustments to the trial balance (5.2)	
Complete the extended trial balance (5.3)	

1 Procedure for preparing an extended trial balance

1.1 Procedure for preparing an extended trial balance

Step 1

Each ledger account name and its balance is initially entered in the trial balance columns.

Total the debit and credit columns to ensure they equal; i.e. that all balances have been transferred across. Any difference should be put to a suspense account.

Step 2

The adjustments required are then entered into the adjustments column. The typical adjustments required are:

Correction of any errors	Depreciation charges for the period	Irrecoverable debt write offs
Allowance for doubtful debt adjustments	Accruals or prepayments of income and expense	Closing inventory

Note: it is always important to ensure that all adjustments have an equal and opposite debit and credit. Never enter a one sided journal.

Step 3

Total the adjustments columns to ensure that the double entry has been correctly made in these columns.

Step 4

All the entries on the line of each account are then cross-cast and the total is entered into the correct column in either the statement of profit or loss columns or statement of financial position columns.

Step 5

The statement of profit or loss column totals are totalled in order to determine the profit (or loss) for the period. This profit (or loss) is entered in the statement of profit or loss columns as the balancing figure. See example 1 for further clarification on the adjustment required.

Step 6

The profit (or loss) for the period calculated in step 5 is entered in the statement of financial position columns and the statement of financial position columns are then totalled.

Example 1

Set out below is the trial balance of Lyttleton, a sole trader, extracted at 31 December 20X5.

	Dr £	Cr £
Capital account		7,830
Cash at bank	2,010	
Non-current assets at cost	9,420	
Accumulated depreciation at 31.12.X4		3,470
Sales ledger control account	1,830	
Inventory at 31.12.X4	1,680	
Purchases ledger control account		390
Revenue		14,420
Purchases	8,180	
Rent	1,100	
Electricity	940	
Rates	950	
	26,110	26,110

On examination of the accounts, the following points are noted:

(1) Depreciation for the year of £942 is to be charged.

(2) An allowance for doubtful debts of 3% of total debts is to be set up.

(3) Purchases include £1,500 of goods which were bought for the proprietor's personal use.

(4) The rent account shows the monthly payments of £100 made from 1 January to 1 November 20X5 inclusive. Due to an oversight, the payment due on 1 December 20X5 was not made.

(5) The rates account shows the prepayment of £150 brought forward at the beginning of 20X5 (and representing rates from 1 January 20X5 to 31 March 20X5) together with the £800 payment made on 1 April 20X5 and relating to the period from 1 April 20X5 to 31 March 20X6.

(6) The electricity charge for the last three months of 20X5 is outstanding and is estimated to be £400.

(7) Inventory at 31.12.X5 was valued at £1,140.

Solution

Step 1

The balances from the trial balance are entered into the trial balance columns.

Account name	Trial balance		Adjustments		Statement of profit or loss		Statement of fin. pos.	
	Dr £	Cr £	Dr £	Cr £	Dr £	Cr £	Dr £	Cr £
Capital		7,830						
Cash	2,010							
Non-current asset cost	9,420							
Accumulated depreciation		3,470						
SLCA	1,830							
Inventory	1,680							
PLCA		390						
Revenue		14,420						
Purchases	8,180							
Rent	1,100							
Electricity	940							
Rates	950							
Total	26,110	26,110						

There are a number of points to note here:

- the accumulated depreciation is the balance at the end of the previous year as this year's depreciation charge has not yet been accounted for

- the figure for inventory is the inventory at the start of the year – the opening inventory. The inventory at the end of the year, the closing inventory, will be dealt with later.

Make sure you total each column at this stage to ensure that you have entered the figures correctly, and nothing has been missed.

Step 2

Deal with all of the adjustments required from the additional information given.

Adjustment 1 – Depreciation charge

The double entry for the annual depreciation charge is:

Dr Depreciation charges account	£942
Cr Accumulated depreciation account	£942

You will need to open up a new account line for the depreciation expense account at the bottom of the extended trial balance.

Account name	Trial balance		Adjustments		Statement of profit or loss		Statement of fin. pos.	
	Dr £	Cr £	Dr £	Cr £	Dr £	Cr £	Dr £	Cr £
Capital		7,830						
Cash	2,010							
Non-current asset cost	9,420							
Accumulated depreciation		3,470		942				
SLCA	1,830							
Inventory	1,680							
PLCA		390						
Revenue		14,420						
Purchases	8,180							
Rent	1,100							
Electricity	940							
Rates	950							
Depreciation charges			942					

Adjustment 2 – Allowance for doubtful debts

There is no allowance in the accounts yet so this will need to be set up. The amount of the allowance is 3% of receivables therefore £1,830 × 3% = £55

The double entry for this is:

Dr Allowance for doubtful debt adjustment £55

Cr Allowance for doubtful debts £55

As neither of these accounts yet exists they will be added in at the bottom of the ETB.

Revision point: If an allowance for doubtful debts account already exists then only the increase or decrease is accounted for as the adjustment.

Account name	Trial balance		Adjustments		Statement of profit or loss		Statement of fin. pos.	
	Dr £	Cr £	Dr £	Cr £	Dr £	Cr £	Dr £	Cr £
Capital		7,830						
Cash	2,010							
Non-current asset cost	9,420							
Accumulated depreciation		3,470		942				
SLCA	1,830							
Inventory	1,680							
PLCA		390						
Revenue		14,420						
Purchases	8,180							
Rent	1,100							
Electricity	940							
Rates	950							
Depreciation charges			942					
Allowance for doubtful debts adjustment			55					
Allowance for doubtful debts				55				

Adjustment 3 – Owner taking goods for own use

If the owner of a business takes either cash or goods out of the business these are known as drawings. Where goods have been taken by the owner then they are not available for resale and must be taken out of the purchases figure and recorded as drawings.

The double entry is:

Dr Drawings account £1,500

Cr Purchases account £1,500

A drawings account must be added to the list of balances:

Account name	Trial balance Dr £	Trial balance Cr £	Adjustments Dr £	Adjustments Cr £	Statement of profit or loss Dr £	Statement of profit or loss Cr £	Statement of fin. pos. Dr £	Statement of fin. pos. Cr £
Capital		7,830						
Cash	2,010							
Non-current asset cost	9,420							
Accumulated depreciation		3,470		942				
SLCA	1,830							
Inventory	1,680							
PLCA		390						
Revenue		14,420						
Purchases	8,180			1,500				
Rent	1,100							
Electricity	940							
Rates	950							
Depreciation charges			942					
Allowance for doubtful debts adjustment			55					
Allowance doubtful debts				55				
Drawings			1,500					

Adjustment 4 – Rent

The rent charges for the year should be £1,200 (£100 per month) therefore an accrual is required for the December rent of £100.

The double entry is:

Dr Rent account £100

Cr Accruals account £100

An accruals account must be added at the bottom of the extended trial balance.

Revision note: The treatment for an accrued expense is to increase the charge to the statement of profit or loss. This ensures that the cost for all goods/services used in the period is captured. We must also recognise a liability known as an accrual.

Account name	Trial balance		Adjustments		Statement of profit or loss		Statement of fin. pos.	
	Dr £	Cr £	Dr £	Cr £	Dr £	Cr £	Dr £	Cr £
Capital		7,830						
Cash	2,010							
Non-current asset cost	9,420							
Accumulated depreciation		3,470		942				
SLCA	1,830							
Inventory	1,680							
PLCA		390						
Revenue		14,420						
Purchases	8,180			1,500				
Rent	1,100		100					
Electricity	940							
Rates	950							
Depreciation charges			942					
Allowance for doubtful debt adjustments			55					
Allowance for doubtful debts				55				
Drawings			1,500					
Accruals				100				

Adjustment 5 – Rates

The charge for rates for the year should be:

	£
1 Jan to 31 March	150
1 April to 31 Dec (800 × 9/12)	600
	——
	750
	——

As the invoice of £800 covers 1 April 20X5 to 31 March 20X6, a prepayment should be recognised for the period 1 Jan X6 to 31 March X6 as this relates to costs incurred outside of the accounting period. (£800 × 3/12 = £200).

This is accounted for by the following double entry:

Dr Prepayments account   £200

Cr Rates account   £200

A prepayment account must be set up at the bottom of the extended trial balance.

Revision note: The accounting treatment for a prepayment is to reduce the charge to the statement of profit or loss, as the expense is too high because it includes a payment for another period's costs; and to set up a receivable account in the statement of financial position known as a prepayment.

Account name	Trial balance		Adjustments		Statement of profit or loss		Statement of fin. pos.	
	Dr £	Cr £	Dr £	Cr £	Dr £	Cr £	Dr £	Cr £
Capital		7,830						
Cash	2,010							
Non-current asset cost	9,420							
Accumulated depreciation		3,470		942				
SLCA	1,830							
Inventory	1,680							
PLCA		390						
Revenue		14,420						
Purchases	8,180			1,500				
Rent	1,100		100					
Electricity	940							
Rates	950			200				
Depreciation charges			942					
Allowance for doubtful debts adjustment			55					
Allowance for doubtful debts				55				
Drawings			1,500					
Accruals				100				
Prepayments			200					

Adjustment 6 – Electricity

There needs to be a further accrual of £400 for electricity.

The double entry for this is:

Dr Electricity account   £400

Cr Accruals account   £400

Therefore £400 needs to be added to the accruals account balance of £100 to bring it up to £500.

Account name	Trial balance		Adjustments		Statement of profit or loss		Statement of fin. pos.	
	Dr £	Cr £	Dr £	Cr £	Dr £	Cr £	Dr £	Cr £
Capital		7,830						
Cash	2,010							
Non-current asset cost	9,420							
Accumulated depreciation		3,470		942				
SLCA	1,830							
Inventory	1,680							
PLCA		390						
Revenue		14,420						
Purchases	8,180			1,500				
Rent	1,100		100					
Electricity	940		400					
Rates	950			200				
Depreciation charges			942					
Allowance for doubtful debt adjustments				55				
Allowance for doubtful debts				55				
Drawings			1,500					
Accruals				500				
Prepayments			200					

Adjustment 7 – Closing inventory

We saw in a previous chapter on inventory that the closing inventory appears in both the statement of financial position as a debit (as a current asset), and in the statement of profit or loss as a credit (a reduction to cost of sales). Therefore two entries will be made in the ETB:

Dr Inventory – statement of financial position   £1,140

Cr Inventory – statement of profit or loss   £1,140

Account name	Trial balance		Adjustments		Statement of profit or loss		Statement of fin. pos.	
	Dr £	Cr £	Dr £	Cr £	Dr £	Cr £	Dr £	Cr £
Capital		7,830						
Cash	2,010							
Non-current asset cost	9,420							
Accumulated depreciation		3,470		942				
SLCA	1,830							
Inventory	1,680							
PLCA		390						
Revenue		14,420						
Purchases	8,180			1,500				
Rent	1,100		100					
Electricity	940		400					
Rates	950			200				
Depreciation charges			942					
Allowance for doubtful debts adjustment			55					
Allowance for doubtful debts				55				
Drawings			1,500					
Accruals				500				
Prepayments			200					
Closing inventory SoFP			1,140					
Closing inventory SPL				1,140				

Step 3

The adjustments columns must now be totalled. Each adjustment was made in double entry form and therefore the total of the debit column should equal the total of the credit column. Leave a spare line before putting in the total as there will be a further balance to enter, the profit or loss for the period.

Account name	Trial balance		Adjustments		Statement of profit or loss		Statement of fin. pos.	
	Dr £	Cr £	Dr £	Cr £	Dr £	Cr £	Dr £	Cr £
Capital		7,830						
Cash	2,010							
Non-current asset cost	9,420							
Accumulated depreciation		3,470		942				
SLCA	1,830							
Opening inventory	1,680							
PLCA		390						
Revenue		14,420						
Purchases	8,180			1,500				
Rent	1,100		100					
Electricity	940		400					
Rates	950			200				
Depreciation charges			942					
Allowance for doubtful debts adjustments			55					
Allowance for doubtful debts				55				
Drawings			1,500					
Accruals				500				
Prepayments			200					
Closing inventory SoFP			1,140					
Closing inventory SPL				1,140				
	26,110	26,110	4,337	4,337				

Step 4

Each of the account balances must now be cross-cast (added across) and then entered as a debit or credit in either the statement of profit or loss columns or the statement of financial position columns.

Income and expenses are entered in the statement of profit or loss columns and assets and liabilities are entered in the statement of financial position columns.

This is how it works taking each account balance in turn:

- capital account: there are no adjustments to this therefore the balance is entered in the credit column of the statement of financial position – the liability of the business owed back to the owner

- cash account: again no adjustments here therefore this is entered into the debit column of the statement of financial position – an asset

- non-current asset cost account: no adjustments therefore entered in the debit column of the statement of financial position – an asset

- accumulated depreciation: (£3,470 + 942 = £4,412) this is the amount that has to be deducted from the non-current asset cost total in the statement of financial position, as it is the accumulated depreciation, and therefore the credit entry is to the statement of financial position – part of non-current asset net book value

- SLCA: no adjustments therefore entered in the debit column of the statement of financial position – an asset

- opening inventory account: entered as a debit in the statement of profit or loss as it increases expenses – part of cost of sales

- PLCA: no adjustment and so is entered as a credit in the statement of financial position – a liability

- sales account: no adjustments therefore a credit in the statement of profit or loss – income

- purchases account: (£8,180 – 1,500 = £6,680) note that the £1,500 is deducted from the initial balance, as the £8,180 is a debit and the £1,500 a credit. The total is then entered as a debit in the statement of profit or loss – part of cost of sales

- rent account: (£1,100 + 100 = £1,200) these two amounts are added together as they are both debits and the total is entered in the debit column of the statement of profit or loss – an expense

KAPLAN PUBLISHING

- electricity account: (£940 + 400 = £1,340) again two debits so added together and the total entered in the debit column of the statement of profit or loss – an expense

- rates account: (£950 – 200 = £750) the balance of £950 is a debit therefore the credit of £200 must be deducted and the final total is entered in the debit column of the statement of profit or loss – an expense

- depreciation charges account: adjustment is entered in the statement of profit or loss debit column – an expense

- allowance for doubtful debts adjustment – another expense account to the statement of profit or loss debit column

- allowance for doubtful debts account: this is the amount that is deducted from receivables in the statement of financial position and is therefore entered in the credit column of the statement of financial position

- drawings account – this is a reduction of the amount the business owes to the owner and is therefore a debit in the statement of financial position, it is a reduction of the amount of overall capital

- accruals account: this balance is a liability in the statement of financial position therefore is entered into the credit column in the statement of financial position

- prepayments account: this balance is an asset in the statement of financial position and is therefore a debit in the statement of financial position columns.

Account name	Trial balance		Adjustments		Statement of profit or loss		Statement of fin. pos.	
	Dr £	Cr £	Dr £	Cr £	Dr £	Cr £	Dr £	Cr £
Capital		7,830						7,830
Cash	2,010						2,010	
Non-current asset cost	9,420						9,420	
Accumulated depreciation		3,470		942				4,412
SLCA	1,830						1,830	
Opening inventory	1,680				1,680			
PLCA		390						390
Revenue		14,420				14,420		
Purchases	8,180			1,500	6,680			
Rent	1,100		100		1,200			
Electricity	940		400		1,340			
Rates	950			200	750			
Depreciation charges			942		942			
Allowance for doubtful debts adjustment			55		55			
Allowance doubtful debts				55				55
Drawings			1,500				1,500	
Accruals				500				500
Prepayments			200				200	
Closing inventory SoFP			1,140				1,140	
Closing inventory SPL				1,140		1,140		
	26,110	26,110	4,337	4,337	12,647	15,560	16,100	13,187

Steps 5 and 6

- Total the debit and credit columns of the statement of profit or loss – they will not be equal as the difference between them is any profit or loss.

- If the credit total exceeds the debits the difference is a profit which must be entered in the last line of the ETB and put into the debit column of the statement of profit or loss columns in order to make them equal.

- To complete the double entry the same figure is also entered as a credit in the statement of financial position columns – the profit owed back to the owner.

- If the debit total of the statement of profit or loss columns exceeds the credit total then a loss has been made – this is entered as a credit in the statement of profit or loss and a debit in the statement of financial position columns. Finally total the statement of financial position debit and credit columns, these should now be equal.

Account name	Trial balance Dr £	Trial balance Cr £	Adjustments Dr £	Adjustments Cr £	Statement of profit or loss Dr £	Statement of profit or loss Cr £	Statement of fin. pos. Dr £	Statement of fin. pos. Cr £
Capital		7,830						7,830
Cash	2,010						2,010	
NCA cost	9,420						9,420	
Accumulated depreciation		3,470		942				4,412
SLCA	1,830						1,830	
Open. inventory	1,680				1,680			
PLCA		390						390
Revenue		14,420				14,420		
Purchases	8,180			1,500	6,680			
Rent	1,100		100		1,200			
Electricity	940		400		1,340			
Rates	950			200	750			
Depreciation charges			942		942			
Allowance for doubtful debts adjustment			55		55			
Allowance for doubtful debts				55				55
Drawings			1,500				1,500	
Accruals				500				500
Prepayments			200				200	
Closing inventory SoFP			1,140				1,140	
Closing inventory SPL				1,140		1,140		
Profit (15,560 – 12,647)					2,913			2,913
	26,110	26,110	4,337	4,337	15,560	15,560	16,100	16,100

Test your understanding 1

The following is the trial balance of Hick at 31 December 20X6

	Dr £	Cr £
Shop fittings at cost	7,300	
Accumulated shop fitting depreciation at 1 January 20X6		2,500
Leasehold premises at cost	30,000	
Accumulated leasehold depreciation at 1 January 20X6		6,000
Inventory at 1 January 20X6	15,000	
Sales ledger control account at 31 December 20X6	10,000	
Allowance for doubtful debts at 1 January 20X6		800
Cash in hand	50	
Cash in bank	1,250	
Purchases ledger control account at 31 Dec 20X6		18,000
Proprietor's capital at 1 January 20X6		19,050
Drawings to 31 December 20X6	4,750	
Purchases	80,000	
Revenue		120,000
Wages	12,000	
Advertising	4,000	
Rates for 15 months	1,800	
Bank charges	200	
	166,350	166,350

Complete the journal entries for the adjustments below.

Depreciation of shop fittings: £400; depreciation of leasehold: £1,000.

Journal	Dr £	Cr £

Journal	Dr £	Cr £

A debt of £500 is irrecoverable and is to be written off; the doubtful debts allowance is to be 3% of the remaining receivables.

Journal	Dr £	Cr £

Journal	Dr £	Cr £

Advertising fees of £200 have been treated incorrectly as wages.

Journal	Dr £	Cr £

The proprietor has withdrawn goods costing £1,200 for his personal use, these have not been recorded as drawings.

Journal	Dr £	Cr £

The inventory at 31 December 20X6 is valued at £21,000.

Journal	Dr £	Cr £

The rates included in the trial balance relate to the 15 month period to 31 March 20X7.

Journal	Dr £	Cr £

Prepare an extended trial balance at 31 December 20X6.

Extended trial balance at 31 December 20X6

Account name	Trial balance		Adjustments		Statement of profit or loss		Statement of fin. pos.	
	Dr	Cr	Dr	Cr	Dr	Cr	Dr	Cr
	£	£	£	£	£	£	£	£
Shop fittings cost								
Accumulated shop fitting dep'n								
Leasehold								
Accumulated leasehold dep'n								
Open. inventory								
SLCA								
Allowance for doubtful debt 1.1.X6								
Cash in hand								
Cash at bank								
PLCA								
Capital								
Drawings								
Purchases								
Revenue								
Wages								
Advertising								
Rates								
Bank charges								
Dep'n charges								
– Fittings								
– Lease								
Irrecoverable debts expense								
Allowance for doubtful debt adjustment								
Prepayments								
Closing Inventory SoFP								
Closing Inventory SPL								
Net profit								
TOTAL								

Test your understanding 2

Michael carries on business as a clothing manufacturer. The trial balance of the business on 31 December 20X6 was as follows:

	Dr £	Cr £
Capital account – Michael		30,000
Freehold factory at cost (including land £4,000)	20,000	
Factory plant and machinery at cost	4,800	
Sales reps' cars at cost	2,600	
Accumulated depreciation, 1 January 20X6		
Freehold factory		1,920
Factory plant and machinery		1,600
Sales reps' cars		1,200
Inventories, 1 January 20X6	8,900	
Trade receivables and payables	3,600	4,200
Allowance for doubtful debts		280
Purchases	36,600	
Wages and salaries	19,800	
Rates and insurance	1,510	
Sundry expenses	1,500	
Motor expenses	400	
Revenue		72,000
Balance at bank	11,490	
	111,200	111,200

Complete the journal entries for the adjustments below.

Inventories at 31 December were £10,800.

Journal	Dr £	Cr £

Wages and salaries include the following:

        Michael – drawings   £2,400

        Motor expenses   £600

Journal	Dr £	Cr £

Journal	Dr £	Cr £

Provision is to be made for depreciation on the freehold factory, plant and machinery and sales reps' cars at 2%, 10% and 25% respectively, calculated on a straight line basis.

Journal	Dr £	Cr £

Journal	Dr £	Cr £

Journal	Dr £	Cr £

On 31 December 20X6 £120 was owed for sundry expenses and rates paid in advance amounted to £260. Neither of these had been adjusted for in the trial balance.

Journal	Dr £	Cr £

Journal	Dr £	Cr £

Of the trade receivables £60, for which an allowance had previously been made, is to be written off. The closing allowance for doubtful debts is to be reduced to reflect this write off.

Journal	Dr £	Cr £

Prepare an extended trial balance at 31 December 20X6 dealing with the above information.

Extended trial balance at 31 December 20X6

Account name	Trial balance		Adjustments		Statement of profit or loss		Statement of financial position	
	Dr	Cr	Dr	Cr	Dr	Cr	Dr	Cr
	£	£	£	£	£	£	£	£
Capital account								
Freehold factory cost								
Plant cost								
Sales Reps' cars cost								
Accum dep'n								
– factory								
– Plant								
– Sales Reps' cars								
Open. inventory								
Sales ledger control account								
Purchase ledger control account								
Allowance doubtful debts								
Purchases								
Wages and salaries								
Rates and insurance								
Sundry expenses								
Motor expenses								
Revenue								
Cash at bank								
Closing Inventory – SoFP								
Closing Inventory – SPL								
Drawings								
Depreciation								
– factory								
– Plant								
– Sales Reps' cars								
Accruals								
Prepayments								
Net profit								
TOTAL								

1.2 Treatment of goods taken by the owner

In the earlier example we saw how goods taken for use by the owner must be taken out of purchases and transferred to drawings. The double entry was:

Dr Drawings account

Cr Purchases account

With the cost of the goods taken.

There is however an alternative method which may be required by some examinations:

Dr Drawings account with the selling price plus VAT (Gross)

Cr Sales account with the net of VAT selling price (Net)

Cr VAT account with the VAT

As a general guide use the first method when the goods are stated at cost price and the second method when the goods are stated at selling price. If both methods are possible from the information given use the first method as it is simpler.

Test your understanding 3

You have been asked to prepare the 20X0 accounts of Rugg, a retail merchant. Rugg has balanced the books at 31 December 20X0 and gives you the following list of balances:

	£
Capital account at 1 January 20X0	2,377
Rent	500
Inventory as at 1 January 20X0	510
Rates	240
Insurance	120
Wages	1,634
Receivables	672
Revenue	15,542
Repairs	635
Purchases	9,876
Discounts received	129
Drawings	1,200
Petty cash in hand 31 December 20X0	5
Bank balance 31 December 20X0	763
Motor vehicles, at cost	1,740
Fixtures and fittings at cost	829
Accumulated depreciation at 1 January 20X0	
– Motor vehicles	435
– Fixtures and fittings	166
Travel and entertaining	192
Payables	700
Sundry expenses	433

Complete the journal entries for the adjustments below.

Closing inventory, valued at cost, amounts to £647.

Journal	Dr £	Cr £

Rugg has drawn £10 a month and these drawings have been charged to wages.

Journal	Dr £	Cr £

Depreciation is to be provided at 25% straight line on motor vehicles and 20% straight line on fixtures and fittings.

Journal	Dr £	Cr £

Journal	Dr £	Cr £

Irrecoverable debts totalling £37 are to be written off.

Journal	Dr £	Cr £

Sundry expenses include £27 spent on electrical repairs and cash purchases of goods for resale of £72.

Journal	Dr £	Cr £

Journal	Dr £	Cr £

KAPLAN PUBLISHING

Rugg has taken goods from inventory for his own use. When purchased by his business, these goods cost £63 and would have been sold for £91.

Journal	Dr £	Cr £

The annual rental of the business premises is £600; in addition £180 of rates charges paid in August 20X0 covers the year ending 30 June 20X1.

Journal	Dr £	Cr £

Journal	Dr £	Cr £

Prepare an extended trial balance reflecting the above information

Extended trial balance at 31 December 20X0

Account name	Trial balance		Adjustments		Statement of profit or loss		Statement of fin. pos.	
	Dr	Cr	Dr	Cr	Dr	Cr	Dr	Cr
	£	£	£	£	£	£	£	£
Capital 1.1.X0								
Rent								
Open. inventory								
Rates								
Insurance								
Wages								
Receivables								
Revenue								
Repairs								
Purchases								
Discounts received								
Drawings								
Petty cash								
Cash at bank								
Vehicles cost								
Fixtures cost								
Accum'd dep'n								
– Vehicles								
– Fixtures								
Travel								
Payables								
Sundry expenses								
Closing Inventory SoFP								
Closing Inventory SPL								
Dep'n charges								
– Vehicles								
– Fixtures								
Irrecoverable debts								
Accruals								
Prepayments								
Net profit								
TOTAL								

📝 **Test your understanding 4**

1   What is the double entry for a depreciation charge for the year of £640? (record the account name and amount)

Account name	£	£
Debit		
Credit		

2   The owner of a business takes goods costing £1,000 out of the business for his own use. What is the double entry for this? (record the account name and amount)

Account name	£	£
Debit		
Credit		

3   What is the double entry required to put closing inventory into the adjustment columns of the extended trial balance? (record the account names)

Account name	£	£
Debit		
Credit		

4   Does the accumulated depreciation appear in the statement of profit or loss or statement of financial position columns of the ETB?

Statement of profit or loss ☐

Statement of financial position ☐

5   Does opening inventory appear in the statement of profit or loss or statement of financial position columns of the ETB?

Statement of profit or loss ☐

Statement of financial position ☐

Test your understanding 5

Randall

Trial balance at 31 December 20X6

	Dr £	Cr £
Shop fittings at cost	2,000	
Depreciation accumulated at 1 January 20X6		100
Leasehold premises at cost	12,500	
Depreciation accumulated at 1 January 20X6		625
Inventory in trade at 1 January 20X6	26,000	
Receivables at 31 December 20X6	53,000	
Allowance for doubtful debts at 1 January 20X6		960
Cash in hand	50	
Cash at bank	4,050	
Payables for supplies		65,000
Proprietor's capital at 1 January 20X6		28,115
Drawings to 31 December 20X6	2,000	
Purchases	102,000	
Revenue		129,000
Wages	18,200	
Advertising	2,300	
Rates for 15 months to 31 March 20X7	1,500	
Bank charges	200	
	223,800	223,800

The following adjustments are to be made:

1 Depreciation of shop fittings   £100

   Depreciation of leasehold   £625

2 A debt of £500 is irrecoverable and is to be written off; the doubtful debts allowance is to be increased to 2% of the receivables.

3 Advertising fees of £200 have been treated incorrectly as wages.

4 The proprietor has withdrawn goods costing £1,000 for his personal use; these have not been recorded as drawings.

5 The inventory in trade at 31 December 20X6 is valued at £30,000.

Required:

Prepare an extended trial balance at 31 December 20X6.

Test your understanding 6

Willis

Willis extracts the following trial balance at 31 December 20X6.

	Dr £	Cr £
Capital		3,112
Cash at bank		2,240
Petty cash	25	
Plant and machinery at cost	2,750	
Accumulated depreciation at 1 January 20X6		1,360
Motor vehicles at cost	2,400	
Accumulated depreciation at 1 January 20X6		600
Fixtures and fittings at cost	840	
Accumulated depreciation at 1 January 20X6		510
Inventory at 1 January 20X6	1,090	
Receivables	1,750	
Allowance for doubtful debts		50
Payables		1,184
Purchases	18,586	
Revenue		25,795
Selling and distribution expenses	330	
Establishment and administration expenses	520	
Financial expenses	60	
	28,351	34,851

You discover the following:

1   Closing inventory is valued at £1,480.

2   The difference on the trial balance is a result of Willis' omission of the balance on his deposit account of £6,500. Willis transferred this amount on 30 September 20X6 by 31 December 20X6 the account had earned £50 interest, which has not yet been reflected in the ledgers.

3   All non-current assets are to be depreciated at 25% per annum on carrying amount.

4   The allowance for doubtful debts has been carried forward from last year. It is felt that receivables of £30 should be written off and the allowance increased to 5% of receivables.

5   Included in the selling and distribution expenses are £20 of payments which are better described as 'purchases'.

6   In establishment expenses are prepaid rent and rates of £30.

7   Also in establishment expenses are amounts paid for electricity. At 31 December 20X6 £28 was due for electricity.

8   An accrual of £50 should be made to cover accountancy fees.

9   The cash book does not reconcile with the bank statement since bank charges and interest have been omitted from the former, totalling £18.

10   On enquiring into Willis' drawings, you discover that £4,000 of the amount transferred to a deposit account on 30 September 20X6 was then immediately switched to Willis' private bank account.

Required:

Prepare an extended trial balance at 31 December 20X6.

 Test your understanding 7

Data

Amanda Carver is the proprietor of Automania, a business which supplies car parts to garages to use in servicing and repair work.

•   You are employed by Amanda Carver to assist with the bookkeeping.

•   The business currently operates a manual system consisting of a general ledger, a sales ledger and a purchases ledger.

•   Double entry takes place in the general ledger and the individual accounts of receivables and payables are therefore regarded as memoranda accounts.

•   Day books including a purchases day book, a sales day book, a purchases returns day book and a sales returns day book are used. Totals from the various columns of the day books are transferred into the general ledger.

At the end of the financial year, on 30 April 20X3, the balances were extracted from the general ledger and entered into an extended trial balance as shown below.

Task

Make appropriate entries in the adjustments columns of the extended trial balance to take account of the following:

(a) Rent payable by the business is as follows:

| For period to 31 July 20X2 | – £1,500 per month |
| From 1 August 20X2 | – £1,600 per month |

(b) The insurance balance includes £100 paid for the period of 1 May 20X3 to 31 May 20X3.

(c) Depreciation is to be calculated as follows:

| Motor vehicles | – 20% per annum straight line method |
| Fixtures and fittings | – 10% per annum reducing balance method |

(d) The allowance for doubtful debts is to be adjusted to a figure representing 2% of receivables.

(e) Inventory has been valued at cost on 30 April 20X3 at £119,360. However, this figure includes old inventory, the details of which are as follows:

| Cost price of old inventory | – £3,660 |
| Net realisable value of old inventory | – £2,060 |

Also included is a badly damaged car door which was to have been sold for £80 but will now have to be scrapped. The cost price of the door was £60.

(f) A credit note received from a supplier on 5 April 20X3 for goods returned was filed away with no entries having been made. The credit note has now been discovered and is for £200 net plus £35 VAT.

Extended trial balance at 30 April 20X3

Description	Ledger balances		Adjustments	
	Dr £	Cr £	Dr £	Cr £
Capital		135,000		
Drawings	42,150			
Rent	17,300			
Purchases	606,600			
Revenue		857,300		
Sales returns	2,400			
Purchases returns		1,260		
Salaries and wages	136,970			
Motor vehicles (MV) at cost	60,800			
Accumulated depreciation (MV)		16,740		
Office equipment (F&F) at cost	40,380			
Accumulated depreciation (F&F)		21,600		
Bank		3,170		
Cash	2,100			
Lighting and heating	4,700			
VAT		9,200		
Inventory at 1 May 20X2	116,100			
Irrecoverable debts	1,410			
Allowance for doubtful debts		1,050		
Sales ledger control account	56,850			
Purchases ledger control account		50,550		
Sundry expenses	6,810			
Insurance	1,300			
Accruals				
Prepayments				
Depreciation				
Allowance for doubtful debts adjustments				
Closing inventory – SPL				
Closing inventory – SoFP				
Totals	**1,095,870**	**1,095,870**		

Note: Only the above columns of the extended trial balance are required for this question.

2 Summary

Once the initial trial balance has been taken out then it is necessary to correct any errors in the ledger accounts and to put through the various year end adjustments that we have considered. These adjustments will be closing inventory, depreciation, irrecoverable and doubtful debts, accruals and prepayments. These can all be conveniently put through on the extended trial balance.

The ETB is then extended and the totals shown in the appropriate statement of profit or loss and statement of financial position columns. Finally the profit or loss is calculated and the statement of financial position columns totalled.

Test your understanding answers

 Test your understanding 1

Extended trial balance at 31 December 20X6

Account name	Trial balance Dr £	Trial balance Cr £	Adjustments Dr £	Adjustments Cr £	Statement of profit or loss Dr £	Statement of profit or loss Cr £	Statement of fin. pos. Dr £	Statement of fin. pos. Cr £
Shop fittings cost	7,300						7,300	
Accumulated shop fitting dep'n		2,500		400				2,900
Leasehold	30,000						30,000	
Accumulated leasehold dep'n		6,000		1,000				7,000
Opening Inventory	15,000				15,000			
SLCA	10,000			500			9,500	
Allowance for doubtful debt 1.1.X6		800	515					285
Cash in hand	50						50	
Cash at bank	1,250						1,250	
PLCA		18,000						18,000
Capital		19,050						19,050
Drawings	4,750		1,200				5,950	
Purchases	80,000			1,200	78,800			
Revenue		120,000				120,000		
Wages	12,000			200	11,800			
Advertising	4,000		200		4,200			
Rates	1,800			360	1,440			
Bank charges	200				200			
Dep'n charges								
– Fittings			400		400			
– Lease			1,000		1,000			

Irrecoverable debts			500		500			
Allowance for doubtful debt adjustment				515		515		
Prepayments			360				360	
Closing Inventory SoFP			21,000				21,000	
Closing Inventory SPL				21,000		21,000		
Sub total					113,340	141,515		
Net profit					28,175			28,175
TOTAL	166,350	166,350	25,175	25,175	141,515	141,515	75,410	75,410

Revision point: Take care with the doubtful debt allowance.

Allowance required is 3% of receivables after writing off the irrecoverable debt.

	£
Allowance 3% × (10,000 – 500)	285
Allowance in trial balance	800
Decrease in allowance	515

Test your understanding 2

Extended trial balance at 31 December 20X6

Account name	Trial balance Dr	Trial balance Cr	Adjustments Dr	Adjustments Cr	Statement of profit or loss Dr	Statement of profit or loss Cr	Statement of fin. pos. Dr	Statement of fin. pos. Cr
	£	£	£	£	£	£	£	£
Capital account		30,000						30,000
Freehold factory cost	20,000						20,000	
Plant cost	4,800						4,800	
Sales Reps' cars cost	2,600						2,600	
Accum dep'n								
– factory *1		1,920		320				2,240
– Plant		1,600		480				2,080
– Sales Reps' cars		1,200		650				1,850
Open. inventory	8,900				8,900			
SLCA	3,600			60			3,540	
PLCA		4,200						4,200
Allowance doubtful debts		280	60					220
Purchases	36,600				36,600			
Wages and salaries	19,800			3,000	16,800			
Rates and insurance	1,510			260	1,250			
Sundry expenses	1,500		120		1,620			
Motor expenses	400		600		1,000			
Revenue		72,000				72,000		
Cash at bank	11,490						11,490	
Closing Inventory SoFP			10,800				10,800	
Closing Inventory SPL				10,800		10,800		

Drawings			2,400				2,400	
Depreciation								
– factory			320		320			
– plant			480		480			
– Sales Reps' cars			650		650			
Accruals				120				120
Prepayments			260				260	
Sub total					*67,620*	*82,800*	*55,890*	*40,710*
Net profit					15,180			15,180
TOTAL	**111,200**	**111,200**	**15,690**	**15,690**	**82,800**	**82,800**	**55,890**	**55,890**

NOTE:

*1 – as the factory also includes land, the depreciation charge is (20,000 – 4,000) × 2% = 320

*2 – including an irrecoverable debt expense line and having a Dr and Cr of £60 is an alternative answer

---

 Test your understanding 3

Extended trial balance at 31 December 20X0

Account name	Trial balance		Adjustments		Statement of profit or loss		Statement of fin. pos.	
	Dr	Cr	Dr	Cr	Dr	Cr	Dr	Cr
	£	£	£	£	£	£	£	£
Capital 1.1.X0		2,377						2,377
Rent	500		100		600			
Open. inventory	510				510			
Rates	240			90	150			
Insurance	120				120			
Wages	1,634			120	1,514			
Receivables	672			37			635	
Revenue		15,542				15,542		
Repairs	635		27		662			
Purchases	9,876		72	63	9,885			
Discounts Received		129				129		
Drawings	1,200		63 120				1,383	
Petty cash	5						5	
Bank	763						763	
MV cost	1,740						1,740	
F&F cost	829						829	

Accumulated dep'n							
– MV		435		435			870
– F&F		166		166			332
Travel	192				192		
Payables		700					700
Sundry expenses	433			27 72	334		
Closing Inventory SoFP			647			647	
Closing Inventory SPL				647		647	
Dep'n charges							
– Vehicles			435		435		
– Fixtures			166		166		
Irrecoverable debts			37		37		
Accruals				100			100
Prepayments			90			90	
Sub total					14,605		
Net profit					1,713		1,713
TOTAL	**19,349**	**19,349**	**1,757**	**1,757**	**16,318**	**16,318**	**6,092**	**6,092**

Test your understanding 4

1	Debit	Depreciation expense account	£640
	Credit	Accumulated depreciation account	£640
2	Debit	Drawings account	£1,000
	Credit	Purchases account	£1,000
3	Debit	Closing inventory – statement of financial position	
	Credit	Closing inventory – statement of profit or loss	
4	Statement of financial position		
5	Statement of profit or loss		

KAPLAN PUBLISHING

Test your understanding 5

Extended trial balance of Randall at 31 Dec 20X6

Account	Trial balance Dr £	Trial balance Cr £	Adjustments Dr £	Adjustments Cr £	Statement of profit or loss Dr £	Statement of profit or loss Cr £	Statement of fin. pos. Dr £	Statement of fin. pos. Cr £
Fittings	2,000						2,000	
Accumulated depn 1 Jan 20X6		100		100				200
Leasehold	12,500						12,500	
Accumulated depn 1 Jan 20X6		625		625				1,250
Inventory 1 Jan 20X6	26,000				26,000			
Receivables	53,000			500			52,500	
Allowance doubtful debts 1 Jan 20X6		960		90				1,050
Cash in hand	50						50	
Cash at bank	4,050						4,050	
Payables		65,000						65,000
Capital		28,115						28,115
Drawings	2,000		1,000				3,000	
Purchases	102,000			1,000	101,000			
Revenue		129,000				129,000		
Wages	18,200			200	18,000			
Advertising	2,300		200		2,500			
Rates	1,500			300	1,200			
Bank charges	200				200			
Prepayments			300				300	
Depreciation Fittings			100		100			
Lease			625		625			
Irrecoverable debts			500		500			
Allowance for doubtful debts adjustment			90		90			
Closing inventory SoFP			30,000				30,000	
Closing inventory SPL				30,000		30,000		
Sub totals					150,215	159,000		
Net profit					8,785			8,785
Totals	223,800	223,800	32,815	32,815	159,000	159,000	104,400	104,400

Test your understanding 6

Willis

Extended trial balance at 31 December 20X6

Account	Trial balance Dr £	Trial balance Cr £	Adjustments Dr £	Adjustments Cr £	Statement of profit or loss Dr £	Statement of profit or loss Cr £	Statement of fin. pos. Dr £	Statement of fin. pos. Cr £
Capital		3,112						3,112
Cash at bank		2,240		18		.		2,258
Petty cash	25						25	
Plant and machinery	2,750						2,750	
Accumulated depreciation		1,360		348				1,708
Motor vehicles	2,400						2,400	
Accumulated depreciation		600		450				1,050
Fixtures and fittings	840						840	
Accumulated depreciation		510		83				593
Inventory 1 Jan 20X6	1,090				1,090			
Receivables	1,750			30			1,720	
Allowance for doubtful debts		50		36				86
Payables		1,184						1,184
Purchases	18,586		20		18,606			
Revenue		25,795				25,795		
Selling and distribution	330			20	310			
Establishment and admin	520		28	30	518			
Financial expenses	60		18 / 50		128			
Deposit account	6,500		50	4,000			2,550	
Inventory at 31 Dec 20X6								
SoFP			1,480				1,480	
SPL				1,480		1,480		
Deposit interest				50		50		
Depreciation								
Plant and mach			348		348			
Motor vehicles			450		450			
F&F			83		83			
Irrecoverable debts expense			30					
Allowance for doubtful debts adjustment			36		66			
Drawings			4,000				4,000	
Accruals				28 / 50				78
Prepayments			30				30	
Profit					5,726			5,726
	34,851	34,851	6,623	6,623	27,325	27,325	15,795	15,795

Test your understanding 7

Extended trial balance at 30 April 20X3

Description	Ledger balances		Adjustments	
	Dr	Cr	Dr	Cr
	£	£	£	£
Capital		135,000		
Drawings	42,150			
Rent	17,300		1,600	
Purchases	606,600			
Revenue		857,300		
Sales returns	2,400			
Purchases returns		1,260		200
Salaries and wages	136,970			
Motor vehicles (MV) at cost	60,800			
Accumulated depreciation (MV)		16,740		12,160
Office equipment (F&F) at cost	40,380			
Accumulated depreciation (F&F)		21,600		1,878
Bank		3,170		
Cash	2,100			
Lighting and heating	4,700			
VAT		9,200		35
Inventory at 1 May 20X2	116,100			
Irrecoverable debts	1,410			
Allowance for doubtful debts		1,050		87
Sales ledger control account	56,850			
Purchases ledger control account		50,550	235	
Sundry expenses	6,810			
Insurance	1,300			100
Accruals				1,600
Prepayments			100	
Depreciation			14,038	
Allowance for doubtful debts – adjustments			87	
Closing inventory – SPL				117,700
Closing inventory – SoFP			117,700	
TOTALS	**1,095,870**	**1,095,870**	**133,760**	**133,760**

MOCK ASSESSMENT

1 Mock Assessment Questions

Task 1.1 (21 marks)

This task is about non-current assets.

The following is a purchase invoice received by NFS Ltd:

Invoice 60754

To: NFS Ltd 24 Roxburgh Place Newcastle NE6 2HU	Betty's 42 Warwick Street Newcastle NE1 3TT	Date: 28 March 2009
		£
HP Printer	Serial number 571GS90	600.00
Delivery		10.00
Insurance		50.00
VAT @20%		132.00
Total		792.00

Settlement terms: strictly 30 days net

The following information relates to the sale of a vehicle:

Registration number	PQ09 NMH
Date of sale	20 March 09
Selling price excluding VAT	£4,600

- Bytes Technology Group has a policy of capitalising expenditure over £500.

- Vehicles are depreciated at 30% on a diminishing balance basis.

- Computer Equipment is depreciated at 20% on a straight-line basis assuming no residual value.

- A full year's depreciation is charged in the year of acquisition and none in the year of disposal.

(a) Record the following information in the non-current assets register below: (18 marks)

- Any acquisitions of non-current assets during the year ended 31 March 09

- Any disposals of non-current assets during the year ended 31 March 09

- Depreciation for the year ended 31 March 09

Non-current assets register

Description	Acquisition date	Cost £	Depreciation £	Carrying value £	Funding method	Disposal proceeds	Disposal date
Computer equipment							
Mainframe server	17/07/06	14,000.00			Cash		
Year end 31/03/07			2,800.00	11,200.00			
Year end 31/03/08			2,800.00	8,400.00			
Year end 31/03/09							
Year end 31/03/09							
Motor vehicles							
PQ09 NMH	14/09/07	9,000.00			Cash		
Year end 31/03/07			2,700.00	6,300.00			
Year end 31/03/08			1,890.00	4,410.00			
Year end 31/03/09							
EA55 SAR	12/02/08	10,000.00			Part-exchange		
Year end 31/03/08			3,000.00	7,000.00			
Year end 31/03/09							

(b)   Complete the following sentences. (3 marks)

A director of the business _____ (*would / would not*) be an appropriate person to give authority for the acquisition of a non-current asset.

Prior authority should be obtained for capital expenditure

_____.

(*to ensure that the transaction is of an appropriate materiality level / to ensure that the purchase is required for the organisation's benefit / to comply with international financial reporting standards*)

Task 1.2 (17 marks)

This task is about ledger accounting for non-current assets.

At the start of the financial year, the business had fixtures and fittings in the cost account of £35,000. The accumulated depreciation was £4,700 (see opening balances below).

During the year, the business disposed of fixtures and fittings. The original cost of the disposed asset was £1,700 and the carrying value was £1,200. They received a part-exchange value for this of £900 when they acquired new fixtures and fittings with total value of £3,000. The balance of the new purchase was paid for with a cheque.

(a)   Enter the Disposal and Acquisition into the Cost, Accumulated Depreciation, Disposals and Bank accounts below.

Balance the accounts and clearly show either the profit or loss on disposal. (12 marks)

Fixtures and fittings cost			
	£		£
Bal b/d	35,000		

Fixtures and fittings accumulated depreciation			
	£		£
		Bal b/d	4,700

Disposals			
	£		£

Bank			
	£		£

KAPLAN PUBLISHING

(b)   A business acquired a motor van for £10,000 plus VAT of £2,000, paying by cheque. Tick the appropriate box to show whether the account names will appear as a debit or credit entry. (2 marks)

Account name	Debit	Credit
Motor van – cost		
VAT control account		
Bank		

(c)   A business is to charge depreciation of £2,000 for office equipment for the year. What are the accounting entries required? (3 marks)

Account name	Amount £	Debit	Credit

Select account name from: Accumulated depreciation – office equipment, Accumulated depreciation – motor vehicles, Bank, Depreciation charges, Disposals, Office equipment – cost

Task 1.3 (19 marks)

This task is about ledger accounting including accruals and prepayments, and applying ethical principles.

You are working on the final accounts of a business for year ended 31/12/09.

You have the following information. The figures below are net of VAT.

Balance at	01/01/09
Accrual telephone expenses	£90
Prepayment rent expenses	£400

(a)   The bank summary for the year shows payments for rent expenses of £1,600. The £1,600 paid was for rent from 1st March to 31st October 2009. Rent accrues evenly during the year.

Complete the ledger account below clearly showing the brought down and carried down figures as well as the rent for the year that needs to be transferred to the statement of profit or loss. (4 marks)

Rent expenses

Date	Account name	£	Date	Account name	£

(b) During the year £600 was paid out of the bank towards the Telephone expense account. On 31st January 2010, the business received a bill for £150 that related to the whole of November 2009, December 2009 and January 2010.

Complete the ledger account below clearly showing the brought down and carried down figures as well as the telephone expense for the year that needs to be transferred to the statement of profit or loss. (4 marks)

Telephone expenses

Date	Account name	£	Date	Account name	£

(c) Using the figures from your answers in (a) and (b) as well as balances given, complete the Trial Balance extract below as of 31st December 2009. (4 marks)

Account	£	Dr	Cr
Revenue	9,690		
SLCA	4,380		
Drawings	3,150		
Bank overdraft	350		
Accruals			
Prepayments			
Rent			
Telephone			

You are now looking at rental income for the year. Rental income of £2,500 was accrued on 31/12/08.

(d) Complete the following statements: (2 marks)

The reversal of this accrual is dated:

_____

Select from: 31/12/08, 01/01/09, 01/01/08

The reversal is on the _____ side of the rental income account.
Select from: debit, credit

(e) The cash book for the year shows receipts for rental income of £12,550. Rental income of £1,220 for the month of 31 December 2009 was received into the bank on 15 January 2010.

Taking into account all of the information you have, calculate the rental income for the year ended 31 December 2009. (3 marks)

£_____

(f)   Your junior colleague has asked why you are considering the receipt on 15 January 2010. Select the appropriate reason from those given below: (2 marks)

	Acceptable reason	**Unacceptable reason**
The rental income received relates to the year ended 31 December 2009 so must be recognised in that year.		
We have been told to increase the profit as much as we can and the money has come in near the year end so we may as well include it!		

Task 1.4 (23 marks)

This task is about accounting adjustments.

(a)   You are a trainee accounting technician working within an accounting practice. You are working on the accounting records of Widgets Ltd, a business that makes and sells parts for kitchen appliances. A trial balance has been started and is provided on the next page. You have also been provided with details which you are required to consider and make appropriate entries for in the adjustments column of the extended trial balance. (16 marks)

The year-end date is 31 December 20X5.

• The allowances for doubtful debts figure is to be adjusted to 2% of receivables.

• A credit note received from a supplier for goods returned was mislaid.

• It has since been found and has not yet been accounted for. It was for £2,000 net plus £400 VAT.

• Rent is payable yearly in advance. For the 12 months to 31/10/X5 the rent is £12,000, the prepayment bought down has been included in the ledger balance. For the 12 months to 31/10/X6 the rent is £15,000.

- Inventory is valued at cost at £14,890. However, there was a leak in the storage cupboard and £3,000 worth of items has been damaged and need to be written off. No entries have yet been made for closing inventory.

- The electricity bill of £450 for the 3 months ended 31 January 20X6 was received and paid in February 20X6.

Extended trial balance

Ledger account	Ledger balances		Adjustments	
	Dr £	Cr £	Dr £	Cr £
Accruals		1,330		
Advertising	1,800			
Bank	7,912			
Capital		50,000		
Closing inventory				
Depreciation charge				
Drawings	24,700			
Fixtures and fittings – accumulated depreciation		945		
Fixtures and fittings – cost	6,099			
Irrecoverable debts	345			
Allowance for doubtful debt adjustment				
Electricity	1,587			
Opening inventory	5,215			
Prepayment				
Allowance for doubtful debts		485		
Purchases	78,921			
Purchase returns				
PLCA		14,000		
Rent	25,000			
Revenue		145,825		
SLCA	9,500			
VAT control account		11,453		
Wages	62,959			
	224,038	224,038		

(b)   Show the journal entries required to close off the electricity account for the financial year end and select an appropriate narrative.
(4 marks)

Journal

	Dr £	Cr £

Select from: Allowance for doubtful debts, Electricity, Profit or loss account, Rent, Statement of financial position, VAT control account

Journal narrative:

_____

Select from:

Closure of general ledger for the year ended 31 December 20X5, Closure of electricity account to the suspense account, Transfer of electricity for the year ended 31 December 20X5 to the statement of financial position, Transfer of electricity for the year ended 31 December 20X5 to the profit or loss account.

(c)   Your manager has now reviewed the figures in the draft accounts and is concerned about the level of irrecoverable debts. It looks rather low from your manager's understanding from prior discussions with the client. You are under pressure to get the accounts finalised by the client as they have a very important upcoming meeting. Any further investigation into the irrecoverable debts may mean the accounts will not be ready in time.

What would be the appropriate action to take? Please select one.
(3 marks)

Investigate the concerns of the level of irrecoverable debts – any concerns should be addressed to ensure the accounts represent a true and fair view.	
Ignore concerns about the level of irrecoverable debts – if you start looking into it you won't meet the deadline. It is more important to meet the deadline than to worry about irrecoverable debts!	

KAPLAN PUBLISHING

Task 1.5 (20 marks)

This task is about period end routines, using accounting records, and the extended trial balance.

The bank statement has been compared with the cash book and the following differences identified:

1   Bank interest paid of £82 was not entered in the cash book.

2   A cheque paid for £450 has been incorrectly entered in the cash book as £540.

3   Cheques totalling £1,980 paid into the bank at the end of the month are not showing on the bank statement.

4   A BACS receipt of £1,750 from a customer has not been entered in the cash book.

The balance showing on the bank statement is a credit of £5,250 and the balance in the cash book is a debit of £5,472.

(a)   Use the following table to show the THREE adjustments you need to make to the cash book (6 marks)

Adjustment	Amount £	Debit/Credit

(b)   Which of these can be capitalised as part of the cost of a new piece of machinery? (Please note, there could be more than one correct answer.) (3 marks)

	Tick
Delivery charges to transport the machinery to the business' factory	
Insurance for the machinery	
Maintenance costs after machinery has been used by the business	
Essential repairs before the machinery can be used for the first time	

(c) You have the following extended trial balance. The adjustments have already been correctly entered. You now need to extend the figures into the statement of profit or loss and statement of financial position columns. Make the columns balance by entering figures and a label in the correct places. (11 marks)

Extended trial balance

Ledger account	Ledger balances		Adjustments		Statement of profit or loss		Statement of financial position	
	Dr £	Cr £	Dr £	Cr £	Dr £	Cr £	Dr £	Cr £
Allowance for doubtful debts		1,300	600					
Allowance for doubtful debts adjustment				600				
Bank	28,380			500				
Capital		4,530						
Closing inventory			40,000	40,000				
Depreciation charge			20,500					
Office expenses	69,550			500				
Opening inventory	26,000							
Payroll expenses	31,150			150				
Purchases	188,000		900					
Purchases ledger control account		29,900						
Revenue		436,000						
Sales ledger control account	36,000							
Selling expenses	67,000							
Suspense		250	1,150	900				
VAT		9,800						
Vehicles at cost	62,000							
Vehicles accumulated depreciation		26,300		20,500				
	508,080	508,080	63,150	63,150				

Mock Assessment Answers

Task 1.1 (21 marks)

(a) Record the following information in the non-current assets register below: (18 marks)

Non-current assets register

Description	Acquisition date	Cost £	Depreciation £	Carrying value £	Funding method	Disposal proceeds	Disposal date
Computer equipment							
Mainframe Server	17/07/06	14,000.00			Cash		
Year end 31/03/07			2,800.00	11,200.00			
Year end 31/03/08			2,800.00	8,400.00			
Year end 31/03/09			2,800.00	5,600.00			
HP Printer 571GS90	28/03/09	610.00			Credit		
Year end 31/03/09			122.00	488.00			
Motor vehicles							
PQ09 NMH	14/09/07	9,000.00			Cash		
Year end 31/03/07			2,700.00	6,300.00			
Year end 31/03/08			1,890.00	4,410.00			
Year end 31/03/09			0	0		4,600.00	20/03/09
EA55 SAR	12/02/08	10,000.00			Part-exchange		
Year end 31/03/08			3,000.00	7,000.00			
Year end 31/03/09			2,100.00	4,900.00			

(b)   Complete the following sentences. (3 marks)

A director of the business would be an appropriate person to give authority for the acquisition of a non-current asset.

Prior authority should be obtained for capital expenditure to ensure that the purchase is required for the organisation's benefit.

Task 1.2 (17 marks)

(a)   Enter the Disposal and Acquisition into the Cost, Accumulated Depreciation, Disposals and Bank accounts below.

Balance the accounts and clearly show either the profit or loss on disposal. (12 marks)

Fixtures and fittings cost			
	£		£
Bal b/d	35,000	Disposals	1,700
Part exchange	900		
Bank	2,100	Bal c/d	36,300
	38,000		38,000
Bal b/d	36,300		

Fixtures and fittings accumulated depreciation			
	£		£
Disposals	500	Bal b/d	4,700
Bal c/d	4,200		
	4,700		4,700
		Bal b/d	4,200

Disposals

	£		£
Fixtures and fittings	1,700	Accumulated depreciation	500
		Part exchange	900
		Loss on disposal	300
	1,700		1,700

Bank

	£		£
		Fixtures and fittings	2,100
Bal c/d	2,100		
	2,100		2,100
		Bal b/d	2,100

(b) A business acquired a motor van for £10,000 plus VAT of £2,000, paying via cheque. Tick the appropriate box to show whether the account names will appear as a debit or credit entry. (2 marks)

Account name	Debit	Credit
Motor van – cost	✓	
VAT control account	✓	
Bank		✓

(c) A business is to charge depreciation of £2,000 for office equipment for the year. What are the accounting entries required? (3 marks)

Account name	Amount £	Debit	Credit
Depreciation charges	2,000	✓	
Accumulated depreciation – office equipment	2,000		✓

Task 1.3 (19 marks)

(a) Complete the ledger account below clearly showing the brought down and carried down figures as well as the rent for the year that needs to be transferred to the statement of profit or loss. (4 marks)

Rent expenses

Date	Account name	£	Date	Account name	£
1/01/09	Bal b/d	400	31/12/09	Statement of profit or loss	2,400
31/12/09	Bank	1,600			
31/12/09	Bal c/d (W1)	400			
		2,400			2,400

(W1) Rent paid from 1 March to 31 October = £1,600 for 8 months.

Therefore monthly amount is £1,600/8 = £200.

Rent accrued November and December = £200 × 2 = £400

(b) Complete the ledger account below clearly showing the brought down and carried down figures as well as the telephone expense for the year that needs to be transferred to the statement of profit or loss. (4 marks)

Telephone expenses

Date	Account name	£	Date	Account name	£
31/12/09	Bank	600	1/01/09	Bal b/d	90
31/12/09	Bal c/d (W1)	100	31/12/09	Statement of profit or loss	610
		700			700

(W1) Bill of £150 received after the year end on the 31 January

Telephone accrued November and December = £150 × 2/3 = £100

(c) Using the figures from your answers in (a) and (b) as well as balances given, complete the Trial Balance extract below as of 31st December 2009. (4 marks)

Account	£	Dr	Cr
Revenue	9,690		9,690
SLCA	4,380	4,380	
Drawings	3,150	3,150	
Bank overdraft	350		350
Accruals			500
Prepayments			
Rent		2,400	
Telephone		610	

You are now looking at rental income for the year. Rental income of £2,500 was accrued on 31/12/08.

(d) Complete the following statements: (2 marks)

The reversal of this accrual is dated: 01/01/09

The reversal is on the <u>debit</u> side of the rental income account.

(e) The cash book for the year shows receipts for rental income of £12,550. Rental income of £1,220 for the month of 31 December 2009 was received into the bank on 15 January 2010.

Taking into account all of the information you have, calculate the rental income for the year ended 31 December 2009.(3 marks)

£11,270

(£12,550 + £1,220 - £2,500)

(f) Your junior colleague has asked why you are considering the receipt on 15 January 2010. Select the appropriate reason from those given below: (2 marks)

	Acceptable reason	Unacceptable reason
The rental income received relates to the year ended 31 December 2009 so must be recognised in that year.	✓	
We have been told to increase the profit as much as we can and the money has come in near the year end so we may as well include it!		✓

Task 1.4 (23 marks)

(a)   Extended trial balance (16 marks)

Ledger account	Ledger balances		Adjustments	
	Dr £	Cr £	Dr £	Cr £
Accruals		1,330		300
Advertising	1,800			
Bank	7,912			
Capital		50,000		
Closing inventory			11,890	11,890
Depreciation charge				
Drawings	24,700			
F&F – acc dep'n		945		
F&F – cost	6,099			
Irrecoverable debts	345			
Allowance for doubtful debt adjustment				295
Electricity	1,587		300	
Opening inventory	5,215			
Prepayment			12,500	
Allowance for doubtful debts		485	295	
Purchases	78,921			
Purchase returns				2,000
PLCA		14,000	2,400	
Rent	25,000			12,500
Revenue		145,825		
SLCA	9,500			
VAT control account		11,453		400
Wages	62,959			
	224,038	224,038	27,385	27,385

(b) Show the journal entries required to close off the electricity account for the financial year end and select an appropriate narrative.
(4 marks)

Journal

	Dr £	Cr £
Profit or loss account	✓	
Electricity		✓

Journal narrative:

Transfer of electricity for the year ended 31 December 20X5 to the profit or loss account.

(c) What would be the appropriate action to take? Please select one.
(3 marks)

Investigate the concerns of the level of irrecoverable debts – any concerns should be addressed to ensure the accounts represent a true and fair view.	✓
Ignore concerns about the level of irrecoverable debts – if you start looking into it you won't meet the deadline. It is more important to meet the deadline than to worry about irrecoverable debts!	

Task 1.5 (20 marks)

(a) Use the following table to show the THREE adjustments you need to make to the cash book (6 marks)

Adjustment	Amount £	Debit/Credit
Adjustment for (1)	82	Cr
Adjustment for (2)	90	Dr
Adjustment for (4)	1,750	Dr

(b) Which of these can be capitalised as part of the cost of a new piece of machinery? (Please note, there could be more than one correct answer.) (3 marks)

	Tick
Delivery charges to transport the machinery to the business' factory	✓
Insurance for the machinery	
Maintenance costs after machinery has been used by the business	
Essential repairs before the machinery can be used for the first time	✓

(c) You have the following extended trial balance. The adjustments have already been correctly entered. You now need to extend the figures into the statement of profit or loss and statement of financial position columns. Make the columns balance by entering figures and a label in the correct places. (11 marks)

Extended trial balance

Ledger account	Ledger balances		Adjustments		Statement of profit or loss		Statement of financial position	
	Dr £	Cr £	Dr £	Cr £	Dr £	Cr £	Dr £	Cr £
Allowance for doubtful debts		1,300	600					700
Allowance for doubtful debts adjustment				600		600		
Bank	28,380			500			27,880	
Capital		4,530						4,530
Closing inventory			40,000	40,000		40,000	40,000	
Depreciation charge			20,500		20,500			
Office expenses	69,550			500	69,050			
Opening inventory	26,000				26,000			
Payroll expenses	31,150			150	31,000			
Purchases	188,000		900		188,900			
Purchases ledger control account		29,900						29,900
Revenue		436,000				436,000		
Sales ledger control account	36,000						36,000	
Selling expenses	67,000				67,000			
Suspense		250	1,150	900				
VAT		9,800						9,800
Vehicles at cost	62,000						62,000	
Vehicles acc dep'n		26,300		20,500				46,800
NET PROFIT					74,150			74,150
	508,080	508,080	63,150	63,150	476,600	476,600	165,880	165,880

INDEX

KAPLAN PUBLISHING